Fire
on the
Ganges

Celebrating
30 Years of Publishing
in India

Praise for *Fire on the Ganges*

'Vividly told and richly detailed, Radhika Iyengar's *Fire on the Ganges* is an untold story that will shape our collective understanding of India.'

— **Sonia Faleiro**, author of *The Good Girls*

'You might think of Manikarnika as a place for the dead. This fine book is a reminder that the burning ghats are a place for the living.'

— **Amitava Kumar**, author of *The Blue Book*

'In this vivid work of slow journalism, Radhika Iyengar guides us into the brutal world of the Doms, a sub-caste of Dalits, or "untouchables", who have tended the corpses and lit the funeral pyres in Banaras for as long as anyone can remember. By observing their world with a keen, unflinching eye, Iyengar is able to render the lives of her subjects with compassion and insight while delivering a story that is both uplifting and heartbreaking. *Fire on the Ganges* is the work of a first-rate reporter and a gifted writer, whose narrative moves like the river, slow and deep, to the ancient rhythms of Indian life.'

— **Don Belt**, former senior editor, *National Geographic Magazine*

'A worthy illustration of show-don't-tell, *Fire on the Ganges* leaves you both hopeful and anxious about the possibilities of breaking through the barriers imposed by the caste system, for those who are placed at its very bottom. The Dalit community of corpse burners in Varanasi, Doms, have featured in literature and film before, but Iyengar's work stands out for its dogged curiosity and immersive storytelling.'

— **Snigdha Poonam**, author of *Dreamers*

'*Fire on the Ganges* is a complex and atmospheric account of life on the ghats that welcome death. A book of humanity and intimacy, hope and resilience, Radhika Iyengar has chronicled that which is often overlooked—the enduring power of the voice. This is oral history at its finest.'

– **Aanchal Malhotra**, oral historian and author of
Remnants of a Separation

'With the narrative drive of a novel, this is a non-fiction book that illuminates a profession, a tradition and a society. An absolutely fascinating read!'

– **Tabish Khair**, critic and author of *The Body by the Shore*

'Deeply reported, thoroughly researched, with writing that leaves your skin cold, *Fire on the Ganges* is a book about the hum of life arranged around death. It will teach you about growing up sleeping amid corpses waiting to be lit, stealing shrouds and carrying the stench of death lodged deep inside your fingernails. It will force you to wonder whether life is often crueller than death.'

– **Mansi Choksi**, author of *The Newlyweds*

'At once sobering and enlivening, *Fire on the Ganges* is a compelling account of how the Doms both contribute to, and are overlooked by, a "new India" that has lost its lustre. Radhika Iyengar makes her subject spring to life through her eye for detail and her immersion in the world she's writing of.'

– **Amit Chaudhuri**, writer, musician and author of *Sojourn*

'Their alleged impurity is integral to what is the holiest city for Hindus. Radhika Iyengar's narrative non-fiction on the Doms of Varanasi peels the layers of this socio-cultural irony. With admirable elegance and empathy, she tells stories of a community that has not been spared caste prejudice despite their traditional "prerogative" of cremating Hindus at the most auspicious ghats along the Ganga. For all the changes in the name of development in the Prime Minister's constituency, the female members of the Dom community remain worse off as they are as much in thrall to patriarchy.'

– **Manoj Mitta**, author of *Caste Pride*

'Deeply alarming and yet never alarmist, Radhika Iyengar's *Fire on the Ganges* is essential reading—wise, sensitive and unsettling.'

– **David Hajdu**, author of *A Revolution in Three Acts*

Fire
on the
Ganges

Life among the
Dead in Banaras

RADHIKA IYENGAR

An Imprint of HarperCollins Publishers

First published in India by Fourth Estate 2023
An imprint of HarperCollins *Publishers*
4th Floor, Tower A, Building No. 10, DLF Cyber City,
DLF Phase II, Gurugram, Haryana – 122002
www.harpercollins.co.in

2 4 6 8 10 9 7 5 3 1

P-ISBN: 978-93-5699-467-6
E-ISBN: 978-93-5699-466-9

Typeset in 12/16 Adobe Garamond at
Manipal Technologies Limited, Manipal

Printed and bound at
Thomson Press (India) Ltd

To my family

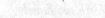

'Were the Creator
Concerned about caste,
We'd arrive in the world
With a caste mark on the forehead.'

Kabir says.

– Essential Kabir,
Translated by Arvind Krishna Mehrotra

Contents

Prologue

Death

2016

THE NIGHT HER husband was cremated, Dolly Chaudhary was not allowed to visit his funeral pyre. Her anklets, which once tinkled when she ran to meet him, were silent. She cried as she collapsed into the arms of her female relatives. The community believed that women were too weak-hearted to be present at cremations. Dolly watched his burning corpse from a distance, from the outer boundaries of Manikarnika Ghat—the land of the dead. It was the open-air cremation ground where her husband had stood countless times as a corpse burner, setting dead bodies alight, and where he himself now lay. Dolly's husband, Sekond Lal Chaudhary, had died mysteriously by falling off a bridge.

While the city of Banaras (Varanasi) sleeps, Manikarnika Ghat, one of the most important Hindu cremation sites in the world, is alive with its burning pyres. This is where death asserts itself as the last witness to life.

I

The Neighbourhood

DOLLY CHAUDHARY DOES not know her age. Each time she has been asked that question, she has answered wearily in Hindi, 'I was born the year Indira Gandhi was killed. I don't know when that was; you do the maths.'[1]

In the afternoons, when the summer heat is unbearable, Dolly walks around in her one-room home, braless. Occasionally, she will tug at the sleeves of her blouse so that she can air her armpits. The pallu of her sari rests loosely over her forehead, slipping every now and then at will. Her body moves with a slight hunch, suggesting years of childbearing. She lifts her nylon sari till her knees and tucks it between her legs before squatting on the floor. Her three-year-old daughter, Vidhi, who was born months before Dolly's husband died, clings to her, sucking on two fingers.

In 2019, thirty-five-year-old Dolly is a young widow with five children. To make a living, she has recently opened a shop in her small home. When Dolly hears a tap on the two-panelled, wooden door of her house, she gets up to crack it open from the middle. Outside, in the narrow lane, a young boy, around ten, stands barefoot. He cups a five-rupee coin in his palm. 'Beedi,' he says casually, with practised ease. He has done this before. Dolly reaches behind the makeshift shop counter precariously placed near the door, picks up a small packet of brown leaf swirls stuffed with tobacco and pulls one out. The boy takes it, leaves the coin on the threshold and disappears into the house next door. 'His father is one lazy fellow,' Dolly mutters under her breath. 'Can't even buy his own beedis.'

Dolly leaves her door open as she watches her sixteen-year-old neighbour emerge from the house opposite hers with a pitcher, breaking through a dense cluster of flies hovering in the lane. She is going to fill water from the community tap.

The Doms, a Dalit sub-caste, inhabit the inner arteries of the city, hidden from the main alleyways of Banaras. Chand Ghat, where Dolly lives, is primarily a Dom neighbourhood, home to a small community of corpse burners. Their profession involves cremating the dead and they are considered 'untouchable' by a majority of dominant-caste Hindus. The Dom locality, therefore, is isolated and unseen—unless you go looking for it.

The neighbourhood itself, though, is alive—bustling through the humdrum of the everyday. You can reach it by following a labyrinth of narrow alleys, hemmed in by walls plastered with drying dung cakes or exhibiting hand-drawn art. Chand Ghat consists of a cluster of mud-and-brick buildings, painted in candy hues of blue, baby pink, lemon and pea green. Each house is nameless, bearing no address or number plate on its door. Most families in the neighbourhood live in cramped, one-bedroom accommodations. At night, temporary partitions are put up with bedsheets draped on ropes to make smaller rooms within.

Against the hard blue sky, electrical wires weave in and out in a tizzy from the rooftops. Monkeys swing from one balcony to another, disturbing drying clothes in their wake. The long-tailed acrobats traverse the wires with efficiency. Children fling pebbles at them to scare them off. The monkeys hiss wildly, displaying their sharp teeth.

The ground below is a collection of cracked and wobbly stone slabs. They rattle as young boys on bicycles ride by, petrifying the goats that crowd the lanes. In an open courtyard-like space, a toddler sits on a parked motorbike. He narrows his eyes and plays with the handle bar: 'Vroom! Vroom!' he sputters. Older boys play gali cricket, while young girls watch them shyly from a distance. Other children play around a solitary hand pump that has fallen into disuse over the last twenty years or so. In the evenings, old men emerge from their homes to light beedis, drink tea and play card games. They discuss their day in Bhojpuri, the local language.

The Dom women—young or old, married or widowed—mostly remain hidden within their dimly lit homes, cooking and cleaning utensils. In Chand Ghat, an invisible boundary exists between the Chaudhary and the adjoining Yadav colonies. Both communities, however, know where that boundary begins. If a married Dom woman wants to walk beyond this line, she must pull her veil down to her chin and wait for her husband or another male family member to accompany her.[2] Young and unmarried women cannot walk off alone on a whim either. 'It's simply not allowed,' an elderly lady from the Dom community once told me. 'It's for their own protection. Our women can easily be swayed by the advances of jobless flirts who wander about.'

Women in this community are constantly under surveillance. Like elsewhere in India, a woman takes her husband's name once she is married. From then on, a Dom woman is socially and financially dependent on him for the rest of her life. Without her husband, it is believed within the community that a woman has no essence of her own.

Dolly takes a deep breath. 'I now feel that marriage ruined me. Tell me, who am I without my husband?'

Three years ago, in 2016, when Dolly heard the news of her husband's death, she felt the ground beneath her fall away. She had imagined slitting her wrists or hanging herself with his belt, but the thought of her five children, including her newborn, convinced her otherwise. Some part of her, though, died that night. According to the people close to her, she has changed drastically since her husband's death. They say what remains now is but a weak shadow of her former self.

'Three people went together. Two came back alive, one died,' she tells me as she reaches for a plastic container and drops the five-rupee coin in it. 'Does something like that happen in an accident, where only one dies and the rest survive?'

There is deep pain in her eyes. 'My husband fell off a bridge from a great height, but none of his bones were broken. There was not a single scratch on him. We found his body, but no one had the brains to figure out what exactly happened.'

2

Charcoal, Smoke and Tangerine

In 2019, AAKASH Chaudhury stands in his flimsy rubber slippers and observes his feet. They have assumed the colour of charcoal; deep cracks mark the edges of his soles. The ground beneath him radiates heat. He is standing among clusters of burning pyres, waiting for a corpse to disintegrate into ash. The sounds of the wood snapping and splaying, of bones splitting in the fire, are sharp. If you gaze at the pyre long enough, the crackle gently fades into the background—it becomes a hum that is strangely familiar and comforting.

A fibula juts out from a nearby pyre, almost defiantly. Aakash picks up a bamboo stick and stabs the bone into subservience. The corpse encased within the hand-built structure of wood and straw shifts limply. Flakes of ash, disturbed by his nudge, take flight. They sting his eyes and settle on his lips. Aakash coughs and turns away to spit. His ashy saliva lands on the ground. *Splat.*

The afternoon sun burns his back. His mahogany skin is covered in ant-sized heat boils.

For a thirty-year-old man, Aakash has a scrawny frame and looks at least a decade younger. He wears an oversized vest, which begins inches below his neck, and pants, which he rolls up while at work. From a string around his neck dangles a reedy iron pendant that he uses as a toothpick to tease out the bits of betel leaves wedged between his teeth. A thin, scarlet-hued gamchha is usually fastened around his waist or wrapped around his head. The tail-end of this gamchha is often used by him to wipe the sweat off his face. The whites of his eyes are discoloured—a pale hue of mustard.

In his lifetime, Aakash has seen 'all sorts of bodies—deformed, mutilated, broken': corpses with smashed skulls, severed limbs, gunshot wounds, knife-torn torsos with guts spilling out. He has cremated those who died by suicide, either by hanging or self-immolation. Over the years, Aakash has admitted wanting to vomit while working at the ghat. 'It's the sight of melting flesh that is revolting,' he says in Hindi. 'That is why most Dom men drink alcohol or chew gutka.[1] We kill our senses before getting down to work.'

A majority of boys in the community grow up watching their fathers and uncles consume copious amounts of liquor. It is only a matter of time before they too begin drinking. 'A bottle of beer costs about one hundred and forty rupees,' a sixteen-year-old who works at the ghat informs me. 'I have it every now and then, and I regularly chew gutka. My mother has no idea and neither does my father.'

At Manikarnika Ghat, the working conditions are debilitating and torturous. Not only are Aakash and his co-workers subjected to extreme dehydration, but also, if the winds are strong and fierce, their skin and hair are often singed by the scorching wayward flames.

'We don't have a choice; we have to drink. We work with dead bodies,' explains Aakash. 'We have to smell such terrible things that we feel sick to our stomachs. Alcohol makes things bearable. At least our breath smells of liquor and not of a decaying corpse.'

Extreme exhaustion, heat and smoke inhalation (among other things) put an enormous strain on the cremators' bodies. To cope, the men spiral into prolonged bouts of excessive drinking and drug consumption. It is not uncommon, the community members say, for Dom men to die at an early age, usually by the time they are in their sixties. Aakash's father too was an alcoholic who died of liver cirrhosis in 2019. He was sixty-five.

The first time Aakash cremated a corpse, he was thirteen or fourteen years old. 'It was a man's body,' he recalls. 'Back then, I didn't know what to do. The body wasn't catching fire. The corpse had a lot of water in it.'

Normally, a corpse takes around three hours to turn to ash. However, the cremators explain that bodies that have been tormented by illnesses for weeks or months, and have been injected with intravenous fluids and glucose in hospitals, take longer—usually six to seven hours. '*Saari lakdi jal jayegi, magar chamdi jalegi nahin.* All the wood will burn, but the skin won't melt,' says Aakash. 'It makes us work doubly hard. I've seen bodies come in with bloated bellies that burst open when the fire tears through them. When that happens, the water drowns the fire out. That's why burning such bodies takes time.'

Aakash has a predilection for candour. He describes incidents in his life in a steady, unflinching tone—difficult incidents that have been internally normalized. It is a defence mechanism to cope with the bleak every day of his existence.

He grew up at Manikarnika Ghat. As a child, he used to walk to the ghat to deliver lunch to his father. 'I was probably eight or nine years old at the time—I can't remember the exact age,' Aakash says, shrugging. Before heading back, he would pick up some charred wood from the extinguished pyres and haul it home.

The wood was used by his mother for cooking. While the food cooked, smoke would fill his small home. It pressed against the ceiling and clung to the walls. It hung thick in the air for at least half an hour before it cleared, leaving behind sooty patches on the clothes, a crusty layer on the furniture and walls, and a lingering, choking smell in the house. Even today, many in the community still use charred pyre wood to fuel their makeshift stoves on which food is prepared.

Using the wood Aakash brought home, his mother made the rotis. Even when she was pregnant with his younger sister, she laboured before the firewood. When there was not enough food in the house, she would forgo her share to her husband. To satiate her hunger, she would break a clay cup into tiny pieces, crush it into a powder, mix it with water, swivel it around in her mouth and spit it out.

'Most of us did it just for the swaad, the taste,' Dolly explains later.

Many pregnant women in the Dom community have a calcium deficiency. Occasionally, they eat chalk, clay or granular sand. 'If we eat betel leaves, we don't feel like eating much. It kills our hunger for some time. Like that, when we are expecting, we eat a bit of mitti, clay. There is no harm. When I was pregnant, I ate it too,' says Dolly.

Aakash stabs at the pyre once again. The flames leap up, forming an eddy of smoke. The sun is high; the gold-flecked Ganges gleams. Paper kites flit across the cerulean sky. Boats, plumped up by pilgrims and tourists, move slowly across the water. Thick columns of unused pyre wood, easily 7–10 feet high, stand as gatekeepers to the solemn ground. Wood labourers stack the logs one over the other with acquired efficiency as though building larger-than-life Jenga towers.

Men here are a constant, watchful presence. A tea-stall owner listens to the radio while brewing a pot of milky ginger tea. Swaying from side to side, labourers carry heavy logs on their backs, warning people to move out of their path with rhythmic staccato alerts: '*Aye! Side ho*! Give way!' Priests offer spiritual advice to grief-stricken families. Street barbers walk about with portable kits, setting up makeshift salons anywhere. One of them runs his blade across the lathered chin of a client. Onlookers squat on the stone steps nearby, taking slow drags from their beedis. A few men stand solemnly with their hands clasped behind their backs, watching the funeral pyres in the distance. Young men, about seventeen or eighteen years old, stroll in search of foreign tourists: 'Boat? Show you around ghats if you like?' one offers. Most of these men can converse in broken English—a valuable skill picked up on the job as tourist guides.

Much of Manikarnika Ghat is covered in swathes of ash and small mounds of trash. If you walk across the cremation ground, you will notice plastic bags strewn about, crumpled packets of beedis, broken bottles, trampled marigolds, the odd lone slipper, shards of broken glass, nails and splintered bamboo remains. Flies swarm everywhere. Brindle stray dogs scamper, nosing their way through the debris. Crows and cows give each other company. Every ten minutes or so, you will hear a group of four or five men chanting, '*Ram naam satya hai*'—God's name is the truth—as they deliver corpses on bamboo stretchers. Temple bells peal in the background; axes tirelessly cut through the firewood.

In the land of the dead, there is life all around.

A few metres away a corpse is being readied for its last rites. Two men peel away a dazzling red cloth that covers the body. Each corpse is brought wrapped in a kafan, a shroud, either saffron or scarlet hued with golden tinsels stitched along the border. When the body is ready to be cremated, the cloth is removed, bundled up and carelessly thrown aside.

A child with matted hair lingers nearby. He does not belong to the mourning party. He stays mostly out of sight, but his eyes remain transfixed on the shroud. Suddenly, when the men are not looking, he lunges towards it, grasps a corner between his forefinger and thumb, and runs off in the other direction, the cloth trailing behind him. The boy is lucky—the men barely notice the disappearance of the tangerine-coloured drape.

'I used to do that when I was a kid,' Aakash says, playfully biting his tongue and breaking into a cackle. When he was nine years old, he was a part of a small group of children who were shroud pickers at the ghat. 'We used to steal shrouds, just like that boy.'

The children would scour piles of abandoned cloth to find good-quality shrouds, which they would later sell to a shopkeeper for a meagre sum of a few rupees a piece. The shopkeeper recycled them by washing, drying and ironing each piece, packing them in cellophane packets, and reselling them to grief-stricken customers.

'I would earn about fifty or sixty rupees in a day,' Aakash says. 'It was nothing, but it was something.

'The first time I visited Manikarnika Ghat, I was scared out of my wits,' he laughs embarrassedly. 'There were too many dead bodies and I was so young. Later, once I began working here, I immediately realized this was the only place where I could make a living. It wasn't possible to find work elsewhere because of my caste. Then, what did I have to be scared of? Dead bodies meant money. If I was scared, I couldn't earn. So, I just had to decide not to be fearful any more.'

Aakash began taking late-night shifts, which some of the other boys did not. 'I was working at 1 a.m. or 2 a.m. even, and I worked non-stop. Before I knew it, the fear disappeared from my body completely,' he says.

By the time Aakash was ten, he had earned the reputation of being a bully. He was clever, tactful, quick and competitive. In the words of his friends, he was 'a troublemaker', 'a naughty boy'—loud, rebellious and easily provoked. There were times when, in order to make a quick buck, Aakash would try to steal the shrouds that his friends had painstakingly collected. The children would break into fights, flinging abuse, threats and spittle everywhere. Shirts were torn and noses were bloodied. At times, the brawls seemed engineered—perhaps a channel for the boys to vent their frustrations. As one of them put it, working at the cremation ground was a 'majboori', necessity. 'Unless we steal the shrouds, we won't get any money. And if there is no money, how will our households run?'

Stealing shrouds is illegal. If Aakash and his friends weren't quick on their feet, they were caught by men from the mourning parties, who would grab them by their collars and slap them around. Sometimes, out of spite, Dom men who felt that the children were bothering their clients would pick up the pile of shrouds amassed by the kids and throw them in the fire. This never deterred the children, though. Within minutes they were back, combing through the litter for the elusive tangerine cloth.

'Having grown up doing what we did, how could we possibly be afraid of death?' asks Aakash.

'No other city on earth is as famous for death as is Banaras,' writes scholar Diana L. Eck. Manikarnika Ghat is often called 'Maha Shamshan'—the Great Cremation Ground. Eck describes it as 'the sanctuary of death, with its ceaselessly smoking cremation pyres'.[2]

From where the Ganges curves northwards, Banaras rises as a city with its striking stone minarets and temples. Its feet are firmly anchored in the river, chiselled into the enduring ghats: formidable steps of stone, built centuries ago as sacred bathing sites situated on the western riverfront. Today, they are weathered, discoloured and chipped, yet every day thousands of pilgrims continue to pour in from different corners of the world to visit the ghats and bathe in the Ganges.

The city's interiors are dense with movement. Locals will tell you in jest: 'Subah-e-Banaras, shaam-e-Banaras, jab dekho tab jam Banaras. Morning in Banaras, evening in Banaras, at all times there's a traffic jam in Banaras.' Low-rise buildings with their run-down facades line either side of the busy roads. Hole-in-the-wall eating joints sell oil-soaked fritters and chaat next to garment shops where blonde-haired, white-bodied mannequins in sequined, light-catching ethnic attire are on display. Shoppers, mostly Indian women, jaywalk excitedly, undaunted by the threatening noose of untamed traffic. Hawkers on the streets sell everything from colourful toddler caps to faux flowers. Tailors sit idle with measuring tapes draped around their necks. Government-approved bhang shops thrive next to sweet shops flaunting rows of local desserts inside brightly lit, glass-panelled counters.[3] Striking billboards praise politicians, while posters slapped onto the public walls state: 'I Love Banaras'. Autos blare Bhojpuri music as they go by. Motorcycles, bicycles and man-drawn rickshaws cross-weave. Confusion and congestion reign.

Banaras, where religion and modernity vie for supremacy, is considered one of the holiest cities in India. It is also where Lord Shiva is believed to reside. Some say that the city is perched on Shiva's trident, and that the crescent shape of the river is, in fact, the luminous moon that bejewels the god's wild, matted hair. One of Shiva's revered Jyotirlingas is protected within the inner sanctum of the city's Kashi Vishwanath temple.[4] It is one of the more famous lingas in the country. Shiva's presence, therefore, is believed to be all-encompassing in the city.

The city itself is over 3,000 years old. Mark Twain famously pronounced it 'older than history, older than tradition, older even than legend, and looks twice as old as all of them put together!'[5] A Scottish clergyman named Norman Macleod, who visited Banaras in the late 1800s, marvelled at the city's celebrated reputation. 'Benaras is to the Hindoos what Mecca is to the Mohammedans, and what Jerusalem was to the Jews of old. It is the "holy" city of

Hindostan.'[6] Fascinated by Banaras, Macleod described the ghats as being 'alive with devotees',[7] and confessed to being 'amused by this antique drama—so strange, so un-European, so old-world'.[8]

The 'drama' continues to this day, particularly at the burning ghats. Countless Hindu families prefer to have their loved ones cremated at either of the city's cremation sites—Manikarnika Ghat or Harishchandra Ghat. Corpses from wealthy households are flown across thousands of kilometres so that their last rites can be performed in the holy city. Not just air, the deceased travel by cabs, trains and buses as well. In fact, in the 1980s, anthropologist Jonathan Parry noted that thriving transport services like the 'Last Rites Mail', 'Heaven Express' and the 'more prosaically named "Corpse Waggon"' delivered the dead to Banaras.[9]

It is at Manikarnika Ghat, the locals say, that Shiva whispers the taraka mantra, the ferryboat mantra, into the ears of the dead, before escorting their souls to heaven.[10]

'Death, in most places, is feared,' a local once remarked as I sat upon the steps of Manikarnika Ghat with my notebook. 'Here, it is celebrated.'

And it is here that moksha or mukti—the liberation of one's soul from the endless cycle of death and rebirth—can truly be attained.

3

The Monolith of Caste

BANARAS IS A city where caste still maintains a stronghold. Locals will tell you that this age-old stratification, which defines one's place in Hindu society according to their family's socio-religious identity, is waning. However, as things slowly unfurl around you in the city, you will begin to feel, deeply, the caste system's clawing presence. It is in the subtleties of a gesture or a nod, in the incessant probing into one's ancestral past. It is so unapologetically normalized that unless you are an outsider, it doesn't tug at your conscience. Headmasters at local schools, who consider themselves liberal-minded, have unflinchingly asked about my caste during my work visits. Often, upon receiving a non-committal response, they have requested that I spell out my full name. In India, while each caste is distinguished by its hereditary occupation, historically, surnames have been used as caste identifiers.

Once, I invited a few Dom children to my guest house to share a meal. The manager, a local who recognized the children from their neighbourhood, pulled me aside and asked if, instead of using their ceramic crockery, food could be served to the children in pattals—plates made with dried leaves—which would be thrown away after.

Hindu society is divided on the basis of the caste system.[1] Perched at the top of this caste pyramid are Brahmins: priests and scholars. Below them is the warrior caste, Kshatriyas. The third, Vaishyas, are traders and farmers, and on the lowest rung of the pyramidal order are Shudras: servants or labourers. As a conceited local priest at a Hanuman temple once explained, 'In the granthas, the four varnas have been stated thus: the Brahmin protects religion, Kshatriya protects the Brahmin, Vaishya arranges food for the Brahmin and Shudra cleans after the Brahmin,' stressing on the Brahmin's apex stature.

The Ati-shudras or Avarnas are considered castaways—'outcastes'. They are designated so low that they are placed outside the caste system.[2] In many parts of the country, Avarnas continue to be thought of as 'downtrodden', 'unworthy', 'polluted'—'untouchables'.

For as long as one can remember, dominant castes have denied the 'outcastes' their right to land and water (including the use of public wells), and entry into shared public spaces, like temples. They have controlled their access to food and compelled them to live in separate settlements.[3] This tyranny of oppression and humiliation is sanctioned in Hindu society. Highly offensive words such as 'Bhangi', 'Chamar' and 'Chandal' were and are still used as slurs to identify and address those who belong to 'lower castes' in certain parts of the country.[4]

These 'outcastes' are more commonly known today as Dalits. According to the 2011 Census of India, they form 16.6 per cent of the country's population.[5] In Sanskrit, the word 'Dalit' literally translates to those who are 'broken' or 'scattered'. 'The term "dalit" was popularized by the Dalit Panthers,' write K. Satyanarayana and Susie Tharu in *The Exercise of Freedom: An Introduction to Dalit Writing* (2013). 'Today, it is the most favoured mode of referring to this group ... It is a name that untouchables have given themselves.'[6]

For generations, Dalits have experienced not only physical abuse, but psychological trauma as well. In nineteenth-century Kerala, for instance, they had to adhere to a lexicon different from that of the rest. While conversing in Malayalam, a Dalit could not say 'I'; instead, they had to refer to themselves as '"adiyan" (your slave) or "adiyangal" (one who lies at your feet),' writes Vinil Baby Paul, a department member at the Centre for Historical Studies, Jawaharlal Nehru University. 'Their house was called "chala" (small dirty hut). They spoke of their children as "kitanagal" (calves),' he continues.[7]

Dalits were believed to be so 'impure' that even sincere acts of bravery and kindness were deeply criticized. Social reformer and economist, Dr B.R. Ambedkar meticulously made a note of such incidents. In a collection of his writings and speeches (published posthumously in 1989), he draws attention to *Bombay Samachar's* December 1936 issue, which reported an incident where a child had unwittingly fallen into a well in a village in Calicut (now Kozhikode). Despite the desperate plea of the mother, no one stepped up to rescue the child until a passer-by jumped into the well and pulled the child to safety. 'Later, when the people asked the benefactor who he was, he said, he was an Untouchable.

Thereupon instead of being thankful [sic], the man was fully abused and assaulted as he had polluted the well,' the report says.[8]

In March 1927, to assert their Dalit identity, Ambedkar rallied over 10,000 supporters to join him in a seminal movement in Mahad, Maharashtra. The non-violent procession marched to the Chavdar water tank, where Ambedkar encouraged everyone to drink from it. Dalits were prohibited from even being in the vicinity of the tank, let alone using the water. This pivotal moment in Indian history came to be known as the Mahad Satyagraha or the Chavdar Tale Satyagraha.

Of course, 'upper-caste' Hindus considered this act sacrilegious and were deeply offended. Deeming the tank 'polluted' and its water unfit for consumption, a puja ceremony was performed by Brahmin men to 'purify' the reservoir. Cow dung and cow urine along with milk, butter and curd were used to 'sanitize' the tank.[9]

Almost a century later, the situation has still not changed. On 18 November 2022, 'upper-caste' individuals cleaned a water tank with cow urine in a village in Karnataka after a Dalit woman drank water from it.[10] In Rajasthan's Jalore district, a nine-year-old Dalit boy was allegedly thrashed by his 'upper-caste' schoolteacher Chail Singh for mistakenly drinking water from an earthen pot that belonged to Singh. The boy, Indra Meghwal, succumbed to his injuries on 13 August 2022, two days before the country celebrated seventy-five years of Independence.[11]

Ambedkar could not have put it more succinctly when he told Gandhi in 1931:

You say I have got a homeland, but still I repeat that I am without it. How can I call this land my own homeland and this religion my own, wherein we are treated worse than cats and dogs, wherein we cannot get water to drink? No self-respecting Untouchable worth the name will be proud of this land.[12]

At the Bombay Presidency Mahar Conference held on 31 May 1936, Ambedkar described the many atrocities that Dalits were subjected to. If they wore 'superior-quality' clothes or walked in shoes, they were beaten. If they refused to discard dead animals, they were thrashed. If they bought land for cultivation, their houses were set on fire.[13]

In his undelivered speech, *Annihilation of Caste* (15 May 1936),[14] Ambedkar wrote: 'There cannot be a more degrading system of social organisation … It is the system which deadens, paralyses, and cripples the people, from helpful activity.'[15]

Over eight decades have passed since. Although untouchability was outlawed in 1950 due to the relentless efforts of Ambedkar (one of the key architects of the Indian Constitution), Dalits continue to be the victims of caste-based crimes. The enactment of the Scheduled Castes and Scheduled Tribes (Prevention of Atrocities) Act, 1989, made offences involving (but not limited to) 'forcibly tonsuring of head', 'removing clothes' and parading them naked, dumping 'excreta, sewage or carcasses' on their property or making them wear garlands of footwear—illegal and punishable.[16] The atrocities, however, have not ebbed.[17] In parts of the country, it is still believed that if an 'untouchable's' shadow falls on a member of the 'upper caste', the latter must bathe immediately.

———•——

The Doms carry with them an enduring sense of inferiority—one that is yoked to the persisting acts of oppression by 'upper-caste'

Hindus. It is so deeply entrenched and remains so subliminal that it has an overpowering hold over their lives.

The first time I visited a Dom home, the elders placed their palms together in a gesture of salutation and tucked their shoulders inwards to make their bodies smaller, so that they did not take up too much space in my presence. They sat at a distance, squatting on the floor, while insisting that I take the plastic chair, borrowed especially for me from a neighbour who was financially better off. It took several minutes to convince them that I was perfectly comfortable sitting on the ground beside them.

One of the elders told me that during his childhood, he had to call out to the people on the streets, requesting them to move out of the way: '"*Bhaiya hatt ja, hum aawat hai.* Brother, please move, I am coming," we would say. Only then could we walk there. If our shadow fell on them, we would be beaten up, shouted at.'

'Even today,' Dolly tells me afterwards, when I ask her about this, 'if we walk in the same lane as an upper-caste Hindu, chances are that he will abuse us. And if we touch them by mistake, they criticize and threaten us.'

'Have you ever answered back?' I ask.

'Of course not,' she replies, mildly affronted. 'For generations, our elders haven't said anything. What will we say now? We just bow our heads and carry on walking in silence.'

She continues, 'There is a certain shop owner who refuses to touch us. If we buy anything from his shop, he demands that we keep the money on the table and step back. He doesn't want to risk our fingers accidentally touching him. If he has to return some change, he'll tell us to cup our hands so that he can drop the money into our palms.'

Her voice rises as she says defiantly, 'I've stopped buying things from him now.'

While the elders have suffered in silence for many years, Dolly's own protests are non-existent. It is the generation after hers, though, that is more outspoken and willing to make its voice heard. It is in their eyes that you can see the city's caste monoliths slowly crumbling. They have ambitions that steer them off the path that has been set for them. They are driven, eager to somehow become more than what society dictates.

4

Modern Love

IN THE MORNINGS, before stepping out of his home, Lakshaya Chaudhary scoops a generous amount of hair gel and smears it into his hair. He takes his tousled hair, mottled with burgundy, gently between his fingers, pulls it towards the ceiling, and then sideways. Twice a day, he applies cream on his face and then lightly pats it with powder. He gazes into the mirror, tilts his head slightly and lifts his square jaw to look into his eyes: dark orbs brimming with confidence. A roaring silver-plated lion's head attached to a thick silver band sits on the knuckle of his left forefinger, and from his right wrist dangles a gold-lacquered bracelet: material markers of wealth. A thin silvery wire, almost invisible to the eye, has been passed through his earlobe to pass off as an earring. Tattooed, and five-feet-four-inches tall, Lakshaya struts about in thigh-hugging jeans and T-shirts that often encourage adventurism. Today, on a hot summer day in 2019, his T-shirt instructs in English, 'Make more mistakes'.

When Lakshaya was born twenty-five years ago, his mother was relieved. His dewy, pale skin was lighter than the dark complexions of the men in their community. In a country that overwhelmingly equates fair skin with good looks, Lakshaya's colouring is an asset. It has led him to believe that he will always have an edge over others from his community.

Lakshaya grew up watching his older brother work hard as a corpse burner. His childhood memories are singed with experiences of stealing shrouds, plunging into fisticuffs to defend his pile, sleeping at the cremation ground among corpses waiting to be lit and watching his mother being incapacitated by a grave illness. She survived, but hospital bills skinned his father's savings to the bone, leaving them poorer than ever.

By the time Lakshaya was an adolescent, he had decided that he would live a life different from the Doms. He wanted to do things the elders in his community had never dreamt of. The possibility of marrying a woman of his choice irrespective of her background was one of them.

———————

In Banaras, the Doms can be easily recognized by their surname: Chaudhary. The community marries its own, compelled to keep in line with the diktats of the Hindu social order. The caste system fiercely promotes and protects endogamy. India has a fevered history of unchecked violence—including lynchings and honour killings—against many of those who have dared to transgress. For generations, therefore, caste hierarchy has been maintained by not only practising untouchability, but also policing exogamy. Although it is legal for an individual to marry outside their caste in India, in many parts of the country it is still considered impermissible. In fact, it has been reported that only 5 per cent of marriages are inter-caste.[1]

Haresh Kumar Solanki, a Dalit, had married Urmila Jhala, a Rajput (Kshatriya) in early 2019. The marriage was opposed by Jhala's family. In July 2019, Solanki was hacked to death by his wife's family members near his in-laws' home in Varmor village, Gujarat. Jhala was pregnant at the time.[2]

In another incident, a Jat woman's brothers gunned down her Dalit husband and his family at their home in Haryana.[3] The woman, who was nine months pregnant, was also shot in her belly and left to die. She was rushed to the hospital, where miraculously she gave birth to a baby boy and survived. When she was discharged from the hospital, she quietly returned to her parents' home and dropped charges against her brothers.[4]

For the past seven years, Lakshaya has been in a serious relationship. 'Her name is Komal Pandey,' he says politely, showing me his girlfriend's photograph on his phone while running his other hand through his metallic, waxy hair. 'She's a Brahmin.' When I ask him whether he is anxious about a potential backlash from Komal's family, he says, 'Times are changing. I hope our story will be different.'

———

Lakshaya believes that his childhood memories are of little value. There is a keenness in him to rearrange his life around the present rather than bury his head in the past.

He shrugs. 'What is there to tell?

When he was seven years old, his father pushed his small body out through the doorway and told him to go work at the ghats.

The house was drowning in a financial crisis; it was all hands on deck. Lakshaya has been in survival mode ever since.

At Manikarnika Ghat, he befriended other boys, like Aakash, who picked shrouds wearing faded shorts and half-buttoned shirts. Profanities galloped on their tongues. Each time a new swear word was learnt, it was used at the end of every sentence with great relish. The heat was crippling and the humidity left their scalps prickly.

The children learnt the value of money very early on. 'Sometimes, I burned corpses too, just to make some extra cash,' Lakshaya says. 'Initially, it all felt good. Suddenly, I was earning and it helped pass the time.' Lakshaya worked tirelessly, just to hear the clink of the coins in his shorts' pockets at the close of the day. 'As I grew older, though, I realized that the job was terrible. We were constantly at the receiving end of abuse and beatings from other men who worked at the ghat.'

Shroud-picking is an acquired skill. Lakshaya and the other children had to be swift on their feet and deft with their fingers. If slow, they were sometimes caught by older men who would try to snatch the shroud, engaging them in a tug of war. The boys' small bodies would betray their sense of strength, and they would hit the ground hard, often scraping their thighs.

Once, Lakshaya watched Aakash, who was ten or eleven at the time, steal a shroud that lay on the ground. Aakash waited patiently, looking for the perfect window to lunge. Suddenly, he leapt towards the shroud, grabbed it and darted in the other direction. His slippers slapped against the ground; his ashen hair rose and fell in sync with his scamper.

A few men began running behind him. One of them yelled, 'Catch him!'

Aakash steered intuitively, jumping over dogs lazing in the sun. The men hastily circled around him. Before he knew it, Aakash had run straight into them. A thick-armed man caught hold of him, pulled him by the collar and pinned him against a brick wall. Then he dragged Aakash to the riverfront, lifted his small body and threatened to throw him into the river.

The boy screamed, 'Arre, arre, don't! Don't you dare!'

Soon, the commotion intensified. People began to gather around them. When the man realized that there were too many eyes on him, he lowered Aakash to the ground. Before walking away, he wagged his fat finger and grunted, 'Don't keep doing this shit, boy, I'm telling you.'

Aakash caught his breath before running off to meet Lakshaya and the other boys, who had watched the events unfold from a distance. A smirk lingered at the side of Aakash's lips. He pulled back his shoulders to broaden his narrow chest. He felt victorious. Lakshaya glanced at Aakash's feet and noticed that they were covered in patchy burns. He must have accidentally burned himself while running too close to a lit pyre. Before Lakshaya could draw his attention, Aakash had already picked up a few stray marigold petals from the ground, squashed them and spread the ochre paste on his wounds.

Getting injured at Manikarnika Ghat is not uncommon. While on the job, the children would accidentally cut their foot on a shard of glass, unknowingly step on a nail, or on hot ash freshly spewed by the surrounding pyres. Since they could not afford to consult doctors, they alleviated the pain with marigold paste; they learnt this on the job. Sometimes, if they were lucky, their mothers would soak pieces of cloth in warm kerosene oil and dab them on their burns.

Aakash placed his hands on his waist and spat on the ground. He had watched the older men at work do so and thought it exhibited manliness. 'So, what now? What's next?' he asked, acting as though nothing had happened. Even if he had been petrified of the man who had nearly thrown him into the water, Aakash did not show it. He wanted everyone to know that he was fearless. Sometimes this fearlessness transformed into arrogance.

'Aakash was a bit of an asshole,' says Lakshaya, sitting cross-legged on the floor of his home. 'When we were young, the other kids and I were all smaller in size, so he would bash us up. The kind of work we did and the filth we worked in, these fights were inevitable.'

Lakshaya pauses a moment to assess the room and then changes the subject. 'Now things have changed. I don't do that kind of work anymore. Never will. Plus, when you have a girlfriend, your expenses rise exponentially. You have to up your game,' he says with a dry laugh.

Initially, Lakshaya struggled to find better-paying employment. One of his first jobs after leaving his shroud-picking life was spotting excited tourists with plump wallets who were waiting to be ferried across the Ganges. One of his friends from the Mallah caste (a community of boatmen) put him on the job.

Every evening, Dashashwamedh Ghat comes alive during the Ganga aarti, a religious performance that is a famous tourist attraction. After attending the aarti, tourists often want to explore the waters at night. Lakshaya recalls the magical experience of the boat pulling away from the dock and sinuously cutting across the river's smooth back. He would row the boat farther and farther away from the bank, until the riverfront, lit by tungsten lamps, became a thick, glittering band of light. Above, the sky was a heavy canopy of darkness. 'We would row from Harishchandra Ghat to Manikarnika Ghat,' he says. 'And my friends and I would tell the tourists about each spot.'

Lakshaya worked with a group of ten to fifteen boys. Each boat had two or three kids assigned to it. At the end of the day, the collected earnings were divided and Lakshaya would pocket Rs 200–300. In 2019, working as a tour guide, he is shin-deep in the business of religious tourism, and is making three, occasionally four, times that amount. Through an established, sinewy network of a-friend-who-knows-a-friend, Lakshaya has worked his way up. He has formed 'settings' with drivers who 'work at hotels in the city's cantonment area'.

He explains, 'They bring the tourists to me, and I take them sightseeing to the auspicious spots in the city. Ganga aarti, the ghats, the temples and so on.' Lakshaya chaperones his clients to the Kashi Vishwanath temple—the city's religious centre for Hindus—where he introduces them to a 'Brahmin' at the temple who assists them with the darshan. During our interaction, Lakshaya used Brahmin interchangeably with 'pundit'—a priest—which underscores how deeply caste is embedded in the religious lexicon.

In a day, he earns about Rs 900–1,200. 'Sometimes, if my clients are generous, they give a big tip. Those are the good days. Those days I can earn almost three to four thousand rupees,' he says.

Lakshaya is saving the money to fund his wedding in the future and eventually open a sari shop.

Although Komal belongs to a dominant caste, her family has struggled financially for years. Komal grew up in Chand Ghat, in the neighbouring Yadav colony; her rented house at the time was not too far from Lakshaya's home. Every now and then, Lakshaya bumped into Komal in the narrow by-lanes. He loved her soft smile, her full lips and her delicate nose. He would watch her as she walked away, his eyes never leaving her.

Komal came from a broken home. Her father beat her mother with clenched fists and the nights were filled with her mother's screams. Komal had no one to turn to. So, when Lakshaya, a sweet-faced boy, beaming with confidence and eagerness mixed in good measure, wished to befriend her, she willingly agreed. She was looking for hope; everything else was immaterial.

In 2013, Komal's father abandoned their family. Her mother, harried by the demands of paying household bills and buying groceries, took on a job as a cook, working around the clock in other people's homes. At that time, Komal, a girl with an ambitious mind, insisted on studying.

'I started working seriously because I wanted to help Komal monetarily,' Lakshaya says. 'I spend most of my money taking care of her, so that she can attend college. Like a husband takes care of his wife, I look after everything. Though we are not married yet, whatever I earn is for her.'

5

The Transgression

LAKSHAYA'S SISTER DOLLY, however, has no husband to take care of her. A deep sense of sadness engulfs her home. Its moss-coloured walls are riddled with pockmarks. Vidhi, her three-year-old daughter, often busies herself scraping off the paint and gingerly licking the wall with the tip of her tongue. From the ceiling hangs a lone bulb with an exposed wire. At night, when the bulb glows, small translucent-winged creatures dance around it, leaving Vidhi mesmerized.

Through a process of push-and-shove, space has been made for almost everything. Aluminium and steel pots are stacked on a long, narrow stone slab attached to the wall. A lumpy mattress rests on a single bed. Beneath it is a large metal trunk, which stores winter clothes, photo albums and other essentials. Summer clothes hang from iron hooks, piled on top of each other. A plastic tray that holds a toothbrush and a wiry tongue cleaner is fixed to the wall. A small ceiling fan whirs at a freakishly high speed. This is its only setting: the regulator is faulty. In a corner of the room hangs a tiny mirror. A thin film of dust has settled over it. When Dolly was still Sekond Lal's wife, she would spend hours before it, admiring her features while she combed her hair. Now she rarely looks at herself.

In 2019, three years after her husband's death, Dolly has aged. Her black eyes have become stony and her cheeks have sunk in. She bundles her long hair in a clumsy lump at her nape. She wears no jewellery, except for a wiry nose ring, a pair of anklets and two blood-red glass bangles. Perhaps, through this state of unkemptness, she tries to deflect the prying eyes of men. As a young widow, she is vulnerable.

Ten days after Sekond Lal died, Dolly's in-laws told her they could no longer support her. 'You are of no value to us,' they said. 'Fend for yourself and live on your own.' Dolly was too shaken, too weak to question her mother-in-law, who instructed her to pack her belongings and leave. She quietly returned to her parents' home, where her father gave her a small room on the ground floor despite the protests of her brother Ajay, who lived in a room above hers.

Ajay, though younger than her, is the eldest of the boys. He didn't want to slice off a portion of his meagre earnings to feed half a dozen extra bellies, even if they were his own blood. He had a wife and children of his own to look after.

Lakshaya, Dolly's younger brother, was more accommodating. However, he refused to be seen with her beyond the boundary of Chand Ghat. 'I have an image to maintain,' he tells me later.

Lakshaya, who was already working as a guide at the time, wanted to be seen in public by his clientele as a high-class man. He did not want to be associated with anyone or anything that might remotely remind people of his Dom background.

Dolly unconsciously grinds her jagged teeth, rimmed crimson from excessive paan-chewing. 'At that time, there was no one I could really depend on, except my parents, who were already old,' she says.

In order to allow Dolly to live comfortably with her children, her parents packed their bags and moved 150 kilometres away to another house. Barely able to make ends meet, however, Dolly was forced to part with three of her children. She sent one to live with her aunt and packed off two to live with her parents. The eldest, a son, and the youngest, Vidhi, remained with her.

Like all the girls in the community, Dolly was raised to believe she would always be taken care of. As a child, her father had looked after her expenses. Her parents never encouraged her to study, nor did she feel the need to. She was brought up to believe that her husband would take care of her once she was married. When she became a widow, Dolly realized she needed to earn. She disliked the idea of being dependent on her brother Ajay.

'But if I got a job, people in the community would ridicule him, saying that he couldn't take care of me,' she explains.

Still, Dolly knocked on the doors of 'upper-caste' homes, asking whether they had cooking and cleaning jobs. Whenever she identified her neighbourhood or told them her surname, the individuals would take a step back. No one was comfortable giving her work, except that of scrubbing toilets.

'I am, after all, a "low-born",' she says, echoing a belief that has been seared into her since childhood.

To be able to feed her children comfortably, Dolly needed to earn at least Rs 4,000 a month. The 'latrine job', as she called it, would earn her a meagre sum of Rs 550.

In India, a majority of safai karamcharis, manual scavengers, are Dalits. Among them, it is primarily the women and girls who are engaged to clean latrines, drains and toilet pits, and rid dominant-caste homes of faecal sludge and other waste.[1]

'We are the Chaudharys of Manikarnika Ghat,' Dolly's neighbour Mirchi tells me on another day, while we are sitting in her home, drinking tea from small plastic cups.

Mirchi is a thirty-six-year-old woman with almond eyes, long dark hair and a pepper tongue. 'People still consider us "untouchables". If we touch people like this'—she pokes my knee with her finger—'they immediately run off to take a bath. It's because of our caste that almost nobody gives us a job.'

A working woman is an anomaly in Chand Ghat. That a woman can earn a living and be self-reliant is an alien concept for the community. 'It's just not in our tradition. It's unacceptable,' Mirchi informs me. '*Log galat nazar se dekhtein hain.* People look at you in the wrong way.' If a woman leaves the house on her own, the community wonders if there are any strange men in her place of work or if she is going to meet someone secretly. 'If a woman goes out to earn money, her husband's masculinity is questioned,' she continues. 'The community ridicules him, saying that he is incompetent. In some instances, the husband might do nothing, just eat and drink all day, and live off his wife. Or he might say, "Okay, you're earning. Clearly you don't need me. So, earn and live by yourself." Basically, their ego gets hurt.'

When women are married, their husband's name is inked on their right forearm. 'Underneath his name, a small symbol of the sun is drawn.' Mirchi stretches out both her forearms over her lap for me to inspect. 'On our left arm, a tiny crescent moon is tattooed to signify that we are married. Even our chin is tattooed with a dot. All these are the markers of a married woman.' Of course, the men who are married don't have to get anything done. There are no moon or sun symbols on their arms or dots on their chins. 'They are free to do what they like,' she says.

If a woman steps outside the boundaries of Chand Ghat for any personal work, unchaperoned by a male family member, gossip takes flight. Whispers circle like birds of prey. 'She is thought to be a "randi", a whore.' Mirchi settles the pallu of her sari over her head. 'That's the way we talk in our community.' People wonder why a woman must venture out of the house alone. Married women walking about in public without a veil covering their faces are frowned upon.

The women, unfortunately have no means to defend themselves. 'There is not a single girl who has studied beyond the eighth standard. Not one,' Mirchi informs me. Since government schools offer free education to children till the eighth standard,[2] along with planned mid-day meals, most parents allow their daughters to study. But permission comes with an early expiry date. Once a girl turns fourteen, her movement is curtailed, and she is withdrawn from school. Within the Dom community, the paucity of funds, household responsibilities and the pressure to marry at an early age, often thwart many girls' basic right to education.

'In our community, when a girl turns fourteen, she starts to become a burden on the parents. They feel it's their responsibility to get her married off as soon as possible,' Mirchi says, playing with her anklet. 'Nobody cares if the girl wants to study. People here think that a girl should quickly wrap up her studies and get married. If she is educated, they believe she will fall in love with any man and run off. Nobody wants that. That will ruin her honour and ours.'

Some girls are emotionally blackmailed by their parents. 'My father used to ask me to stay at home with my mother because: "Who will look after her and help her with the daily chores?"' Mirchi recalls. 'Today, I have no desire to study. I was never interested in studying even at a very young age. I don't even want to work outside my home,' she admits.

Despite difficulties, Dolly did manage to pick up a few cleaning jobs that did not involve scrubbing toilets. Leaving her children in the care of her reluctant sister-in-law for hours, however, soon proved to be a challenge. It led to incessant nagging and, subsequently, time-consuming arguments. Fed up, Dolly decided to take matters into her own hands: she would open her own shop. Dolly quietly collected her gold nose ring, silver anklets and bangles in a pouch and sold them in the market for Rs 5,000.

'I felt naked that day,' she recalls.

She saved some money, kept some aside to buy vegetables for the night's meal and with the rest bought a few products to sell.

Finally, on a cold day in January 2019, Dolly opened her shop in her parental home. Since her home was not large enough to accommodate a full-fledged outfit, she made do with a makeshift one, which could be easily dismantled at any time. It was pitched right by the door. A scarlet clothesline was fastened to nails on the walls on either side and small packets of biscuits, chips and bhujiya, along with shampoo sachets, were hung on it neatly. The clothesline sagged slightly under their weight. A somewhat broken cardboard carton containing Frooti tetra packs, packets of beedis and more eatables was placed right below it.

Hers is the first shop to be owned by a woman in the community. Dolly did not realize it at the time, but it had the potential to disrupt the patriarchal status quo. Tradition dictates that women cannot earn. Within the Dom community, only men are allowed to make a living; women are considered 'too naïve', incapable of exercising financial autonomy. As long as Dolly was doing minor, part-time cleaning jobs, the community was fine with it; she was a widow and a single mother, after all. Owning a business, however, was a different ball game altogether.

Dolly's 'transgression' birthed sharp-edged chatter. Though neighbours bought products from her shop because it was convenient, disgruntled whispers began to hint at overall community displeasure.

One afternoon, Dolly left her children with her sister-in-law and stepped out to buy supplies. When she returned home, an uncomfortable, cloying smell hung in the air. Someone had flung fistfuls of faeces into her home through the iron-grilled window. Cow dung, still warm, was splattered everywhere.

Dolly bit her tongue to swallow her scream. She stopped herself from stepping outside to make a noise. As a young widow, Dolly could not afford to create a scene in front of the entire community. Battles had to be picked. She quietly squatted on the floor and scooped and swept out the muck before washing it off with a bucket of cold water.

6

Fleeing the 'Crabs'

THE FIRST DAY 24-year-old Bhola Chaudhary walks into his university in Ludhiana, Punjab, in 2018, he feels a shift in the trajectory of his life. Unfamiliar territories induce a sense of anxiety and discomfort in most people. In such situations, Bhola thrives.

Bhola is broad-shouldered and stands about five-feet-four-inches tall. He has thick lips, black hair with a side-parting and a neatly trimmed line of fuzz above his upper lip.

No one in the university knows him. No one knows the name of his neighbourhood, or that he has spent his childhood waking up engulfed in smoke, watching his mother roast aubergines on the firewood, while the rice water hissed and frothed over. No one knows that the floor he slept on burned under him every summer night, or that he had to elbow his siblings for space, or that the stench of their sweat lacing the air had often helped him drift off to sleep.

His classmates would never know, as he has known, the sting of being shooed away from a public temple by a bespectacled, silver-bearded priest raining abuses on him—*rat-a-tat-tat*— prayer beads swaying from his wrist as he mouthed each insult.[1] Or how he braced himself every time dominant-caste passers-by on the streets frowned and growled: 'Oi, Domva! Move it!'—as though his entire bloodline were a despicable slur.

His classmates would never know—and he would never tell them.

So far, Bhola is the only individual in his community who has been able to leave Banaras to study at a private university.

———

For the Doms, private education is but a distant dream. For those who can somehow rise above the debilitating poverty that cripples the community, access to quality learning is almost non-existent. Their only options then are the local Hindi- and English-medium government schools, where the standard of education is subpar at best.

In 2016 and 2017, I visited a few government schools that neighboured Chand Ghat. They were all in a disappointing state: dilapidated windows, chipped paint, textbooks piled on corner desks gathering dust. One of the classrooms I entered had a solitary tube light that strained to brighten the room. The children squinted to read.

A schoolgirl was assigned to show me around. 'It has been over a week but no one has attended to the tube light,' she informed me shyly, once we were out of her teacher's earshot. She also said that the school faced frequent power cuts and that the teachers were rarely interested in teaching. The girl fiddled with the coarse red ribbon woven into her braid as we climbed to the second floor of the building. The staircase had no railing, nor was it well-lit. I had to use the torch from my cell phone to carefully ascend. Children hurtling down the stairway could easily fall or injure themselves.

Schools such as this one, demotivate many students from attending. Although several children from the Dom community are enrolled here, they are but names on the register; most of the time they do not attend. Their parents prefer that they work at the ghats instead and earn money to contribute towards the household finances.

⸻

As a child, Bhola hated Chand Ghat. He nurtured simple dreams: to attend school and leave Chand Ghat for good. He would ask his mother to pack him off to faraway lands full of magic and mystery. He was a ship ready to sail, but was repeatedly told that his caste would keep him moored.

'This is where you are born and this is where you will die,' his uncles would tell him each time he expressed a desire to run away. The fish-lipped bullies and naysayers cackled at his ambitions: 'You are a Dom, boy, and will always be one.'

In the years to come, Bhola would liken his community to crabs teeming in a deep pot—each desperate to climb out, but the moment one managed to make some headway, the others would aggressively tug it back down with their claws. 'They would tell me: "We will let you take one step ahead and then pull you two steps back,"' Bhola recalls.

Prevailing over one's circumstances, then, came down to one's inner zeal. Bhola refused to have a plan B. He would work hard to nurture a life different from the one he was living. His story would be the fresh ink on the palimpsest of his family's history.

———

So, when Bhola is finally in Ludhiana, miles away from Banaras, he decides to be anyone but a Dom. He will start afresh. It will be for him a second birth.

It is in Ludhiana that he develops and finesses the art of storytelling: plucking himself out of his reality and planting himself in an invented narrative of his choosing. He uses his imagination to mould a past he never had. When his classmates ask about his family, Bhola says he has two brothers and one sister. In reality, he has four brothers and four sisters; they are nine siblings in all. When they ask what his eldest brother does for a living, Bhola says that Mohan owns a successful sari business in Banaras. In reality, his brother—like his father, his grandfather, his great-grandfather and the generations before them—tames glowing pyres under the bright silver moon, and watches the ruby-red flames swallow bones whole and spit out ash.

'To protect one lie, I have to follow it up with fifty others,' Bhola tells me in 2019, his expressive eyes alert under his heavy brows. 'I have to make a lot of things up.' At his university, his classmates inquire about his family, his surname, his roots. 'They ask if Chaudharys are Yadavs. I say, "Yes." Whatever they assume, I agree with them. I never correct them,' he says.

There are times when Bhola twists facts or invents stories about who the Chaudharys were back in the day. 'I tell my classmates that the rajas referred to themselves as "Chaudhrana" and that's why the wealthy call themselves Chaudharys today.'

Bhola recounts how he had stepped out one evening with a classmate to have crisp, sweet jalebis from a street-side vendor. His classmate bumped into an acquaintance and introduced Bhola as a 'pundit' (a Brahmin). Bhola smiled and then pushed an entire jalebi into his mouth. 'I remember laughing inside,' he says. He was consumed by a sense of accomplishment. Bhola had been able to pass off as a dominant-caste individual. 'Why would I correct him? What would I gain from it? I just nodded and kept quiet.'

In India, though Chaudhary is spelt only one way in Hindi (in Devanagari script), it is written in different ways in English— Chaudhari, Chaudhary, Chowdhury, Chaudri and Chowdury are some of the many variations, permutations and combinations. Historically, 'Chaudhary' was an honorific title given to the heads of land-owning communities in India. It loosely translates to 'holder of four', where the number indicates the scale of the estate. While the title is not exclusively associated with a specific community, it was earlier reserved for the dominant castes. However, one of the Doms told me that since Chaudhary is understood as 'headman', and the Doms command ownership of the cremation grounds in Banaras, they use 'Chaudhary' as their surname.

None of his classmates at the university challenge Bhola about his identity or background. He has learnt English and polished it to the best of his abilities, consciously forming the words before rolling them off his tongue. He dresses sharply with fastidious care: his clothes are always fresh and crease-free, his shirt is neatly tucked into his pants and his shoes are buffed. His moustache is painstakingly contoured, and his hair is well-greased, combed and parted to the side. He daubs face cream on his cheeks during winter, applies rose water in the summer and sculpts his arms using weights. In his shirt's breast pocket, Bhola carries a small jar of Vaseline. Every time his lips feel dry, he dabs a bit of the gel. Chapped lips indicate poor hygiene and he frowns upon those who pull at the skin of their lips with their teeth. The uneven crevices are not pleasing to the eye. For his hostel room, Bhola has even invested in products beyond his budget, such as an electric iron and a tea kettle.

Appearances, which he has built with artful care, have to be kept up.

Speaking English is important to him. People naturally assume that one belongs to a 'higher caste', he believes, if they are fluent in the language. At college, sometimes when Bhola speaks too quickly, he drops conjunctions. His friends, who have a better grasp of the language, often chuckle and tell him that his mouth has a tendency of stifling words before they are even born. Such insensitive comments never blight Bhola's desire to learn. Instead, he asks them for the correct way of speaking. Then he repeats it many times in his head, careful never to forget.

The pressure to behave as though he belongs to the middle-class universe, however, is immense. '*Hamesha bachh ke chalna padta hai, bahut bachh ke.* I always have to be careful around people, very careful,' he admits. 'I don't let anyone know what or who I am. I don't let them know that I am a Dom, that my worth is nothing.'

———

Bhola carries with him a palpable desire to blend in—to be one with others, to be invisible, to not stand out. Once, when he was still in school, he and I had visited a restaurant in Banaras for dinner. I watched him make thin, unsteady incisions into a paratha with a knife, then stab the piece with a fork and put it in his mouth. I wondered why he had not torn it with his hands and eaten it the way it is traditionally eaten.

He told me that the diners at the restaurant were all privy to a shared knowledge of how to perform in public spheres— skills that individuals born into a certain caste and class, would organically pick up in their childhood. His parents, on the other hand, had never eaten at a restaurant. Bhola had to learn everything on his own. 'You know, how to sit, speak, drink and eat in public spaces,' he explained.

Over the years, by watching YouTube videos and observing others around him, he has learnt what he considers 'middle-class mannerisms'. Now, in college, Bhola has picked up the correct angle at which a fork is supposed to be held and has studied the carefulness with which soup was scooped out of a bowl with a spoon.

—•—

Bhola is not ashamed of his roots or his family, but he fears the unforgiving repercussions that may arise from telling anyone his truth. If they know, he will probably be humiliated and ostracized. His perfect grades will be undermined and credited to the reservation quota. In one fell swoop, his accomplishments will be negated and he will be labelled 'undeserving'.

It is why Bhola fiercely guards his past and lives in the present. Some classmates have been suspicious of him. 'I have a few friends here who've become close over time,' he says. 'They wonder if I really am who I present myself to be. They sense that I am hiding something, that I am someone else. In fact, a friend once asked me, "Bhola, what is it? Why are you so secretive?" I laughed it off by saying, "Everything is okay, don't you worry."'

Bhola's necessity for caution, however, is not rooted in imagination. Comb through newspaper archives and Dalit literature and you'll mine countless stories of Dalit students who have been tortured, humiliated and/or abused. In his memoir, *Akkarmashi* or *The Outcaste* (1991), Sharankumar Limbale, who grew up in the 1960s, describes how, once a week, his teacher tasked a young Limbale with coating the school-cum-temple walls and floors with cow-dung paste.[2] During the classes, the Mahar students were made to sit at the back, behind the dominant-caste students, at the temple's entrance.[3] Often, Limbale was the subject of ridicule when his 'upper-caste' classmates flung stones at him and shouted, 'Mahar!'[4]

In *Joothan* (1997), celebrated author Omprakash Valmiki, who also grew up in the 1960s, relays painful memories of going to school. He recounts how the headmaster forced him to sweep the building's playground instead of allowing him to attend classes with the other children.[5] And how, when he grew older, his Chemistry teacher purposely barred him from conducting lab experiments due to his caste, as a result of which Valmiki failed his Chemistry board examination.[6] In one way or another, Valmiki noted in his memoir, his identity as a Chuhra, a community traditionally known for manual scavenging, always got in the way.[7]

Similar incidents continue to occur even today. For instance, there are reports on Dalit students being expected to sweep classroom floors, pick up garbage and scrub toilets in a school located on the outskirts of Jaipur.[8] In Bengaluru too, a headmistress was booked for allegedly forcing Dalit students to wash utensils and clean toilets.[9] If the students refuse, they usually are punished and publicly humiliated.[10] It is widely observed that students from oppressed castes are often 'othered' and discriminated against on educational campuses across India.[11]

In 2016, Rohith Vemula, a PhD candidate, hanged himself in his university hostel's room in Hyderabad after being penalized for allegedly attacking a privileged-caste student named Nandanam Susheel Kumar, the leader of the right-wing student body Akhil Bharatiya Vidyarthi Parishad. 'My birth is my fatal accident,' Vemula wrote in the note he left behind, pithily summing up his life.[12] His death sent shockwaves across the nation and made headlines.

Yet, even now, not much has changed in the country. In March 2017, Muthukrishnan Jeevanantham, a Dalit scholar at New Delhi's Jawaharlal Nehru University, died by suicide. A few days before his death he had written on his Facebook page, 'There is no Equality in M.phil/phd Admission … there is only denial of equality …'[13] In Indore, in 2022, a sixteen-year-old Dalit girl was harassed by dominant-caste individuals who were angered by the fact that she was attending school. The same day, the girl's family was brutally beaten up by baton-wielding men. A video of the incident was circulated online.[14]

Which is why, years ago, when he was studying in a private school, Bhola fearfully protected his identity. His classmates were younger, lighter-skinned and not lacking in physique as he was. Bhola looked distinctly different from the others, which meant he would have to work twice as hard if he wanted to 'fit in'. Once, during a class at school, when the teacher was explaining a chapter on the caste system and the back-breaking labour sewage workers performed, Bhola caught his classmates sneering.

Though he felt deeply hurt, he chose to remain quiet and feign indifference. Yet, far away from home, he yearned for companionship and the freedom to be able to trust someone and share secrets. Once, in naïveté, he pulled down his walls in order to comfort a dominant-caste schoolmate from an underprivileged background who shared his woes with Bhola in the privacy of their dorm room.

'He was someone whom I deeply trusted. He had come crying to me because he was struggling with issues at home,' Bhola recalls. 'He told me that he had been through a lot in life. And I wanted to support him. I admitted that I too had suffered a lot and revealed almost everything about my life—that I am a Dom, that I used to pick shrouds for a living, what my conditions were and how we lived. In hindsight, that was a huge mistake.'

Hours later, the classmate had circulated Bhola's closely guarded secrets to 'every possible schoolmate'. Almost everyone in school turned on him after that. '*School mein bahut hungama ho gaya tha mere caste ko le kar.* There was a lot of drama at school due to my caste,' Bhola says. 'Many of my classmates began talking offensively to me. They would say, "Move away, saale, you are a Dom. We shouldn't touch you." Occasionally some would say it in jest, but they said it all the same.'[15]

Such experiences have left deep incisions in Bhola's memory—he remembers them vividly. In public, Bhola walks tall and appears confident, but in private, when he is feeling vulnerable, he reiterates what he feels within: '*Meri kuch aukaad nahin hai.* I am worth nothing. Anyone who learns my truth begins distancing themselves from me.'

It is the only reason Bhola has been resolute on his path, single-mindedly studying, regardless of all the times he has been insulted or mocked. 'I have heard jibes everywhere. It doesn't matter if they're educated or illiterate—people try to pull me down wherever I go. I have suffered a lot of humiliation in school. One day, though, I will give everyone an answer. When I become someone, when I earn my worth, I'll show them who I truly am.'

7

The Matriarch

BACK IN CHAND Ghat, Bhola's mother, Kamala Devi, has other plans for him. She draws her sari's pallu over her head and sits cross-legged on the floor, near the firewood. It is a late summer morning in 2019 and lunch is being prepared. Her forearm rests on her knee as she picks up a knife and begins to cut an onion. Translucent lavender slices plop onto the ground.

Kamala Devi is working on the terrace, which has been walled on three sides and has a balcony-like opening on the fourth side that overlooks Aakash's home. The roof is layered with tin sheets and covered with black plastic. The terrace is used as a kitchen, a bedroom and a bathing area. A single bed takes up most of the space, leaving just a narrow strip in front. This is where Kamala Devi sits and cooks. Above the bed, saris, pants and shirts hang from hooks on the wall.

At night, the terrace transforms into a bedroom, where a few of the family members sleep. A sturdy iron ladder descends into a second room. Four saggy mattresses, folded into space-saving halves, lie limply on another single bed. At dusk, the mattresses are spread over the floor for people to sleep on. Miniature figurines of Hindu gods huddle on a tiny shelf built into the wall. Apart from the bed, a small television set and the deities, the room is sparse. A bathing bucket stands on a metal trunk; a broom rests in a corner; an exposed bulb hangs from the ceiling.

Below this is another compact room with an en-suite Indian-style bathroom that requires squatting. This is the bathroom all the family members use. The room has a double-bed, which swallows most of the space. When Bhola's father was alive, eleven family members coexisted in these three extremely small rooms. Today, seven people and two children live here; Kamala Devi's eldest son, Mohan, and his wife and children occupy the room with the bathroom. Bhola's close friend Shortcut comes over every now and then to sleep: his own home is too small to accommodate everyone.

Kamala Devi is an imposing matriarch. In a community where women tend to fade into the shadows, she announces her presence with her waddling yet assured gait. Her face is lugubrious and her movements heavy with fatigue. A frown pinches her dense brows together. Her hair, tucked securely under her pallu, sits like a band of grey wool on her forehead. Thick veins run beneath the translucent, papery skin of her hands; spidery scarlet vessels crawl across her calves and ankles, and disappear.

Now in her early fifties, Kamala Devi is tired of slaving before the fire, dicing okra, peeling potatoes, scrubbing utensils and washing clothes. She wants to retire from housework, and hopes for a daughter-in-law who will take over the chores, oil her hair and massage her calves at night.

'Mohan's wife is no good. She has a tongue of her own,' she remarks, suggesting that is reason enough to scout for another daughter-in-law. She wants Bhola to marry and bring home a bride who is humble and submissive—someone she can order around. 'It's time to settle down,' she tells him every time he visits home during the holidays.

Even though Kamala Devi exudes armoured confidence, she worries about the future. She wants Bhola to stay in Banaras with her. 'There are times when I want Bhola to return home. I just want to call him back,' she says, sitting on the floor with her legs folded. For years, she has questioned her son's desire to study. 'We have too much suffering here. I want Bhola to leave his studies, earn and contribute towards the household now. I want him to marry and settle down. He stays far away from us, so he doesn't know what we go through every day. The family has many expenses. We are a poor community.'

As much as his mother's exhaustion disturbs him, Bhola politely brushes off her requests, resolutely focused on his larger goal in life. 'I won't marry until I have a steady job,' he has told her. Although Bhola has uprooted himself from his community for the sake of a better future, he faces resistance from all fronts: his mother, who wants him to marry and return home; his community, which doesn't believe he can make it; and the larger society itself, that will try time and again to ensure that he does not overreach.

⁂

Decades of wisdom are knitted into Kamala Devi's forehead like thick lines. When she talks, she slips in and out of Hindi, occasionally rattling off in Bhojpuri, a language she is more fluent in. One afternoon, I make the mistake of inquiring about her late husband. 'What was his name?' I ask.

Kamala Devi stiffens and stares at me quizzically, before turning to her young twelve-year-old neighbour. He has invited himself in to sit with us and listen to our conversation; he helps translate the Bhojpuri bits. In Chand Ghat, doors remain open during the day. Everyone is related one way or another; children walk in and out of homes at will.

'Keshav Chaudhary,' says the boy, jumping in to rescue us from an awkward pause.

Kamala Devi relaxes her shoulders and smiles. 'Yes. All my life, I have never said my husband's name,' she says. 'Out of respect, women never do. Ever.' Kamala Devi emphasizes the last word, holding my gaze intently, as though tutoring me on the etiquette of marriage.

Our conversation segues organically, slipping into the past as she unravels stories about her childhood or the moment when she first understood what being a Dom meant. 'I think I knew from the day I was born,' she says. 'I always knew. You can ask any toddler and they will tell you the same thing. They know what caste they belong to.'

The children know because of the frayed hand-me-downs, the taunts hurled at them by passers-by on the streets, the firewood they scavenge from the cremation ground and lug back home.

'I have never felt any discrimination,' Kamala Devi continues, 'because I have always followed the rules. As women, we don't mingle with other castes. We live within the community and stay within the premises of the house. I have never spoken to anyone outside my community. I know my place.' Kamala Devi has lived a life tethered to Chand Ghat, rarely stepping out or interacting with anyone.

Like most Dom women of her generation, Kamala Devi never opened a textbook. Even if her father had considered enrolling her in school, she believes it would have been a waste of time. 'I just got lost in growing up, playing, learning the household chores, getting married, having children. That was the assigned path,' she says. 'We had to live by the rules, which meant that as soon as a girl became a woman, she had to be married off. That's the only way she can preserve her izzat, her respect,' Kamala Devi explains. 'It's insulting for the family if their daughter goes out alone or doesn't have a suitable man to marry her by a particular age. So, we urge the girls to marry early to ensure they have a secure future, safe from insults.' Her words echo the overarching paternalistic point of view of the community: by marrying the girls young, they are doing *them* a favour.

Kamala Devi's own parents wedded her a lifetime ago: her hair was still raven dark, her waist was still narrow and the insides of her thighs had not yet felt the trickle of menstrual blood. She was thirteen, a young bride whose small palms had been stained burgundy with mehndi for a man she knew nothing about, not even his name. 'He was much older, of course, but I never asked his age. My job was to get married,' she says, her eyes glinting like a pair of black sapphires. Once married, Kamala Devi immersed herself in the goings-on of the house while obeying her in-laws, never talking back, keeping her voice low and '*hamesha ghoonghat kar ke rahu*'—always keeping the veil drawn over her face. 'That was what my life was about,' she says, unconsciously rocking back and forth.

Within a few years, Kamala Devi was pregnant. In the years that followed, she gave Keshav a trinity of daughters, a quartet of sons, then another daughter and, in the end, another son. Overall, Kamala Devi birthed nine children: four daughters and five sons. She could not attend to all of them at once. They were loud and demanding, and she was alone. 'I wanted my children to have a better life, but poverty made me helpless,' she says.

'Somehow, my children grew up,' she adds, a tone of finality in her voice.

Kamala Devi's irascible husband, Keshav Chaudhary, died in 2011. When he was alive, he ruled his home with an iron fist. The certainty of debt gnawed at him and he drowned his frustrations and fears in countless bottles of alcohol, claiming it to be the only balm that made his existence bearable.

When Keshav returned home after work, Kamala Devi feared his nightly rages. Keshav's day was often soured by the increasing number of cremators at Manikarnika Ghat—cocky young men with hot blood, fast feet and grasping eyes. Some nights, when he'd stumble into the house disgruntled and wildly drunk, often at three or four in the morning, Kamala Devi prayed that he would not pick an excuse to grab her by the neck or drag her by her hair on a manic whim.

Bhola recalls one night in particular. Having returned home inebriated, Keshav stumbled around in the dark and bumped into things. The noise did not wake Kamala Devi, who was fast asleep in a corner, exhausted after putting her children to bed. Keshav saw his soggy, cold dinner and grunted.

Kamala Devi was hauled out of bed. 'Wake up, woman,' he growled. He wanted a fresh meal. 'Cook!'

Kamala Devi quietly sat up, fixed her hair and prepared the food. After she had served him, she sat at a distance. Keshav tore the dry chapatti, dipped it into the watery dal and swallowed without blinking. The meal was insipid. He turned and looked at her. 'Tassttelessss,' he slurred, his tone dismissive. Picking up the water pot, he emptied it over the entire meal. Then he staggered towards the door and tossed the food outside.

Keshav was a man of paradoxes. Even when food was cooked at home and kept aside for him, he threw it away for the flimsiest of reasons. It did not bother him that there were some nights when his wife and children went to bed on empty stomachs. Sometimes, in desperation, Kamala Devi would break dry bread into smaller pieces, sprinkle sugar on them and hand them to her children to eat.

That night, Kamala Devi watched her husband turn around and take determined strides in her direction before lunging at her and clutching her blouse. He thrashed her until she fell and lost consciousness.

One never knew when his father's wrath would consume him, Bhola recalls, but it happened often, and when it did, it was his mother who suffered the most. '*Kai baar haath kaat diya, sirr phadh diya, Mummy behosh ho jaati thi, seedhi se gir jaati thi— bahut times. Ek ya do baar nahi.* There were times when her palm would be slashed, her head would be bashed, Mummy would faint, be pushed down the ladder—this happened many times. Not once or twice.'

One of Kamala Devi's daughters, Mitthoo, who says she was ten or twelve years old at the time, remembers watching her mother run out of their home barefoot once, pleading desperately, while her plait unravelled behind her. She almost tripped on the hem of her sari. Keshav caught up with his wife in the alleyway, dug his fingers deep into her hair and threw his fist into her back. Neighbours huddled outside their homes and lingered, but no one came forward to help Kamala Devi.

'People laughed; they enjoyed it,' Bhola says, recounting his father's violent episodes. 'My mother screamed at the neighbours: "What are all of you looking at? Mind your own business. Don't interfere in our matter!"' But the neighbours did not withdraw into their homes. 'They heckled my father, saying, "Are you seeing the way she talks? You don't beat her up enough!"'

Goaded by the men who berated him, Keshav threw another blow at his wife that day. When she lay on the ground, bleeding, Bhola heard his father telling her: 'Your head is becoming too big—the way you talk back nowadays …'

'Maybe it was because we were so poor,' Bhola says, his words bookended with self-conscious sighs, as he tries to explain his father's behaviour. 'We had no money and once he was drunk, he was never in his senses. He didn't know what was going on.'

8

The Rumour

IN 2002, A man had stood outside Dolly's parents' home in the middle of the night, drumming up a commotion. Amidst an audience of mosquitoes, a drunk Sekond Lal declared, 'I love her! I love her!'

Sekond Lal was Dolly's second cousin. As a teenager, he would visit Dolly's home—like most cousins do—to fly kites on the terrace and play hide-and-seek, to chase her and tickle her ceaselessly when she was caught. Dolly frowned when he yanked her braids. When he bothered her too much, she cursed him under her breath, hoping that his hair would crawl with lice. They would play kanche, a game of glass marbles, while squatting on the brown earth—their feet dusty, their eyes brimming with mischief, their squeals full of cheer.

'We had the usual brother–sister relationship,' Dolly recalls fondly. 'He used to call me behen and I used to call him bhaiya.' Sekond Lal, however, had no such platonic feelings towards Dolly.

He had been in love with her since a very young age. When he heard of her rishta, her engagement, he was heartbroken. Dolly had been promised to another man in their caste—a fellow with a stable job and a decent income. 'He was a compounder at a government hospital,' she says. The man lived in another Dom colony a few kilometres away.

At that time, Dolly did not particularly care for Sekond Lal. Nor did she care for the compounder to whom she had been promised. 'Neither of us had seen each other. I didn't know what he looked like; he didn't know what I looked like.' Dolly was simply performing her role as an obedient daughter ready to marry anyone her father deemed fit.

An arranged marriage is a given for most adolescent Dom girls, unless they elope with their lover. 'We had to marry wherever our rishta was fixed—even if the man was blind, an amputee, one-legged, broke, sick, old. We had to ... because our father had chosen him,' Dolly says.

By the time Sekond Lal's theatrics reached their peak, the entire community had stirred awake. Necks craned out of windows and doorways. It took only a few moments for everyone to hypothesize that Dolly *might* be having an affair with Sekond Lal. 'Why else would a man embarrass himself like this?' they wondered. The drunken performance had worked. This was now a matter of shame for Dolly's family.

A few days later, a dark rumour began to fester. When Dolly stepped out of her house to fill water from the community tap, she sensed her neighbours watching her. When she turned around to make eye contact, they immediately looked away. Murmured conversations were prematurely stifled.

Within the next hour, the rumour spread like wildfire. When it finally fell on Dolly's ears, she could not believe what had happened.

It would change her life forever.

———

Someone, somewhere, said something.

No one knew when or where the rumour began, but in the dead of night, it slithered like a dark shadow across the cold grounds of Chand Ghat, under doorways and into the ears of those with wagging tongues.

Someone, somewhere, had heard something: that Dolly Chaudhary had had a secret abortion.

Imaginations ran wild; gossip chased its tail. Was this true? Was this why Sekond Lal had created the commotion the other night? What about the poor compounder? Had she no shame?

By late afternoon, the rumour had made its way to other Dom colonies. A few hours later, Dolly's father's busy schedule was turned on its head by an untimely knock on the door. It was his future son-in-law, the compounder.

———

It is 2019. Dolly and I are sitting in one of her neighbours' homes. Its blue walls are flushed by the white glow of a tube light. Dolly looks at me as she tries to remember that moment when the compounder had entered her home. I watch as she makes an effort to recollect flecks of memory, like someone raking up wilted leaves from ground that has long been left undisturbed.

'The compounder sat my father down and calmly explained, "I am sure that your daughter is pure. I can believe that, you can believe that, but this community will never believe it. If we do get married, we will live out our entire lives being ridiculed and disrespected. It's best that your daughter gets married where the scandal took root,"' Dolly recalls.

Having said his piece, the compounder saw himself out. The cup of ginger tea with its wrinkled skin was left untouched. The engagement was off.

When Dolly speaks of the compounder, her eyes soften and a faint smile widens her lips. She builds him up to be a kind man, a blessed man—one who never suspected her fidelity, even though her own community whispered behind her back. She was grateful that at least someone, who wasn't her family, believed in her innocence. I am reluctant to point out that at the end of the day, the compounder too wanted nothing to do with her. That he too had turned his back on her.

Outside, dusk has fallen.

Dolly takes a deep breath. She pushes her head forward and looks directly at me. 'Would you believe me? Now that I've told you my truth, isn't there a doubt in your mind? Aren't you wondering if there is a possibility that I did do it?'

Without waiting for a reply, she pinches her throat and says in a raised voice, 'But I swear on Bholenath that nothing like that happened.'[1]

'But who spread the rumour?' I ask. 'Was it Sekond Lal?'

'No,' she says. 'It was someone else.'

9

The Most Beautiful Girl

WE CONTINUE OUR conversation in Dolly's home. The door
has been left ajar. The air is languid. Evening has slowly set in,
turning the pale blue of the sky into an inky hue. Dolly sits on
the ground with her legs stretched out. Her toes peek from under
her dull brown sari. She is lost, reminiscing. Her mother, Geeta,
who is visiting her for a few days, sits next to her in a candy-
orange nylon sari. Geeta has a quiet presence. She speaks clearly,
but almost inaudibly, forcing one to incline one's neck towards
her to hear her. Unlike Dolly's, Geeta's hair is neatly coiled into
a bun: oiled, combed and separated by a streak of deep orange.
Earrings dangle from her earlobes and her eyes betray the deep
sense of sadness she holds within.

Aakash, who is walking home after work, pops his head
through the open doorway. 'What is happening?' he asks.

Dolly ignores him. She is still thinking about Sekond Lal.
Aakash takes a few steps back from the threshold and leans

against a bike parked in the lane. He is curious and decides to listen to our conversation.

Dolly looks into the distance, almost vacantly. Then, she reveals the innocent relationship that Sekond Lal shared with her when they were kids. 'Out of affection, he used to call me "Rani behen". My maternal grandmother had given me the nickname "Rani", which means queen. I would grow up to become his.'

In Chand Ghat, the monsoons were terrible. Galis overflowed with cloudy water. Open sewers gushed grey, transporting balls of discarded hair, belly-up cockroaches and dregs of spit, among other things. Roofs, which often leaked, sang to the tune of rain: drumming, pattering and petering out. Skeletal spiders with their fine needle legs canvassed the walls, and plump rats scurried about, leaping over arms and heads.

Once, perhaps to escape the torrential downpour, a snake had crept into Dolly's home, smuggling itself through the house's drainage. One of Dolly's younger siblings spotted it and immediately pulled out a straw-toothed broom to beat the reptile to a pulp. Dolly was horrified. 'Don't kill it! Don't kill it! It's the monsoons,' she cautioned. 'Don't commit a sin. It's Bholenath's day!'[1] By the time her sister looked up from the task at hand, the snake had slipped back down the drain and disappeared, leaving behind a slender wet patch with a vanishing end.

The eldest among her siblings, Dolly was the naïve, trusting one. She did not have a mean bone in her body. She did not have street smarts, she felt, nor did she care much for them. Her main concerns were to cook well, clean well, feed well, marry and serve well. She lived a life measured by superstitions and a blind acceptance of the lines that mapped her palms—always arching, falling, weaving, splitting, halting.

When she was young, Dolly was considered the most beautiful girl in the mohalla. Her smooth, oval face, accented by high cheekbones, was the colour of sun-seared sand. Her thick hair was woven tightly into a long braid that dangled in the hollow between her bony shoulders. A gold chain rested on the gentle incline of her breasts; earrings dangled from her ears; her anklets, made of 'pure silver' and heavy with sound, called attention to her slender feet.

Dolly tells me that she wore earrings and anklets worth at least Rs 6,000–7,000 when she was young. 'My father did not have many financial troubles back then. I was the only one he spent his money on since my brothers and sisters were very young at the time,' she says.

Dolly would innocently play in the gali, displaying her father's wealth. It was easy advertising, a calculated move by her father to remind everyone in the community that they were better off—a class above. It was also a way of ensuring Dolly got many suitors when it was time to get her married. To describe their neighbours as envious of them would be an understatement.

Her parents owned a black-and-white television set with a cable connection, a fan and a small air cooler; other houses in the mohalla did not. During summers, mangoes were a luxury, not something every household could afford; most Doms subsisted on a single meal a day. Yet, mangoes were available in plenty in Dolly's house. Her siblings and she frequently gorged on the fleshy fruit with relish, giggling as they squished the seed between their fingers and traced the yellow trickle from their wrists to their forearms with the tips of their tongues.

In the evenings, her family would watch television, slumped against the wall, while the neighbourhood children gathered outside their ground-floor window, clutching the window grating, elbowing and hustling for space, desperate to catch a glimpse of the Bollywood film playing on the screen.

When food was scarce at Bhola's home, on his mother's insistence, he would amble over to Dolly's house, where he ate the leftover food Geeta offered. Before Bhola left, however, Dolly's father always found an errand for him to carry out in lieu of the meal.

When Dolly's younger brother Lakshaya got tired of wearing certain clothes, his mother donated his old clothes—frayed, faded, forgettable—to Bhola's mother, who would mend them and slip them on her sons. Other times, Bhola's mother would walk up to a tailor and get shorts made for her boys using the garish shroud fabric. Bhola and his brothers would wear them to weddings and on festive occasions.

The Doms in Chand Ghat have never had much. Dolly's family though, in comparison, had enough: her grandfather was a maalik who owned a seat in the pari. As I learnt over the years, 'pari' is a rota system monopolized by wealthier Doms who are known as maaliks or bosses. They hire Dom corpse burners and preside over the goings-on at the cremation grounds. When her grandfather died, Dolly's father and her uncles inherited their respective seats in the pari.

Within the Dom community, there exists an unchallenged power equation. Wealthy maaliks hold the maximum number of pari. Under each maalik, one or two managers are employed to do the organizational, clerical work—which includes bookkeeping, overseeing the performance of Dom workers and, sometimes, offering the sacred fire to clients when the maalik is not present. Then, there are the labourers, like Aakash and Mohan, who handle corpses and perform the strenuous funerary work on ground.

The maaliks, though few in number, command immense social and economic clout over the majority of Dom labourers working under them. These Dom labourers work in shifts. A shift may consist of four days, nine days or even eleven days at a stretch. During each shift, a corpse burner works between sixteen to twenty hours a day. He is not permitted to work throughout the month, which leads to an overall unstable and pitiable monthly income.

A maalik can mortgage, sell, buy or gift his pari. This transaction can be done only within their caste. During a financial crisis, a Dom may mortgage his pari; if he is unable to accumulate sufficient funds to buy it back, he may have to forfeit it altogether.

Everyone kept a close eye on the family. Dolly was an attractive young woman whose father had deep pockets. She was the perfect potential bride in a community committed to marrying its young through an arranged liaison. Those with eligible sons advertised their availability through the occasional name-dropping. Dolly feels that there were some families who fervently wished for a day when something unspeakable would befall her family, so that the world would be fair again.

Sekond Lal's mother, Saroj, was Dolly's aunt—her father's cousin. She was married to an unambitious man content in his government job, where he supervised sweepers. When she learnt that her son liked Dolly much more than just as a second cousin, she felt as though the universe had set a plan in motion especially for her. But she knew that she would have to be quick and tactful. She approached Geeta with an unusual proposition. When the time was right, she told Geeta, Dolly would be betrothed to Sekond Lal.

'We will keep the rishta within our family,' Geeta remembers Saroj leaning in and whispering to her while gently pressing her forearm.

At the time, Geeta, who has a soft voice and a compliant demeanour, nodded quietly in acquiescence. Although a cautious woman, she seldom questioned blood—Saroj was her husband's relative. Not to mention that she was also intimidated by her. Thus, a verbal pact was made, which seemed unbreachable at the time. Sekond Lal and Dolly were destined to be together: bound by blood, bound by promise, bound by fate. Nothing could possibly go wrong.

When hopeful mothers from the community asked Geeta to consider their sons as possible suitors for Dolly, she politely turned them down, informing them that Dolly's match was already made. Geeta took immense comfort in knowing that she wouldn't have to run from house to house, desperately searching for a husband for Dolly. By God's grace, things had fallen into her lap.

By the late 1990s, however, the family's savings began to dwindle. There were three major events to which Dolly attributes her family's riches-to-rags story. After Lakshaya's birth, Geeta underwent a reversible birth-control procedure that involved surgically inserting a Copper-T into her uterus. The doctor instructed Geeta to visit again in a few years to get the IUD replaced. Perhaps it was because her husband was unable to find time to take her to the doctor again or perhaps she got busy with family life; for some reason Geeta let the cautionary advice slip her mind. She carried on until complications began to make themselves known: sharp, mysterious pains in her abdomen, accompanied by fever, which arrived and disappeared unannounced. After medical tests, the family learnt that Geeta was suffering from a severe internal infection. Dolly believes that the negligence towards changing the Copper-T as directed is what caused the problem. They treated the infection in time, but a lot of money was spent to meet hospital expenses.

The second incident was Ajay's fall. Her brother had a habit of showing off. He possessed a false sense of invincibility while imagining himself to be a badass Bollywood hero, chasing kites, jumping from one terrace to another. One day, the daredevil, all of ten, lost his footing and fell off the terrace. The neighbours found him. 'We had to rush him to the hospital,' Dolly says. Ajay survived, but Dolly estimates that her father had to spend 'Rs 1.5 lakh on him'.

The third blow came when a very young Lakshaya, perhaps five years old at the time, fell and broke his hand. He neglected this and the infection in his hand worsened to a point where the doctor informed his family that the hand would have to be amputated. His father, however, consulted a friend, who took them to another doctor for a second opinion. This doctor cleaned the wound, and over a period of time, the hand healed and the limb was saved. However, by the time Lakshaya recovered, the family was in a tight monetary fix.

'Things just kept getting worse, one after another,' Dolly says. 'When poor luck strikes, what can you do? We became as good as beggars.'

Some years later, once Geeta had recovered and Dolly had reached the 'marriage-appropriate' age set by the community, Geeta visited Saroj's home to remind her of their pact. Saroj was crouched over her small choolah, flattening dough between her palms, stretching it with her fingers, before slapping it onto the hot tawa to make chapattis. When the subject was brought up, Saroj smiled, but Geeta noticed her sister-in-law stiffen. Saroj rolled her shoulders outwards, commanding more space in the room.

Geeta lucidly narrates the exchange as though it happened yesterday. 'Saroj told me, "*Hum shaadi nahi karenge.* I will not get them married."' She shifts uncomfortably; her voice quavers. 'I could not believe my ears,' she says. 'I told her that my daughter was grown up now; where else would we go to get her married?'

One's vulnerability is another's advantage. Saroj patiently heard Geeta's plea, gently patting her knee while tactfully spinning the chapatti on the choolah with her other hand.

'Don't worry,' she reassured Geeta. Perhaps Saroj had felt empowered by the fact that she had four sons, or maybe she thought this was how she could move forward in life—socially, financially. Either way, she finally said, 'We are family. Chalo, I will agree to this wedding and I will talk to my husband ... but you must give us twenty thousand rupees.'

Geeta remembers feeling her spirit sink into the ground. She had three daughters, all of whom were unmarried. Committing a large sum to Sekond Lal's family would compel her to give similar monetary gifts to the grooms who would wed her other daughters.[2] The family was no longer wealthy.

'*Humari itni aukaad nahi hai.* We cannot afford to pay such an amount. It's a big ask,' a flustered Geeta told Saroj.

She recalls how Saroj sat quietly, with pinched lips, as though she had sucked a lemon. 'Then, it's settled,' Saroj had replied curtly, slapping another chapatti onto the tawa. 'This wedding is impossible.'

'And just like that,' Geeta says, clicking her fingers, 'Saroj called off the wedding.' She takes a deep breath. 'But you know, my daughter was pretty and had a good head on her shoulders, so we decided to get her married elsewhere.' Through word of mouth, Geeta and her husband found a rishta for Dolly: the compounder, who stayed in another Dom colony. The news of the betrothal spread quickly. When Saroj heard about it, she was furious.

'That woman was greedy,' Dolly says in a dry, brittle tone. '*Unko sirf daulat ki havas thi.* All she cared about was money. Back then, she thought that if I married her son, she would get a fat dowry in return. When she realized that I wouldn't be marrying him, she could not bear the thought of it.'

10

The Only Willing Man

SEKOND LAL FELL in love, the community members tell me, with Dolly's bright eyes and her warm smile. There was an incomprehensible lightness to her being—a spirit-lifting aura that made him believe that with her around, anything was possible. That with her by his side, he could take on the world. Dolly, on the other hand, was oblivious to her cousin's feelings, and had lived out most of her teen years in comfortable ignorance.

Upon hearing news of her engagement to the compounder, Sekond Lal was inconsolable. His mother's refusal to honour their betrothal agreement—a decision swayed by greed—angered him. Dolly says that Saroj needed to fix the situation. She had not expected Dolly's parents to find another suitor so quickly. The embarrassment of being snubbed and outplayed, of watching a potential and sizable dowry slip from under her nose, filled her with resentment. To reweave her plan that was quickly unravelling, Saroj adopted subterfuge.

'So, she cooked up a rumour that I had aborted her son's unborn child,' Dolly alleges in a loud voice.

'*Jhoota ilzaam!* It was a false accusation!' Geeta declares hotly. Despite the passage of time, her intuitive maternal need to clear her daughter's name is as strong as ever.

In Chand Ghat, it didn't matter how ludicrous the rumour sounded or who started it. It didn't matter if there wasn't any tangible evidence to prove it. No one asked questions; no one challenged it. The gossip was juicy and everyone wanted a lick of it. The scandal was a desired distraction from one's own monotonous existence.

Overnight, Dolly's life became one she no longer knew. She went from being a hopeful bride-to-be to a woman who had an 'illicit affair' with her cousin, secretly conceived his child and then supposedly murdered it in cold blood.

'When I first heard the rumour, it felt as though a sharp arrow had pierced my chest, torn my heart and then left my body,' Geeta recalls despondently. '*Uss aurat ne samaaj mein aisey izzat bech di.* That woman publicly sold our honour and humiliated us. *Batao, kaun bikki hui izzat se shaadi karega?* Tell me, who will want to marry someone whose honour has been stained?'

Geeta is still for a moment, quiet, as though her voice has perished somewhere in the hollow of her throat. Her eyes well up. Then she begins to talk again: 'The rumour she cooked up was unthinkable. How could a woman be so wicked as to spread such ghastly gossip about her own niece? It was only a matter of time before the rishta with the compounder was broken.'

In the room upstairs, with its painted green walls, is a small mandir built for Dolly by her father upon her insistence when she was very young. The mandir has a pantheon of deities, including figurines of Hanuman and Durga. At least four times a week, Dolly would sit at the altar and offer prayers, palms joined together in silence. The day the rumour brought about a seismic shift in their lives, Dolly swore never to visit the shrine again.

'She rejected God,' says Geeta. 'She stopped believing in him. My poor girl did not even light incense to grace the altar any more. It was too painful for her.'

'Can no one challenge an unfounded rumour?' I wonder aloud.

Aakash, who has been standing quietly all the while, draws closer to the door's threshold. 'We belong to a small, uneducated caste. A rumour here spreads like wildfire. Everyone has a wagging tongue. If I stand here and clap my hands,' he says, bringing his hands together with a resounding *thwack*, 'the sound will travel. Everyone in the lane will hear it. Like that, once a rumour has left one's mouth, there is no stopping it. And once a girl's name is ruined, it's ruined. There is no going back. No one questions a man, though; his name is never ruined.'

Geeta nods. 'No one wanted to believe that Dolly was innocent.'

Dolly sits quietly while the two of them speak. A few moments later, she tells me that she wishes she had studied more. If only she knew how to defend herself, things would have been different. If only she had rushed to a doctor's clinic, got a report and thrown it at that 'vile woman's face'.

Dolly's body is hunched as she wraps her arms around her knees. 'At that time, my parents also did not know what to do.

It didn't occur to them to get the report either. With one lie, my entire life changed,' she says. '*Badnaami ho gayi.* I lost my honour.'

A plastic clip holds Dolly's uncombed hair together. She hasn't washed her face in days. All her time is spent worrying about her children and making sales at her shop. 'I was so naïve,' she continues as she recalls how harsh and unforgiving people can be. 'I had no knowledge, so I just kept quiet. I never said anything. That was my mistake.'

Dolly takes a deep breath. Tears well in her eyes. She wipes her cheek with one hassled sweep and sucks her lower lip. A shudder runs through her body. Then, Dolly composes herself. Over the last few years, she has learnt a thing or two about how the world preys upon the weak. As a widow and a mother of five, Dolly tries to mask her vulnerability, pretending to be battle-ready.

'But today, if anyone dares to say anything about my children, I will tear their eyes out and bury them in the ground!' she hisses in a challenging voice, slamming her fist on the cement floor.

———

When the compounder called off the wedding, no other man in the community was willing to marry Dolly.

Except Sekond Lal.

Community members will tell you that Sekond Lal genuinely loved Dolly. He was the kind of man who wanted to hold her hand and look after her. After the gossip had taken the community by storm, he chanced upon her in an alley.

'Just once ... say you will marry me,' Dolly remembers him telling her softly. 'I will let no harm befall you. I will give up the world for you,' he promised. 'However you want to live, I'll let you. I won't expect anything from you. I'll keep my parents and you separate, if you wish. Speak to your family, please ... Tell them that you have agreed to marry me.'

Dolly, who was confused and surprised by this unexpected proposal, brushed him off, reminding him that she did not have a say in whom she married. 'No girl in our community has ever told her parents what to do,' she had said. 'We don't marry out of love. If you want to marry me, come to my house.'

Sekond Lal promised Dolly that he would talk to his parents and convince them to change their minds. There was something gentle and genuine about him. Here was a man, she thought, who was willing to accept her despite the wretched gossip. Was Sekond Lal in cahoots with his mother? The thought did cross her mind, but she had no time to mull over it.

When Dolly told her father about Sekond Lal's proposal, the family felt there was a ray of hope. Due to their social vulnerability, Dolly's father had no option but to approach Sekond Lal's family. When Sekond Lal's parents were asked to reconsider, money was brought up again. Finally, Geeta's two uncles decided to help them by contributing Rs 10,000 each.

Sekond Lal's family was elated. Dolly's parents got the wedding cards printed. The wedding would take place in 2004.

For the next six months, Dolly and Sekond Lal spoke little with each other but said a lot through their prolonged silences, brief glances and lingering smiles. No letters were folded into neat squares and secretly slipped into hands; no songs were hummed in another's presence, but when Dolly stepped onto her terrace to hang clothes under the big yellow sun, Sekond Lal would make haste and run upstairs to his grandmother's terrace, which coincidentally faced Dolly's. Once upstairs, Sekond Lal would absently scratch his neck or swing his arm like a cricket bowler to mask his feelings of awkwardness.

Dolly could sense his eagerness to speak to her. Unable to think on his feet and unsure of what to say, Sekond Lal would start small. He would begin with 'Hi-Hello', and then proceed to ask her how her day had been. In return, Dolly would smile slightly with an educated reserve that young brides-to-be are taught to possess.

Each morning, before heading out to the cremation ground from his house, Sekond Lal would call out into the air: 'I'm leaving for work!' In her heart, Dolly knew the message was meant for her. She would feel an inexplicable rush—something she could not describe in words—but would immediately leave everything she was doing and dash to her window to catch a glimpse of him. 'I would make any excuse to my mother just to see him off,' Dolly recalls. 'At that time, our relationship wasn't much … It was just the beginning.'

The dynamics of their relationship had changed. They were no longer children running about, striking marbles on the clumpy earth, but two adults who were going to spend the rest of their lives together as husband and wife.

Two months after Dolly and Sekond Lal's wedding date was fixed, word got around that Sekond Lal's older brother was supposed to marry Aakash's older sister. Dolly's parents were shocked.

'We told Sekond Lal's family that if they took twenty thousand rupees from us, they should take the same amount from Aakash's family,' recalls Geeta.

That conversation did not sit well with Saroj and her husband. 'Saroj told us, "No, no, we can't take money from them. They are poor,"' remembers Geeta. 'But we were poor too! Here was a woman who had wanted my daughter to marry her son in the first place, then refused to go through with the engagement, cooked up a rumour and still expected me to pay her for accepting my daughter! Eventually, we did not give them any money. It was just on her son's insistence that the two got married.'

Even then, Dolly recalls, 'My father had to mortgage his pari seat in order to afford the wedding.'

One of Dolly's neighbours, Shortcut, remembers the wedding that took place in 2004. 'Her parents threw the most extravagant one,' he says.

It was the most dazzling event that Chand Ghat had seen in a while. Even though the groom's family did not receive any cash, the groom went home with a black-and-white television set, two single beds, a pair of ceiling and table fans, a trunk full of steel utensils and a Godrej singar-dani.

However, even that gesture was not enough to soothe the anger Sekond Lal's parents had begun to nurture within. Their wishes had not been met: they had been denied the money they had demanded. Their foolish son had turned them into a laughing stock by hastily marrying a girl they did not approve of. Their bitterness against Dolly and her family—that would remain for years after Sekond Lal passed away—had only just begun to fester.

Getting the bride tattooed with sun and moon symbols is a long-held tradition among the Doms. It is considered auspicious. But Dolly refused to get herself tattooed. It was too painful for her. Years later, when Sekond Lal died in 2016, whispers awoke from slumber: Dolly had become a widow too early, the community speculated, because her forearms had remained bare.

Over the years, several spats arose between the two families. Bhola told me once that during one such heated altercation, which resounded through the mohalla, a slip of the tongue revealed that Saroj had planted the rumour.

11

A Five-Rupee Coin

FOR MANY DOM parents, school after a certain age seems to be a waste of time.

One day in 2001, without warning, Bhola's father, Keshav Chaudhary, stopped paying Bhola's fees—Rs 2 a month—at the local government school where he was enrolled. For the next few months, Keshav kept stalling, giving his son false assurances that he would pay the fees the next month, but never did. In school, the teacher would call Bhola out, refusing to let him attend the class unless the fees was paid. By the end of the fourth month, Bhola was forced to drop out. At home, he did not question his father's behaviour. Even as a seven-year-old, Bhola knew that no emotional outbursts would make a difference. Poverty was a reality, and money a desperate need.

A few days later, Kamala Devi held him by the hand and took him to a wholesale shop. The manager there needed a runner—someone to deliver steel utensils and tableware to smaller shops.

The pay was Rs 20 for a twelve-hour shift. Sometimes the shifts could, and did, last longer. Bhola was immediately hired.

The day Bhola earned his first wage, he knew that his life had altered forever. He picked up one of the coins and stared at it. The five-rupee coin, with its lost sheen and bruised edge, weighed heavy in his small palm. It signified something momentous: Bhola was no longer a burden in his family of eleven. He had become a breadwinner.

———

A few months later, he joined his elder brother Mohan at Manikarnika Ghat since the pay was better. Mohan taught him the business of shroud-picking.

'*Bachpan mein hum ek rupay ke liye bhi tarastey the.* As children, we were desperate to earn even a rupee,' Bhola says. That desperation birthed in him a need to be frugal. He began saving one-rupee coins; the day he amassed a hundred of them, Bhola was elated. Since then, being thrifty has come to be deeply ingrained in him. It is a habit he knows will remain with him for the rest of his life.

While children his age chased kites, Bhola chased shrouds. The more he collected, the more money he made. He dreamt about shiny drapes wrapped around corpses, and wondered how something that sparkled so brightly when the sunlight kissed it could hide something so cold and still beneath it.

Aakash would weave tales about the masaan, the cremation ground, cautioning younger shroud pickers from working there late. At night, he said, when the moon was an upturned silver bowl and all was quiet in the cremation ground, the corpses would rise clumsily from slumber. They would stumble across the masaan, dragging their broken, bony parts behind them, waiting to snatch one of the kids. Wide-eyed, the children listened to these stories, full of dread. 'Aakash used to say such things because he was chalaak, clever,' Bhola says. It was a sure-shot way of eliminating competition.

Bhola himself was afraid to work at the masaan post the spell of dusk. Yet, in the mornings, when the big, bright sun revealed itself from behind the dregs of pollution, he had no excuse not to work.

One afternoon, while working, Bhola found an empty gunny sack and tied it around his head to protect himself from the heat. His skin had darkened. Nearby, a man wielded a bamboo log, skilfully working on a burning corpse. The corpse looked terrifying: its bone-white teeth still intact, its eyes seared shut. The air was thick with smoke.

Bhola wanted to puke. He had not eaten much. He ran to the riverside and watched an eagle ride a thermal lift. It would ascend and then drop and glide, before attempting to ascend and swoop down again. It was free, untethered—an aerial cartographer charting its own path. It had the kind of freedom Bhola yearned for. Before he knew it, tears were streaming down his face. He wondered what sins he had committed that God was punishing him with a cruel life.

Bhola's morning had begun at 4 a.m., when Shortcut, who was two years younger than him, had jolted him awake. 'Come on, we're already late!' he had whispered, tugging at Bhola's shirt. Bhola's other siblings sleeping beside him on the floor were slowly stirring awake, but Shortcut wanted the two of them to be the first ones to rush out.

Shortcut lived a few houses down the alley and was the youngest among the boys who worked at Manikarnika Ghat. By blood, he was Bhola's nephew; by relationship, Shortcut said Bhola was his 'best friend'. Every dawn, like clockwork, he would wake up between 3 a.m. and 4 a.m. Shortcut did not need an alarm; often it was a wicked dream that did the job. He would then run to Bhola's home. Many Dom families left their doors slightly ajar through the night, especially during the summers. The houses were poorly ventilated and the indoors would become terribly oppressive if the doors remained latched. 'We were poor people,' Shortcut says, shrugging. 'Who would want to steal anything from us?'

Once he arrived at Bhola's home, Shortcut would search for Bhola, who would be sleeping in a corner. Bhola's father dozed near the doorway. Shortcut would tiptoe over Keshav Chaudhary, carefully pushing aside the man's feet in the dark. There were times when he had accidentally tripped over Keshav and fallen. Bhola's father was monstrous when he awoke. 'Oi, rascal! Run away quickly!' he would snarl. 'Else I'll find a stone to bash your head with!'

That day, Bhola woke up, startled. At first, his small body felt like lead—too fatigued and heavy to move—but he managed to push himself to his feet. There was no time to splash water on his face or change clothes; they had to hurry. More time at the masaan meant more money.

'*Ek tarah ka nasha bann gaya tha voh.* It had become an intoxication,' Shortcut admits, when he talks about foraging for shrouds as a child.

Outside, everything was blanketed in a thick layer of darkness. Daylight was yet to make an appearance. The boys quickly made their way through Chand Ghat. A solitary street light flickered in the distance. Brown-winged moths whirled under it—a mesmeric, golden blur. The narrow gali ahead was deserted. A stray dog appeared out of nowhere and started barking. Two other indie dogs caught up with him, lifted their bony heads and began to howl.

'What if they've seen a ghost?' Shortcut asked fearfully, trying to keep his voice low.

Bhola said nothing. He grabbed Shortcut's hand and sprinted in the opposite direction, swerving to take the longer route.

'Hurry!' Shortcut yelled, one foot chasing the other. 'We have to make sure that the ghost doesn't catch us!'

Bhola held on to the waist of his shorts, which were threatening to slip off. 'Forget about the ghost,' he answered, breathless, heels kicking against his bottom. 'We have to make sure we reach the cremation ground before the Rajghat boys do!'

At Manikarnika, the competition was fierce. There were at least twelve to fifteen other boys who wanted exactly what they did: a sprawl of salvaged castaways—tasselled, patterned, bordered; made of cotton, silk and faux silk; in radiant hues of gold, orange and deep red. The Rajghat boys, in particular, were always competing with them. They were unafraid to rouse trouble and took delight in grabbing and pushing the younger boys from the Chand Ghat gang when the older ones were not around.

When Bhola and Shortcut arrived, the ghat itself was poorly lit, but clusters of pyres glowed fiercely. A snaggle-toothed boy was already sifting through a pile of shrouds dumped near the river. The other Rajghat boys hadn't arrived yet. Bhola signalled to Shortcut to ignore the kid and inspect other parts of the cremation ground. They had to find the spot that had the most number of good-quality shrouds.

Shortcut was still learning the ropes. He was short and skinny, with a trusting disposition. Being the youngest in his family, he had lived a relatively cocooned existence, brought up to believe in the niceness in everyone, until proven otherwise. He was reticent, while the other boys were wild and raucous. He stuck close to Bhola, often lacing his fingers with the older boy's as a habit. He was willing to follow Bhola anywhere, and Bhola went where there were shrouds.

The first time Shortcut saw a corpse, he was five years old. The body had just arrived from the post-mortem building. The dead man's face was slashed; his left eye and sunken belly had been sewn up. He was also missing a hand. At the time, the little boy was aghast. For weeks to come, the corpse's ghoulish face would visit him every night, starring in the most twisted nightmares. But Shortcut could not stay at home and sulk even if he wanted to. For one, his family needed the money, and second, he would be laughed at by his older and meaner teammates. All things considered, it was best if Shortcut feigned some kind of valour.

Going forward, to avoid seeing the faces of the dead and their dismembered pieces, the boy promised himself that he would learn how to become 'high-speed' on his feet and keep his eyes on the ground when the corpses arrived.

The kids became experts at sorting. Deep red shrouds with circular gold motifs and shimmering tassels are the most sought after. The kids nicknamed it 'godhva' because it looked similar to the rich cloth that is draped on a mare's back at a wedding. The cloth was the 'fancy', unrivalled kind. 'This shroud would be placed on a person who came from a "high-fi" home—a rich man's home,' Shortcut says. If bargained well, a godhva could be resold to the shopkeepers for Rs 15, which was a high resale price for the shroud pickers.

A cotton shroud resold at Rs 10 per piece. The children called it 'oonwa'. It wasn't as shimmery as the godhva, but it was the next best thing. 'It had patterns made of gold-coloured thread,' Shortcut describes. Then, there were iridescent gold and silver shrouds, which were abundant and plasticky in appearance. They were dubbed 'papad' due to their annoyingly crispy feel. At the time, papads resold for Rs 2-3. Most of the time, there were more papads strewn about at Manikarnika Ghat than godhvas or oonwas.

The truly unsalvageable shrouds were used by them as hauling material. The younger boys, sent by mothers to procure firewood from the pyres for their choolahs, would skilfully pull out the burnt logs of wood using a pair of bamboo sticks and drown them in water for a few minutes, before tying them in the soiled shrouds and walking back home with the bundle.

'Every Dom boy has grown up carrying wood from the cremation ground,' Bhola tells me. 'At times, the weight of the wood was double that of our tiny bodies. Sometimes, we'd even find pieces of flesh stuck to the logs.'

To find a godhva or oonwa took sustained effort. It required standing for long hours amidst raging pyres and keeping an eye on the shroud draped on a corpse closely guarded by shavyatris— male relatives who travelled with a corpse. It required patience and intuition: the ability to anticipate the exact moment when the shavyatris would be distracted, allowing the boys to swoop in and do the deed. The waiting game required strategy. While they waited, the children would be drenched in sweat, their lips dry, their throats parched. As Shortcut puts it, 'It felt as though all the blood had left our bodies.'

Even among the boys at the ghat, Shortcut was the youngest and the shortest. He was seldom given the tougher job of working near the burning pyres. The older boys did the hard work of pilfering the shrouds; Shortcut was in charge of safely securing them in a gunny bag. 'If I was somehow unable to do that or if I left them piled up in one place, our rivals would steal them, or the older Dom men who disapproved of our work would throw the pile in the fire so that we couldn't earn any money from them.'

Shortcut would search for and find castaway cement sacks at the cremation ground—dirty and frayed. On a good day, the children managed to shove twenty, even twenty-five shrouds into the bag. Bhola and Shortcut would collect as many shrouds as possible, sling them onto their backs and head home, where they would freshen up, bathe and eat whatever there was at home. By 10 a.m., the pair was back at the cremation ground for round two, hawk-eyed and nimble, even though their legs ached. Aakash and other children, like Bhola's older brothers, would also arrive by then and begin scavenging for shrouds.

It was the month of May. Shortcut's stomach began to make noises—like a band of balloons sluggishly deflating. He felt dizzy. A stray earthen pot lay near a washed-out pyre. It was marked by a hairline crack near its mouth, probably left behind by a mourning family.

Among many Hindu communities, earthen pots are used during cremation ceremonies. They are, thus, in abundance at the masaan. The boys at the ghat sometimes pick up the used and discarded pots to store water because it stays relatively cool in them.

Shortcut rushed to a leaking tap nearby to fill the pot with water, then he threw his head back and gulped down large mouthfuls. The water was tepid. He'd rather have a belly that was bloated and full than one that was empty. Half an hour later, though, he vomited. The immense heat, the high-paced running around, the thick fumes from the pyres, the fatigue, the hunger— they had all affected him.

Shortcut thought his head would explode. He dawdled and took refuge at their headquarters, which they called 'madai'. In the afternoons, the children spiritedly dug holes in the ground and erected four slender bamboo poles. To protect themselves from the sun, a makeshift canopy was engineered: a scruffy cloth tied to the tops of the poles with ropes. On dry days, the cloth would billow in protest, spurred by hot winds.

The kids often built such shelters where they secured the collected gunny sacks. Beneath this, they lazed, cracked crude jokes, shared samosas if they could afford them that day and sang songs. Sometimes, Aakash wrapped a scarlet shroud around his head and shimmied for entertainment, while the boys cheered and clapped to a beat. It was here that the children had some downtime. They would drift off to sleep, watching the sun—a blinding coin of gold—playing peek-a-boo from behind the wind-buffeted canopy. Their dusty slippers became their headrests and the dizzying hum of flies their lullaby. If older boys like Aakash jumped into the river, younger ones like Shortcut and Lakshaya followed suit.

Meanwhile, Bhola would diligently be on the lookout for shrouds, trying to concentrate on the job at hand. He was unwilling to bequeath his precious time to uninspired floundering. The other boys splashed around in the river, filling their mouths with water and becoming human fountains.

While Shortcut reposed in the headquarters, Aakash nosedived next to him, concealing a small bottle in his armpit. Then, he twisted the cap and pressed the mouth of the bottle to his thin lips.

'What is this?' Shortcut asked, propping himself on his elbow. 'This is nothing, nothing really,' Aakash mumbled before taking another swig.

'Tell me,' Shortcut pestered.

Aakash looked at the boy. His eyes were heavy with sleep. 'This has sharaab, alcohol, in it. I drink sometimes. *Pata hai, sharaab mood badal deta hai?* Did you know alcohol changes the mood?' he said, with a languid sway of his head.

Shortcut groaned and lay down again, remembering the last time Aakash had let him taste something grown-up—something 'mature'. He had hounded Aakash to let him try gutka. Aakash, who usually smacked the younger kids on their heads when they asked for such indulgences, was in an agreeable mood. He pressed the gutka in his moist palms and then offered a pinch. 'Don't swallow it completely,' he advised. Shortcut tasted some and immediately spat it out. He watched the gutka-laced saliva land on the ground. It had tasted awful. He was quite sure he did not want to try the alcohol.

'Go, get to work!' Aakash dictated as he took another mouthful of the alcohol and pushed Shortcut by the small of his back. 'I'll be here for a few minutes.'

Shortcut rose wearily and dusted himself down. He marched towards the pyres and stopped in his tracks when he saw his older cousin Balram standing tall in the distance, stacking corpses with swift ease before setting them aflame. Balram seemed to be in an unbreakable trance.

Later in the day, Shortcut asked him what he was on, hoping there was a magic pill that could boost his own energy too. Balram confessed, whispering about the powers of ganja: 'If I take one or two hits, my mind eases up. Then I can burn many bodies in one go. Otherwise, the fire whips me so terribly, I cannot bear it.'

The nature of the work was such, Shortcut tells me, that unless you took something, you wouldn't be able to perform. 'At that time, I was young and I didn't feel like taking it and I didn't have the knowledge. If I had stuck around, I would have started at some point. It all happens in the company you keep,' he says. But Shortcut had sworn to his mother that he would steer clear of such stuff, even though his elder brother indulged in all forms of nasha: gutka, paan and alcohol.

Most Dom boys who work at Manikarnika Ghat have been co-opted into the drug culture. A thirteen-year-old boy will be able to tell you where to procure what, and at what price. One even drew a map with his fingers poking into the air: ascend the flight of steps, take a sharp left, go past the tea-stall chacha and the sweet-curd shop, take a right into a narrow gali, cross the

house with a large gate, walk for 500 metres, take another left ...
and so on and so forth.

It is well known that substance abuse is more prevalent among
children who belong to low-income households, who work the
streets and labour in harsh conditions. NGOs like Save the
Children note that children working in unorganized sectors turn
to drugs for solace rather than entertainment.[1] It is a way for
them to cope with hunger, debilitating work environments, peer
pressure, and mental and physical abuse. Easy access to and the
wide circulation of alcohol and drugs on the streets make them
particularly vulnerable to addiction.

At Manikarnika Ghat, the children use drugs not because it
is some kind of flex, but because it gives them a certain kind of
inner toughness: a higher threshold for pain and the uncanny
ability to do twice as much work in less time. The drugs energize
them, alter their mood, and allow them to focus on completing
the task, despite their dreadful working conditions. No one tells
them, however, how addicted they can become to the substances
in the long run, how they trigger disorientation, cause erratic
sleep, spur anxiety and paranoia. The children know it is 'bad'
and 'wrong'—they just don't know how bad it can get. By the
time they figure it out, it is usually too late to pull out of the
addiction.

Shortcut and the other children working at the ghat called the
shavyatris, 'jajman', a reverential term. Once, when one of the
boys tried snatching a shroud that was lying near a dead body, a

jajman picked up a bier and thrashed him. He was unable to walk properly for days.

The boys hustled in two groups: one with four of them and the other with three. One or two would distract the shavyatris, while another would snatch the shroud and run. The last member would grab the fabric from the runner and rush to store it someplace safe.

'That was my duty,' Shortcut says. 'To ensure that it was kept safe. Sometimes we would stand around for hours just to get a good-quality shroud. The heat was so intense that I kept praying to God that he should change my life. I fainted often because it was so hot.'

'On days when there weren't enough bodies,' Shortcut admits ruefully, 'we would feel very sad.' At a remarkably young age, the children were inured to grief, fully aware that others' deaths allowed them to survive.

Once, a man snatched a shroud right out of Shortcut's hands. He held the boy's gaze and sneered as he threw the cloth into the fire. Shortcut's eyes welled up. He stood in silence, watching the fabric burn, curl up and disappear. When the man turned his back, Shortcut lifted a wooden stick and drove it into his back.

Aakash, who was standing next to Shortcut, quietly observed the scene. By the time the man looked over his shoulder, a fearful Shortcut had thrown the stick away in panic. The man grabbed Aakash's collar, thinking he was responsible, and began beating him up. Aakash limply took the thrashing without a word. He was a kid full of contradictions: he would tumble into arguments with the younger shroud pickers at a moment's notice, but at the same time, he felt a strong need to protect his own.

The older men who brought in the corpses on biers despised the children who scavenged for shrouds. 'They always said: *Jiske naam ka kapra hai, uski chita ke saath jalna chahiye.* The body with which the shroud came must burn with it,' Shortcut remembers. As a child, he had wondered what use a piece of cloth would be for a dead person, when it could help those who were still alive.

For him, that shimmering drape was a lifeline. It often meant the promise of a decent meal.

12

Hunger

FOOD, EVEN THE lack of it, has been poignantly documented in Dalit literature.[1] For centuries, oppressor castes maintained caste hierarchy not only by practising untouchability, but also by monitoring one's access to food. One's caste determined what one could eat; food was a way of imposing social inferiority upon Dalits.

In his memoir, *Joothan*, author Omprakash Valmiki describes how his mother, sister and brothers worked in cowsheds that belonged to oppressor-caste homes in the 1950s. The air in the sheds, where his family laboured, diligently picking up the dung and washing the ground, always had an overwhelming stench of dung and urine. As remuneration, they were given one roti at noon each day and were annually provided with 12–15 kilograms of grains. Sometimes, half-eaten, stale food—joothan—was also given to his family along with the roti.[2] In another incident, Valmiki bitterly recalls the sting of his mother being humiliated by Sukhdev Singh Tyagi, a dominant-caste man who denied her request for food at a wedding, instructing her instead to scavenge among the pattals thrown away by guests.[3]

In certain parts of Uttar Pradesh, the maize found in cattle excreta was given as remuneration to agricultural labourers belonging to oppressed castes. While trampling on the corn to take it out of the husk, bullocks often ended up consuming some of it. Later, undigested corn present in their dung was separated and given to Dalit labourers, who would take it home in lieu of wages. This was called 'gobaraha'.[4]

Author and poet Sharankumar Limbale also recalls vividly in his memoir, *Akkarmashi* (The Outcaste), how his grandmother carefully collected remnants of undigested jowar grains from cow dung, washed and then dried them in the sun.[5] Once the grains were dry, she ground them and made bhakris.[6]

Traditionally, a 'low-caste', marginalized community in Bihar was tasked with hunting rodents. Rats, therefore, became a prominent part of their diet. Their caste's name, Musahars, literally means 'rat-eaters'.

In his powerful autobiography, titled *Baluta*, author Daya Pawar narrates his childhood experiences of growing up as a Mahar. A Dalit sub-caste in Maharashtra, Mahar translates to 'original inhabitant of Maharashtra'. Despite this, Mahars (a majority of them now identify themselves as neo-Buddhists) in Hindu society were assigned the responsibility of disposing dead cattle, in addition to fulfilling other traditional duties.[7] Due to crippling poverty and limited access to food, the community was often forced to eat carcasses. In *Baluta*, Pawar recounts how the death of a cow, particularly one that fell off a cliff, brought a sense of relief to his community since its meat would be relatively fresh.[8]

———

As observed earlier, dominant castes would use the coarse millet grains to feed their cattle, and occasionally offer some to the labourers—most of whom were Dalits—on the farm. In 2008, scholar and political commentator, Chandra Bhan Prasad co-led a survey titled *Rethinking Inequality: Dalits in Uttar Pradesh in the Market Reform Era*, which focused on the food and lifestyle changes that took place in Dalit households between 1990 and 2007.

In his article published in *The Pioneer*, Prasad notes that during the era of market reforms in India, 'Dalits had stopped eating millets (bajra) and wheat had become their staple diet. Many people wondered why we (Dalits) were celebrating the fact that bajra was no longer our staple diet.' Prasad states that this was because 'there is a humiliation attached to it. Dalits didn't eat millets because they knew about its health benefits. It was eaten by Dalits and other lower castes because it was inexpensive. And anything eaten by the lower caste had low social acceptance.' So for the Dalits, Prasad proclaims, 'coming out of the millet regime was a freedom from humiliation'.[9]

Bhola himself has many memories of eating millet rotis at home as a child. When food was scarce, the children would subsist on a lump of jaggery and one bajra roti each. Kamala Devi would carefully knead the millet dough and pat it between her palms to make small-sized rotis. Sometimes, she would make larger ones on the tawa, split them into smaller pieces and distribute them among her children.

Waxy potatoes were another staple. It is what Bhola has eaten the most in his life. The multi-eyed, dusty-brown, perennial root vegetable was inexpensive and readily available. At home, Bhola would watch his mother sauté finely diced green chillies with onions, garlic cloves and chopped tomatoes in a vessel sizzling with mustard oil. Kamala Devi then dunked three medium-sized, peeled potatoes in it and poured in a potful—or two—of water. Before nightfall, the children would sit together to have potato sabzi, dipping their dry rotis in the spicy, watered-down gravy.

On days when there were no vegetables at home, Bhola's sisters made dal pithori—a family favourite. Flat circular pieces of dough were added to a soupy, canary-yellow dal bubbling away on the fire and allowed to cook through. This somewhat bland dish was later enjoyed as a full meal. To add spice, fat chillies were chopped and thrown into a hot pan with mustard oil, dry mango powder and salt, and consumed as a fiery side dish.

On other evenings, Kamala Devi took a fistful of uncooked mota chawal—coarse rice—and set it aside to boil in a large vessel full of water.[10] Once ready, each child was given a small bowl of warm rice water sprinkled with salt to drink, and a few grains of cooked rice. The children drank the pearly grey, runny soup with relish, before scampering off to play.

Back when he was five or six years old, Mohan was occasionally woken up by his father early in the morning and offered chickpea water to drink. Later, after teaching him how to pick shrouds at Manikarnika Ghat or take a dive in the river, Keshav would treat his son to breakfast by taking him to a small shop that served tawa-toasted bread layered with thick milk cream. These brief father–son bonding moments were special to Mohan. They ceased shortly after the home filled with more siblings and the finances became strained. But on the rare, good days when Keshav returned home with a wide grin on his face and a fat bundle of notes in his pocket, chicken would be bought and cooked in merriment.

Despite being in debt, it was during festivals that Keshav borrowed money from lenders and splurged on his family to celebrate. New clothes and shoes would be bought for the children and special grocery items too. Chicken was not cooked, since that would displease the divinities, but the vegetarian meal was always a feast; Kamala Devi would artfully make soft, fluffy pooris and serve them with tangy paneer curry.

Later in the day, blaring music and dizzying laughter would resound through the lanes of Chand Ghat. After the meal, Bhola and his siblings would scurry down and tear through the crowd to watch entertaining performances in their mohalla: like watching a pair of Dom men (one of them veiled and draped in a red sari, with plastic bangles on his slender wrists) move their hips rhythmically to Bhojpuri music. The children giggled each time they spotted the sari-clad man's bristly black beard peeking from behind the veil.

The family could not afford a refrigerator, though food was seldom leftover. On the rare occasion when a small quantity of dal or sabzi remained, Kamala Devi put it aside in a covered container. If, on certain nights, rats ate some of the leftover food and scrambled away, the family never came to know. 'We were so poor that we were not really bothered by it,' Bhola says. However, if a lizard's tail accidentally plopped into the milk container, or if smooth, grey pods of cockroach eggs dropped into the leftover dal, then the food had to be thrown away.

Bhola was assigned the responsibility of buying vegetables and other supplies from the market. It was a chore his older sisters had earlier performed. However, once they became adolescents, they were no longer allowed to step outside the house unsupervised. After Mohan, the eldest male sibling, began working full-time at Manikarnika Ghat, he could not do the market runs either. Bhola took over from him. Every day, his father would give Bhola Rs 50. Consumables like uncooked dal, onions, potatoes, wheat or millet flour had to be bought in small quantities within that figure. There were days when all his father could hand him was Rs 20, and days when Bhola was handed nothing at all. By the time he was seven or eight, Bhola knew the price of every affordable item on the shelf and was on his way to becoming a well-oiled bargaining machine.

13

A Time of Change Begins

For years, documentary filmmaker Vikram Mathur had wanted to make a film on Banaras but had been unable to find a subject. One day, in 2006, while sitting at Manikarnika Ghat, he noticed one of the boys stealing a shroud and scrambling away. He soon realized that the boy was a shroud picker working in a group with others. Mathur had found his documentary subject.

Three years later, George Grey watched the premiere of Mathur's documentary in New York. The film intrigued him. It wasn't long after watching the documentary that Grey contacted Mathur with the intention of offering financial support for the children's school tuition, uniforms, and hostel fees till the twelfth standard. When they visited the boys' homes with a plan to fully sponsor their education, however, the parents were reluctant. They preferred that the children worked at the ghat, since their earnings went towards the household expenses.

Grey came up with a solution. He asked the parents how much money the kids were making. The parents told him they earned fifty rupees a day. Grey agreed to pay each of the boys' families a lump sum of Rs 1,500 a month on the condition that the children be allowed to go to school. The parents did not hesitate after that.

In 2010, Bhola, Shortcut, Lakshaya and another boy from the community were enrolled at a private school in Cholapur. The school was a few hours away from Banaras. The children were elated, especially Bhola, whose dream of leaving Chand Ghat behind was finally coming true. Days before he left, Bhola approached the man to whom he, as well as the other shroud pickers, sold the purloined funerary drapes. 'I'm going to a hostel far away!' the teenager announced gleefully. 'I will no longer be doing this work.'

The middle-aged man, disgruntled by the fact that he was losing cheap labour, sat Bhola down. '*Tum Dom ho.* You're a Dom,' he whispered hoarsely as he smoothed Bhola's hair with a feigned paternal familiarity. '*Kabhi badloge nahi.* You will never change,' he continued. 'This is Chand Ghat. We don't let anyone climb the ladder. You climb two steps, and we'll pull you down. We will remain here and so will you.'

Bhola was immediately reminded of Shortcut's drug-addled cousin, Balram. He too had studied in a government school and then fled to Mumbai to work at a stationery store—away from the bedlam of the death business to the therapeutic calm of sorting and arranging files, notebooks, and pen and pencil supplies. Each time he returned home for a short holiday, he boasted about how his boss entrusted him with handling the Xerox machine as well. Balram's glittering 'Bombay dream', however, had come to a halting crash the moment he lost his father. When he returned to Chand Ghat to perform the last rites, his mother was inconsolable. Relatives advised him to stay behind for her sake and toil at the cremation ghat to support her financially. Balram had listened.

Bhola comforted himself with the fact that his father was still alive. His eldest brother, Mohan, was helping with the family income too. All he had to do at the moment was look ahead and rubbish all thoughts of doubt.

———

The school in Cholapur embraced all castes and religions. Bhola was sixteen years old at the time; Shortcut was two years younger. Since the boys were away from their community for the first time, they were put in one room at the hostel.

All their lives the boys had slept on cracked floors, sharing mattresses. Insects left plump red bites on their arms and legs; rats colonized their homes; monsoons left behind large, map-like patches on the walls. When the clouds rumbled, Bhola and his siblings, asleep on the terrace, took cover in the room below, squeezing in for space. Shortcut, whose house was far smaller than Bhola's, often went to sleep at his friend's. 'Sometimes we had no place to stay because of the rain, so we would go and sleep in other people's homes,' he says.

In Cholapur, when the children saw their hostel room for the first time, they threw their bags on the ground and rushed in. They kicked off their slippers, jumped on the beds and spun around in the mosquito nets. They held hands and danced on the carpet. Each one had a bed, a clean mattress, fresh bedsheets, pillows and neatly folded quilts. The walls were freshly painted, non-mouldy and seepage-free. The windows were dressed with curtains. There was a dedicated cupboard assigned to each of them.

The school was a magical wonderland: a world far away from the one they belonged to.

The first six months were spent in helping the boys grow accustomed to this new way of life. In school, they were taught meditation, reading, speaking and table etiquette. The Chand Ghat boys were taught separately from the other students. Their initiation into the world of education had to be done tactfully. They knew how to skilfully silence pyres and spot the best-quality shroud from a pile of trash, but oddly shaped letters printed in textbooks seemed alien to them.

Later, when they joined classes with the other students, there was a visible struggle. It embarrassed them that they were older, taller and scrawnier than the others. Sometimes, their classmates would snigger and mock their accent. In the common bathroom, the Chand Ghat boys closely observed the other hostel students. Some of them lathered their faces with translucent gel squeezed out of glossy tubes; others peeled off sweet-smelling orange goo applied to their foreheads. Bhola and the Chand Ghat boys wondered why anyone would spend a lot of money on some orange goo. Back home, they had grown up vigorously rubbing mustard oil on their crown, face, torso and limbs before skinny-dipping in the Ganges—and they had turned out all right. The oil kept their skin supple and gave it a mild yellow tint. Afterwards, they would scrub their hairless bodies with soap bars that cost one-tenth the price of the 'fancy' face washes.

But the Chand Ghat boys were eager to learn. They were willing to adapt to this new lifestyle. Study was an unshakable priority. They paid attention in class and submitted assignments on time. They read past the school hours, even after the evening meal. It felt like someone had finally handed them the reins to their own lives. They were not going to let anything come in their way.

Families were missed, of course, but it was a small price to pay for the comforts. They slept on beds with their arms spread wide and their legs outstretched. They ate three meals a day. Sometimes, when Shortcut wept for his mother, the other boys huddled around him and tried calming him in hushed voices. They would tell him: 'Look, we have a room to sleep in, a clean bathroom to use and fans to sit under. Whatever we are getting to eat right now, we should enjoy. In the future, we might not get this. We have to make the most of this time.'

When the boys returned to Chand Ghat for the summer break, the community noticed a visible difference. The children moved around with a newly learnt confidence, a certain swag. They no longer appeared spindly or scruffy; in fact, the four had put on weight. Time away from the pyres and studying indoors had lightened their skin. Bathing in warm, soapy water had cleared their acne. When the boys strutted through the galis, their neighbours gaped. Some commented that they looked like 'foreigners'. Everyone wanted to know them and speak to them.

To practise—and to show off—they conversed with each other in English, using random words they had picked up over that short period of time.

Mohan, Bhola's eldest brother, was impressed. 'In our community, no one had spoken decent English until then,' he says.

It was not long before the boys began receiving proposals for marriage from several Dom families. However, they told their parents to decline the offers. They wanted to make something of themselves first. One day, when Bhola was sitting at home reading a textbook, one of his brothers told him to go and work at Manikarnika Ghat instead of 'wasting' his time.

'I won't go,' Bhola replied assertively. 'I am never going to work there again.'

14

The Naysayers and the Believers

IN 2012, THE boys were transferred to another school that offered better infrastructure, activities and curriculum than the one in Cholapur. The first day they walked through the new school's impressive gates in Babatpur and crossed the manicured patches of green, they were awestruck by the large campus. The four wanted to pinch themselves to make sure it was not a dream. Bhola closed his eyes and spoke to God: 'You've brought me this far. Please don't let go of my hand now, because I don't want to turn back from here.'

Bhola was determined to stay. He wanted to prove the naysayers wrong—the ones who had shooed him away and told him with unchallenged confidence that a Dom's son could be nothing more but a cremator. He feared that if he failed in school, if he was unable to 'become someone big', his community would sneer and spit on him. 'Look!'—he imagined them jeering—'Look! He had gone to the hostel to study but nothing came of it.'

At school, when introduced to computers for the first time, Bhola's eyes widened. His eagerness to use them was writ large across his face. Looking at the keyboard, he decided to learn how to construct English sentences as fast as possible. To help achieve this, during the weekly computer classes, he grabbed a random book and copied the English words onto the screen. He practised typing on the keyboard. He sent off several emails to people he knew. In every way possible, he tried to get as comfortable as possible with the computers, the internet and the language. Bhola vowed to make full efforts to remain curious and learn everything that would help him succeed in life.

He dove into extra-curricular activities as well. He learnt to play the tabla and harmonium. He became the Cultural Secretary and fulfilled responsibilities as a House Captain. In his spare time, Bhola visited the on-campus gym, hoping the barbells would transform his average-looking physique into something formidable.

Each time the boys returned to Chand Ghat during the holidays, they increasingly felt like outsiders. They struggled to find a place to finish their holiday homework. Back at the hostel, they could spend dedicated hours studying in the quiet of their brightly lit, uncluttered dormitory room. At home, in Chand Ghat, there was no peace. Their fathers coolly sent them off on errands. Neighbourhood lads summoned them to participate in gali cricket; when the invitations were declined, the Babatpur boys were labelled as snobs with an 'attitude problem'. Taps trickled water at odd hours and electricity departed at will.

Outside, beyond the walls of their homes, the galis rang with the playful shrieks of children, the clangour of utensils, high-pitched quarrels over petty matters and the occasional plaintive bleating of goats. To the boys, Chand Ghat seemed stuck, as though suspended in time; it was oblivious to how quickly the world was moving ahead.

A part of them felt different now: as though they were better off than others. Whenever the occasional sibling fight escalated between Shortcut and his elder brother Bunty, Shortcut would deliberately throw in a few English words to startle his opponent. It was a ploy to embarrass Bunty, who readily called himself an 'angutha chhaap', an illiterate. Bunty found no pleasure in being a target for his brother's condescension, but their mother would clap her hands in awe and tell Shortcut how proud she was of his proficiency in the English language. Perhaps education was the golden ticket, she thought, that would catapult her son out of Chand Ghat and into a high-paying job.

Bunty, however, seethed from within. He felt that he deserved the applause. After all, it was he who tackled raging pyres in a hostile terrain and had to put up with the profanity-spewing maalik who exploited him for hours. He did all this to support his family, while Shortcut would eventually return to Babatpur, sleep in his comfortable hostel bed and study in an unthreatening environment. Yet, their mother thought that Shortcut was the messiah who would one day whisk her away from the cremators' ghetto.

In 2016, after scoring above 75 per cent in his tenth standard board exams, Bhola was awarded a laptop under the 'free laptop distribution scheme' initiated by the then state government led by Akhilesh Yadav. In Uttar Pradesh, the scheme rewarded meritorious students who had passed their tenth and twelfth standard exams with impressive marks.[1] Bhola was the only one among the four Chand Ghat boys to receive the laptop and the first person in his community to own one.

And in 2018, he became the first to join a private college outside Banaras.

———

It is while he is pursuing college in Ludhiana that Bhola realizes how far he has come. His friends are an organic mix of boys and girls. All of them come from wealthier backgrounds than his. When they step outside the campus to wolf down milkshakes and gobble on fried bread, they pull out currency notes from their wallets with a relaxed ease that Bhola longs to experience himself.

For them, spending a few hundred rupees here and there is not a big deal, unlike Bhola, who receives a small amount of pocket money every month from Grey and maintains a strict daily budget of Rs 160. At the cafeteria, Bhola buys breakfast for Rs 20 and lunch and dinner for Rs 70 a plate: a thali of spiced dal, steamed rice, vegetable sabzi and roti. His friends sometimes opt for a paneer curry, which Bhola cannot afford. To keep up appearances, he feigns disinterest, telling them that he is not in the mood to eat it.

It is difficult for someone in these circumstances not to spiral into the web of haves-and-have-nots. Bhola is aware of the branded clothes his classmates wear, while the shirts that hang on his back are less than half the cost. 'I wear shoes worth five hundred rupees, while my friends walk in sneakers worth five thousand rupees,' he says. Still, he refrains from spending money on clothes or shoes.

Often, he even bows out of the expensive picnics organized by his college. His friends are disappointed, but he has convinced them that his mother is against the travelling. In reality, however, Kamala Devi is completely oblivious to the life her son is leading miles away from her. Some of his friends have noticed that Bhola always backs out of planned outings. 'They have stopped inviting me now. But what do they know about my financial condition and the circumstances I come from?'

His friends are unaware that he saves his money to buy essentials for his mother. Bhola bought her a rice cooker first and sent it via an online delivery service. On receiving it, Kamala Devi gingerly unboxed the rice cooker and assessed it suspiciously. She caressed its cable with the tips of her fingers, tapped the cooker on its head a few times and then put it aside. She did not use the machine for months, until Bhola returned home from college during his holidays and taught her how to operate the peculiar-looking device by plugging it in. After her initiation, Kamala Devi was ecstatic and impressed. She began cooking everything in it—steamed rice with peas, turmeric-stained lentils and vegetables with finely diced chillies.

Bhola cannot contain his excitement as he tells me this. When he went back to college after that, he immediately ordered a vegetable blender for his mother and had that delivered too. Bhola had always wanted to make his mother proud and happy. Now he feels he can.

Bhola had once believed he would remain rooted in Chand Ghat forever: 'Scavenging shrouds and burning the dead—this is what I thought life was all about. And, like everyone dies, I would one day die too.'

However, he sees his reality slowly altering. He has promised himself that he will never go back to work at the masaan again, nor will he ever burn a body. He will prove the naysayers wrong.

15

Crumpled Paper

IN 2010, KOMAL sat in front of the mirror and ran a wide-toothed comb through her thick dark hair, thoughts waltzing through her mind. She wondered whether she would be able to catch a glimpse of the boy who lived a few houses away in the colony that belonged to the Doms. Although they were Brahmin, her family lived in a rented home in the Yadav colony, adjacent to the Doms.

A few days earlier, Lakshaya had returned to Chand Ghat from his hostel for the holidays. Although the two had never spoken a word to each other, Komal had rushed to her terrace to see him. She watched him make his way through the alley below her home, before he slipped into the gali that led to his house.

Lakshaya was aware of his admirer's existence. There had been moments when he had noticed Komal peeking at him from behind walls—a vantage point she naïvely thought was not-so-obvious. The instant their eyes met, however, Komal would

110

throw her body backwards, quickly removing herself from his line of vision, as if to magically disappear from sight.

Komal's childhood friend Barkha laughs, recalling Komal's inability to mask her feelings. 'The thing is, both Lakshaya and Komal liked each other. Both of them used to look for each other, but Komal was the one who was afraid. She didn't know how to talk to him. If he looked at her, she would run away.' It had turned into a game of hide-and-seek.

For two years, Komal and Lakshaya expressed their interest in a filmy, almost comical manner. Not once, though, was a word exchanged.

———

Finally, in 2012, things started to look up.

One day, when Komal left home to attend tuition classes, she sensed the presence of a distant shadow. She clutched her notebook and quickened her pace. Someone called out to her: 'Listen!' Komal did not stop.

'Arre, listen,' the voice repeated. Finally, the shadow caught up. 'Why aren't you listening to me? Don't worry, I won't murder you!' Lakshaya said, laughing awkwardly.

Komal halted near a small vegetable market in one of the galis. After years of keeping a measured distance, the two finally stood in front of each other. She could feel his nervous breath on her face.

'Why do you run away every time?' Lakshaya asked.

Komal felt her stomach tighten. She shrugged, 'Just like that.'

Lakshaya slid his hands in his pockets and looked at her sheepishly. 'Oh, okay. I wanted to ask you something. Can you give me your number?'

'I don't have a phone,' came the curt reply. Komal could not figure out how to behave around Lakshaya. She acted coolly, trying to appear unapproachable. Secretly, however, she hoped that he would linger.

Lakshaya stepped back and clicked his tongue. For a moment, he did not know what to say. When he looked up, Komal's eyes were glued to the ground. 'Since you don't have a phone, perhaps I can give you my number?' he offered.

Her gaze still downcast, Komal replied under her breath. '*De dijiye*. Please give it.'

Lakshaya smiled. 'Okay!'

When she glanced at him, Komal noticed that the tips of his ears had turned red. She watched him fumble around in his pockets for a moment before searching the ground, as though he was looking for something. He picked up a scrap of paper and straightened it out. Komal offered her ballpoint pen and watched him scribble something hastily.

'His knees were trembling as he wrote,' she recalls, giggling. 'It was as though he would collapse any moment.'

'I was shaking because it was the first time I was giving my number to a girl,' Lakshaya protests.

'Of course, I was nervous too,' Komal admits. '*Pehli bar baat kar rahe the, isliye bahut andar se dhak-dhak ho raha tha*. I was speaking to him for the first time. My heart was pounding.'

Lakshaya folded the slip and handed it to her. 'Give me a missed call,' he stammered. Komal quickly took the note. As he turned around and walked away, Lakshaya wondered whether his wobbly delivery had left a bad impression. That day, his confidence had eluded him; he was taken aback by his inability to mask his giddiness.

Later that night, Komal, who had never used a mobile phone before, wondered what Lakshaya meant by a 'missed call'. She asked one of her neighbours, Simi, for help. Simi was the only person Komal trusted, the only one with whom she had shared her feelings about Lakshaya.

'Just call him from the PCO and then cut the call immediately,' Simi explained.

'But what would be the purpose of that?' Komal wondered. 'Who calls someone and then cuts the line?'

'Arre, he will call you back. That way you won't spend any money on the call. Don't worry. I know these things.'

The next day, Komal made her way towards a shop that offered PCO services. There was a skip in her step and a tune in her head. Komal felt the promise of new possibilities. 'I was very excited,' she recalls. 'I finally had his phone number and I was going to call him. For two years, we had liked each other, but this was the first time I would speak to him on the phone.'

Komal dialled the number, making sure she punched the right digits. The line trilled. Komal's mouth went dry. She hung up. A few seconds later, the phone rang. She hesitantly picked up. 'Hello?'

'Hello!' came a chirpy voice from the other end of the line. 'How are you?'

Komal's voice quaked. 'I'm fine.'

'Listen, I've been wanting to tell you something.'

'What is it?' she asked.

For a moment, there was silence. Komal could hear Lakshaya breathe into the receiver. Then, he said: 'I love you.'

Komal felt a flush in her cheeks. She stood still, clutching the telephone receiver cable so tightly that it left a red mark on her palm.

Lakshaya prodded. 'Come on, you say it too.'

'I don't know. What should I say?' Komal asked nervously. She tensed up, and before she could think of anything to say, she hung up the phone. But as the day progressed, Komal began regretting leaving things unsaid with Lakshaya. She had been too shy, too tongue-tied. When she met Simi in the evening, she instructed her to help fix the situation: 'If you meet Lakshaya, please tell him that I love him too.'

When Komal's message was relayed the next day, a brooding Lakshaya sat up and smiled. He told Simi with new-found confidence: 'Tell her to tell me herself.'

The next day, Komal decided to play a prank. When Lakshaya answered her call, she changed her voice to a piercing falsetto. 'Heellooo? Guess whooo?' she asked.

There was a pause before Lakshaya replied, 'Priya, my love! How are you?'

Komal was taken aback. She lodged the receiver shut and walked off.

Later that day when she was buying groceries, Lakshaya walked up behind her. 'Did you have fun today?' he quipped.

'Go away!' she snapped. 'Go talk to Priyaaa.' The last word was uttered with an exaggerated nasal twang.

'Arre! I just went along with the game you were playing,' he said flirtatiously. 'Did you not want me to?'

Komal elbowed him away. When he saw her face, his tone became conciliatory. He reasoned with her, begged, apologized and even played the role of a heartbroken Bhojpuri hero. The last attempt seemed to work; Komal's anger fizzled as she broke into restrained laughter.

———

Their phone conversations became a ritual—they spoke to each other whenever possible. Lakshaya talked; Komal listened. Often, they would walk along the ghats in the afternoon, when the sun was high and there weren't too many eyes darting about. Their fingers intuitively brushed against each other, never interlacing. In sweat-drenched clothes, Komal and Lakshaya would swig fizzy soft drinks from cold bottles and watch beads of condensation slide down the glass surface. Komal's eyes would briefly meet his and then hurriedly turn away.

When he asked Komal to be his girlfriend—his eyes steady, sure and filled with awe—Komal giggled self-consciously and changed the subject. However, when he carefully leaned in to pluck a bit of white cotton fluff caught in her hair, she blushed because of the intimacy of the act but did not pull away.

As days passed, Komal's reserve slowly ebbed and she began to feel at ease around Lakshaya. Their relationship was growing, evolving. From being a boy whom Komal barely knew, Lakshaya was turning into the most important person in her life. All pretences and inhibitions effortlessly fell away when they were together. If Lakshaya gorged on a samosa, Komal would grab the fried snack from his hand without asking, bite into the crusty pastry and savour its hot potato filling. When she bought a bottle of nail polish and wanted to test its colour, Lakshaya willingly offered his fingernail.

'There was this kind of apnapan, a known kinship, between us,' Lakshaya says.

Tehri was Lakshaya's favourite dish: aromatic golden rice flavoured with spices, potatoes and onions. When Komal cooked it in her kitchen, she would furtively spoon some of it into a plastic bag, tie a knot and slide it out her window on a stick. Outside, on the street, Lakshaya would cup his hands, catch the pouch and disappear.

On her birthday, Lakshaya gifted Komal a watch. It wasn't too expensive, but she knew he had saved up for her. She wore it every day until it stopped working—and even then, she did not throw it away but saved it as a keepsake.

They referred to each other as 'LK'—a marriage of their first initials. It wasn't long before Lakshaya got 'LK' inked on his arm—the letters nestled within the shape of a heart. The tattoo danced each time he flexed his muscles. To Komal, the inky mark on his skin was a promise that he was all in.

16

Everyone Finds Out

WHILE KOMAL AND Lakshaya's relationship blossomed, there were moments when it tottered under the uncomfortable weight of secrecy. If Komal's family or her neighbours learnt about her affair with a Chaudhary boy, they would be outraged. And so, they hid their relationship and kept their lively, excited gaits in check. Even Barkha, Komal's friend who was known to have the nose of a bloodhound, didn't suspect anything.

Komal always met Lakshaya secretly. Decisions relating to their rendezvous would be finalized over the phone. Lakshaya would choose a meeting spot where no one was likely to recognize them or know their names.

On the predetermined day of their meeting, Lakshaya always left Chand Ghat first. About half an hour later, Komal would discreetly follow, accompanied by Simi. On one such day, the girls rode in a shared auto rickshaw and reached a location near the Rajghat bridge. Lakshaya and his friend were waiting for them there. The quartet spent an hour or so roaming about, sucking on ice lollies. When it was time for them to return home, Komal spotted one of the Yadav boys, who had been slyly watching them from afar. Komal was terrified.

'*Woh ladka bahut dusht tha.* That boy was extremely evil,' she says, eyes flashing.

Komal wondered how he had known where they were. On their rickshaw ride back home, her mind spiralled. There would be an uproar within the community, she thought, picturing an ambush. '*Mujhe laga sab gaali-galoch denge.* I thought everyone would curse me. I came home scared, wondering whether there would be a showdown in my mohalla.'

When she arrived, though, there was no clamour. Everything felt eerie: the calm before the storm. Komal knew that her secret was out. She just didn't know who had ratted on her.

———

The thing about secrets is that they need to be kept as such. A secret is a luminous bubble that offers the illusion of protection, a shield from a reality too ugly to confront. Yet, all bubbles are fated to be pricked.

It wasn't long before others learnt that something was going on. It was as though insidious whispers had swished over the dark waters of the river, swooped across the stone steps, gathered strength and surged towards the neighbourhood like wailing sirens.

The Yadavs in her colony had become suspicious.

When Komal was younger and left home for the market, she would politely nod at a middle-aged neighbour who owned a paan shop in her gali. She had been visiting his house since she was a child. It was from his window that Komal would spy on an unwitting Lakshaya as he sauntered through the narrow lane. The shop that belonged to this 'paan-wale uncle' (as she called him) was where the Yadav men smoked and hung out, traded gossip and news. The paan-wale uncle would call out to Komal with a friendly smile each time he saw her passing by. Sometimes, he would request her to pick up items from the market for him and Komal would happily do so.

And so, one day, when the paan-wale uncle suddenly stopped Komal in her tracks, the look on his face far from friendly, she grew anxious.

'*Tum Domva se batiyavat hai?* You speak to a Dom?' he asked her in an abrasive manner with an unwarranted authority.

'No, I don't speak to anyone,' she replied and began to walk away.

'You're lying!' he said accusingly.

'Why would I lie?' Komal asked, noticing her own voice falter.

The uncle's betel-stained fingernails pulled out a folded document from his pocket. He waved it in the air. 'Who has been talking to you then? Whose number is this?'

The sheet of paper carried a list of phone numbers. Komal had not known it then, but the paan-wale uncle had procured the call list from a man who worked at the same PCO shop that Komal frequented.

'I had no idea at the time that the man at the PCO knew him,' she says.

The uncle brushed past her and walked off in a huff. Not long after, everyone in her mohalla knew that she had been secretly speaking to Lakshaya.

'People suspected that there was something going on between us and on the basis of their suspicion they had procured the list,' Komal explains.

To ensure that Komal did not visit the PCO any more, Lakshaya bought her a cheap, cherry-red mobile phone.

———

Their relationship, however, was out in the open.

The day Lakshaya left Chand Ghat to return to his boarding school, Komal's parents showed up at his house unannounced. His father was not around and his mother, Geeta, had just finished bathing. She was surprised by their visit.

Komal's mother pounced on her almost immediately. 'Your son speaks to my daughter. We don't like it. You have to make him understand the situation,' she said.

Geeta narrowed her eyes and launched a counter-attack. 'Can't you rein in your daughter? I stay in my home. I don't step out. How am I supposed to know whom my son speaks to, where he is wandering, where he is going? I don't know all of that.'

Komal's father stood in the doorway, frowning, arms folded across his chest, but he held his tongue. There was no point speaking to Lakshaya's mother. He would speak to the boy's father, man to man.

Back home, however, his wrath descended on Komal. Anger tore open his mouth. 'This is what I've taught you?' he growled. 'To do *such* things?'

In the Yadav colony, the seeds for gossip had already been sown. Wild stories had begun to take root. Stories which, in Komal's father's mind, were obstinate weeds that had to be pulled out. He decided that the ancestral hometown—a hamlet miles away from Banaras—would be a suitable and conservative detention centre for his daughter. Komal would stay there with their extended family until things settled down. City life had encouraged youngsters to become liberal-minded and nurture an appalling disregard for caste 'purity'. It had made his daughter too soft, too weak, too trusting. She wasn't clever or mature enough, he felt, to discern other people's motives. The village air would set her right.

A month into Komal's departure from the colony, another rumour took flight.

⁃⁃⁃⁃⁃

One morning, Geeta heard the clanking of utensils as Ajay's wife washed them. Before she could ask her to stop, someone yelled in the lane: 'Lakshaya has eloped with that Pandey girl.'

In that moment, Geeta wished her ears would turn brittle and break into tiny shards so that she could pretend she had not heard anything. Surely, it could not be true. Lakshaya was at boarding school. Unless—she imagined the worst—he had run away without informing anyone?

Geeta asked Ajay to call the school. Ajay, annoyed at having been disturbed in the midst of his morning tea, irritably dialled the number. When the warden picked up, he requested to speak to Lakshaya immediately. They were informed that the students were in class and any telephonic conversation would have to wait.

'We were so tense,' recalls Geeta. 'We were told that we could only speak to him after eight in the evening, and I had got the news at nine that morning. I could not eat any food. I had to wait.'

Hearing Lakshaya's voice and confirming he was at boarding school was the only way to prove that the rumour was false. If, however, he wasn't there, Geeta feared the seismic repercussions that would follow.

When Ajay called again later that day, it was Bhola who came on the line. 'What happened?' he asked calmly.

Geeta snatched the mobile phone from Ajay's hands. 'I need to speak to my son.'

Bhola told her that Lakshaya had not been feeling well and had decided to sleep early. 'Tell me what has happened,' Bhola said. 'I will give him the message.'

'I need to speak to Lakshaya right now. I want to hear his voice!' she rasped.

'But he might already be asleep,' Bhola reasoned.

'Wake him!'

Ten minutes later, a tired Lakshaya returned her call. 'What happened, Mummy?' he asked, yawning.

17

'No One Will Touch You'

LIKE A TUG in her gut, Komal knew she was destined to be with Lakshaya. Despite protests from both their families, the two continued to see each other over the next few years. During this period, their relationship was primarily long distance, since Lakshaya was still at boarding school. They would speak on the phone when possible. Whenever Lakshaya returned to Chand Ghat for the holidays, Komal's eyes would light up. The two would spend as much time together as they could.

One would think that as time passed, the communities' discontent would abate, but it only intensified. Both the communities frowned upon the 'brazenness' with which Lakshaya and Komal continued to be together. The pair did not realize that their relationship had metamorphosed into something larger than them—that it was perceived as a ludicrous misalliance that drummed up gossip and hearsay.

Komal tucks her hair behind her ear. 'The Yadavs' ego had been hurt—that was the problem,' she explains, recounting what happened years ago.

We are sitting in a house somewhere on the periphery of the city. A standing fan sputters hot air. Outside the window, a tractor drives noisily down a poorly paved path. She waits for it to pass so that she can be audible again.

Komal sits hunched with her knees touching her chin. A shadow of sadness looms over her face. She lets out a deep breath—the kind that fills up one's lungs and remains there when the body is tense, until the air pries open the mouth and escapes. Outside, wiry trees sway and rustle.

'The Yadavs would say things like, "*Yeh log humari paun ki jutti hain.* These people [Doms] belong at our feet. How dare they think that they are the same biradari—standing—as ours?"' What bothered them even more was that she had not chosen the company of a boy from their caste. Komal's 'misconduct' had set a wrong precedent. Taunts began to be hurled at the Pandey family. 'People from our mohalla would tell my father things like, "Your daughter is spoilt. As a Brahmin, she is romancing a Dom. You must control her." We started having a lot of problems at home,' Komal recalls.

As days passed, the rancour grew, brandishing its sharp teeth. In the afternoons when Komal left home to attend coaching classes, chatter would rise and swell in the alleyways. Her neighbours tossed cuss words in the air like spare pennies. 'They would say things like, "This Brahmin girl, motherfucker! What a randi—whore,"' Komal alleges. Their language turned fouler when she wore a pair of jeans. A ragtag gang of Yadav boys lurking about in the gali would snigger and comment as she passed by. 'Look at the way she flaunts her round ass to everyone. Only the desperate likes of her can enjoy that Dom boy.' Sometimes, for fun, they would intimidate her by threatening to strike Lakshaya. In thick Bhojpuri accents they would hiss: '*Aaj maraii*. Today, we will hit.'

Komal was miserable. She did not know how to deflect such loathsome attention. Their relationship was on everyone's lips. 'It was a constant topic of conversation: morning, evening, afternoon. It never stopped,' she recounts.

Days drifted at a sluggish pace. There were times when her neighbours would move closer to her window to heckle. There were days when, eyes glinting with moral superiority, they rebuked her father: 'Your girl is dirtying up the mahaul! She is behaving like a cheap whore!' Komal squeezes her eyes shut when she recalls that moment, shuddering as she repeats the derogatory word.

The neighbours wove lies: that Lakshaya regularly visited Komal's home—a Yadav property—and that she was 'staining' the name of Brahmins across the country. Unable to defend herself, Komal would stifle her cries with her pillow at night, her body quaking, until, harrowed and exhausted, she finally fell asleep.

Komal caresses the edge of her kameez between her fingers. 'Now, you tell me,' she asks, 'even if I loved him, would I dare bring him home—that too to a rented flat? People said terrible things about me, words that I can't even repeat to you.'

It seemed so easy to discredit a woman, to call her names and humiliate her publicly the moment she stepped away from the 'acceptable' path. As a girl, Komal was aware of every rule and had always played by the book. She had carefully arranged her life according to what was expected of her as a girl. She steered clear of misfits, never repeated crude jokes or cackled loudly. She kept to herself, studied hard and earned the admiration of her schoolteachers. Komal always returned home before the clock struck eight. If, for some reason, her watch swept past the time, she would sink into an uncomfortable guilt.

Her only 'fault' had been that she had befriended and loved Lakshaya—a Dom.

Soon, her friends began distancing themselves. When Komal knocked on Simi's door and waited outside her home to accompany her for a tuition class, she overheard Simi's mother telling her off: 'Don't speak to that girl. Stay away from her from now on.' When Simi opened the door, she told Komal that she could not walk with her that day. A few days later, after their tuition class, Komal waited for Simi and her other friends outside the building. 'We will be walking ahead of you,' one of them told her as they stepped out in a group. 'You can come behind us.' And while Simi assured Komal that she would continue to speak to her, she would not risk doing so in front of others.

Eventually, Komal would learn that it was, in fact, Simi who had betrayed her and told her mother about Komal's secret relationship. Simi's mother, in turn, informed her husband, who sent the Yadav boy after them to Rajghat. That was the end of the girls' friendship.

Komal shifts uncomfortably as she reflects on the enormity of the situation. *'Har koi ne mera saath uss time chhor diya tha.* Everyone had abandoned me at that time,' she recalls.

'Did you ever say anything to the Yadavs?' I ask her.

'What could I have possibly said?' Komal asks, with a tone of helplessness. 'The more one said anything, the more they were instigated. *Aas-paas ke log sabhi unke the. Mera kaun tha?*

Everyone around us was one of their people. There was no one to call my own.'

Komal's family lived in a community that was not their own, in a house that was not theirs. 'The Yadavs would have thrown us out had we retaliated,' Komal says. Her family was outnumbered. 'They had huge backing. It wasn't about their strength in Chand Ghat alone—they had immense support in the neighbouring areas as well.'

Once, in 2013, a group of Yadav boys bashed up her younger brother, Aman. Tired of their incessant badgering, he had protested, but the taunts quickly took on an uglier colour. 'The boys were saying things like, "Take a thousand rupees and give your sister to us for a night,"' Aman remembers. 'So, I picked up a brick and struck one of them with it.' The Yadav boys hit back. When Komal's father lodged a complaint, the Yadav community was livid. 'They told my father, "You motherfucker, you complained about us? You set foot here and we'll teach you a lesson,"' Komal says.

While Komal wrestled with the threat from outside, there was also the threat from within. Her father insisted that there was no future for her with the son of a corpse burner. If, in the years to come, she did decide to marry him, her identity would be reduced to that of a 'low-born'. She would no longer be a Brahmin's daughter, but a Dom's wife. He shuddered at the very thought of it. 'You will belong to a caste from whom no one accepts even a glass of water,' he cautioned her. 'We are Brahmins, my girl, but if you become a Dom, no one will touch you.' Her father paused before he issued another warning. 'Even I will sever all ties with you.'

Komal reasoned with him in a soft voice, 'But Lakshaya is a human being too. Think about it, Papa. He has no flaws. The "worst" thing I may have done in your eyes is to speak to him. Papa, I promise, I haven't done anything wrong.'

Despite all the chaos in her life, never had Komal felt so sure about herself. 'My only desire in life at the time was to marry Lakshaya.'

'Why?' I ask her. What was it about him that convinced her to go against the will of her family, against time-bound traditions?

It was the way he looked at her, she says. The way he tended to her needs, spoke to her with a soft lilt in his voice. He had an uncanny ability to calm her, to soothe her tense brow when she was worried. Unlike the men in their neighbourhood who struck their wives, Lakshaya worshipped her. He spoke of a quiet life together and helped Komal envision a possible happy future. They seldom fought, but when they did, he always returned to her.

'When you have found someone who treats you with respect, cares for you, never screams at you, never hits you, never curses you, you don't let go,' Komal replies.

Yet, the two knew that their precious, precarious world—one in which only they existed—could easily crumble.

'Do you think,' I wonder aloud, 'if the two of you had married each other at that time, you might have been attacked in some way?'

'Yes,' Komal says, nodding with certainty. 'They could have done anything. At that time, the situation was such.'

In her book *Gendering Caste: Through a Feminist Lens*, historian Uma Chakravarti explains how women's bodies have been used to control and maintain caste hierarchies. She mentions the observations of social anthropologist Nur Yalman, who argues that Hindu society believes that a watertight way of protecting one's land and women, while ensuring the purity of caste, is by policing the women's bodies and sexuality. In other words, bloodlines and land can be preserved by keeping the women in check.[1]

Chakravarti writes that according to the marriage laws designed by Manu, he 'alludes to 'the "permissible" practices whereby a man from the brahmana/kshatriya/vaisya castes must have his first wife from his own caste but can have one from each of the castes lower than his own too'.[2] The law, of course, fiercely objected to a Brahmin man taking a Shudra woman as his first wife, for such a marriage would 'pollute' the lineage and the hierarchical order.[3]

Unlike a man, however, a woman from a dominant caste could not violate endogamy in any way. She was not permitted to marry a 'lower-caste' man. Such a union, called 'pratiloma', was considered 'unnatural' and 'reprehensible' and was thus forbidden.[4] If performed, it could lead to punishment, which, as suggested in the Dharmashastras, included killing the man who belonged to the oppressed caste, and mutilating the woman, while also deeming her a social outcast.[5]

This centuries-old line of thought, one that holds women responsible for either preserving or polluting bloodlines, has endured the test of time and exists to this day. Caste purity is inextricably linked to a woman's virtue, and, thus, any hint of 'waywardness' on her part is a cause for alarm. The moment a girl is born, she unwittingly inherits the invisible 'duty' of protecting the 'honour' of her family and, by extension, her community. Thus, a woman must be aggressively 'guarded' through surveillance at all costs.

––––

Soon after the unsettling events of 2013, Komal's father walked out of their house, never to return. People speculated that he had deliberately abandoned his family, unable to handle the disgrace his daughter had brought on all of them. Komal's younger brother, Aman, said that his father was mentally unstable and had disappeared in the crowd like a child who had lost their way, while Komal insisted that he had run off to Mumbai to live a different life. He had disappeared once before, leaving her mother, and had come back unannounced, only after three years. The chances of him returning this time, however, seemed bleaker.

Komal's mother was beside herself. She threatened to remove Komal from school and wed her to a boy from their community. 'I will get you married off and you can go live with your in-laws. No more studies for you,' she said one day, hassled and concerned about her inability to afford the upkeep of her children. Marrying Komal off would mitigate the pressure of providing for one child at least. Komal was in the ninth standard at the time.

Lakshaya stepped up and promised to fund Komal's education.

'Just think about it,' Komal says. 'At that time, Lakshaya saved up his money and invested it in my education to make sure I studied. He ensured that I never lacked anything in my life.'

The tension in the neighbourhood, however, continued to mount. Komal's family was now missing the patriarch. Her mother alone could not fight off the Yadavs' vicious insinuations. Komal and her brother were mere teenagers at the time. Lakshaya's own family was pressuring him to disassociate himself from Komal.

Lakshaya had to make a tough decision.

18

The Ultimatum

ONE MORNING, LAKSHAYA'S family was startled by a knock on the door. At the threshold stood a police officer with a scowl on his face. He inquired about Lakshaya's whereabouts. The boy was promptly called downstairs from his room. Moments later Lakshaya stood before the cop, his anxious family members huddled around him.

The inspector stated the purpose of his visit. 'There has been a complaint against you, boy,' he said gruffly. 'Is there a girl named Komal whom you bother?'

Lakshaya's face turned pale. 'No, there is nothing like that,' he replied. The officer looked at Lakshaya's father and instructed him to accompany his son to the local police station. The pair got ready and walked there.

On the way, Lakshaya frantically dialled Komal's number from his cell phone. Komal did not pick up. Lakshaya dialled again. This time, she took the call. When Komal learnt about the situation, she disconnected the line, grabbed her mother and rushed to the police station in a daze. She clarified to the inspector that Lakshaya was not at fault. That they were willingly together. That people in her neighbourhood did not approve of their relationship and were maliciously slinging mud by filing a fake harassment complaint. This had been done to sully her boyfriend's name and scare him off. Komal's mother supported her daughter's statement.

The inspector carefully read both their faces; years of experience had taught him how to detect a lie. He then grumbled something about idle people wasting his time, and let Lakshaya go.

When the young boy stepped outside, he pulled Komal aside. His voice was curt and direct, his sentences carefully clipped. Komal fell apart at his words.

'Will you do one thing I ask of you?' Lakshaya asked, barely able to keep his anger in check. He had been called to the police station to be questioned—it was an embarrassment for him and his family.

'Anything,' she replied.

'Pack your things and leave Chand Ghat,' he instructed.

For a moment, Komal was speechless with disbelief. Her ears burned.

Lakshaya hurried to fill in the steely silence. '*Na tum yahan rahogi, na yeh sab tension hoga.* If you won't live here, there will be no tension. Otherwise, in the future, there will be more drama. It has happened once, it will happen again.'

He looked at her with a remarkable surety. At the age of twenty-two, a cluster of tough life experiences had hardened him, melding a certain perceptiveness into his bones. He had developed a preternatural ability to think practically ahead.

Komal felt as though she were choking on a thousand insects. She struggled to understand what this meant. It infuriated her that Lakshaya was making a life-altering decision without consulting her or stopping to think how it would impact her. Was this the end of their relationship? If she left Chand Ghat, how would she see him every day? He was denying her a future—the promise of a life together in Chand Ghat.

'Say something,' he pleaded.

She replied sourly, 'I won't go.'

'You *have* to,' Lakshaya insisted.

When Komal asked him where she would go without her mother and brother, he told her to take them along. He would make arrangements for another house—one far away from Chand Ghat. For a while now, Lakshaya had been quietly saving the pocket money that Grey had been sending to each of the boys every month at school. Lakshaya told Komal that he would use it to pay the token amount required to reserve the new house for her family. All she had to do was agree.

Komal hesitated momentarily, took a deep breath and then objected one more time.

'Fine. Then we will never speak again,' Lakshaya said coldly before turning to walk away. He did not say goodbye.

When Komal returned home with her mother, she felt lightheaded, ready to crumble. She took a moment to catch her breath. When she called Lakshaya later, he was quiet. Komal tried to reason with him. She told him that what he was asking of her was impossible, unthinkable. He said that people wouldn't stop gossiping until she distanced herself from the chaos. She asked how she would convince her family. He revealed that his own family was pressuring him to break things off with her because history stood as proof that it was always the oppressed castes who bore the brunt of dishonouring scandals. Lakshaya promised Komal that he would do right by her. All she had to do was trust him.

And so, much against her will, she agreed—because she knew he was right. Deep down, Komal had caved even before she had made the phone call. She had grown to love him immeasurably, and had a natural willingness to obey his every word. It was something that had been unconsciously cultivated in her: to acquiesce to the man whom she hoped to wed one day. If she could convince her mother and brother to leave Chand Ghat, she would collect her belongings and never return.

———

At first, Komal's mother scoffed at the very thought of uprooting her family, that too at the behest of a mere boy. She did not trust Lakshaya's ability to scout for a new home for them. Things would not change as long as Komal and Lakshaya continued to see each other, even if they relocated: casteism was everywhere. She told her daughter to forget moving elsewhere and think nothing of it.

As the days progressed, however, the situation in Chand Ghat became murkier. The harassment did not stop. The name-calling and sexual gestures did not stop. Then one night, when it was quiet and dark, a group of drunk Yadav men assembled outside Komal's home and banged on the door. Aman alleges that he heard them screaming: 'We will burn down this house!' With each aggressive thud, their voices rose higher. 'We will not let you live here!' they threatened. By next morning, Komal's mother had changed her mind.

It was on moving day that she publicly acknowledged Lakshaya for the first time. Their neighbours stood around idly, watching Komal and Aman wobble and falter as they tried to carry bags and slide trunks out of their home. When Komal's mother noticed Lakshaya darting in their direction, her gaze— stern whenever she saw him—softened.

She wiped the sweat that had settled under her lips and hesitated for a moment, before calling out. 'Come here. Come help us with our luggage, please,' she requested Lakshaya. 'Help us take out all the remaining things from the house.'

To this day, Komal feels giddy as she recounts that moment: 'It was like right before leaving the mohalla, my mother made sure that she *showed* everyone that Lakshaya was a part of our lives.'

When the family moved into their new home—a small, rented space with yellow walls and a tiny window—the harassment finally stopped. It was 2016.

The same year, Lakshaya dropped out of school. He would work extremely hard to support Komal's education. Bhola scoffed at Lakshaya's reckless decision, convinced that he had traded his education, his future, for a childish crush—one that Bhola felt would fizzle out in the days to come. Shortcut would describe Lakshaya's behaviour as remarkably flippant, suggesting that those who are given things for free, often take them for granted and forget their value. Deep down, however, Lakshaya felt responsible for Komal, as though it was because of him that she had been forced to leave Chand Ghat. To him, the decision wasn't frivolous; it was pragmatic.

19

Business as Usual

DOMS ARE KEEPERS of a sacred flame—supposedly burning for centuries—over which they have sole ownership. Lighting each funeral pyre with the Doms' fire is considered not only auspicious but also crucial. Without it, it is alleged, a devout Hindu will not receive moksha, liberation from the cycle of death and rebirth. Thus, it is at the cremation ground that the Doms' ritualistic significance is elevated and remains unchallenged.

A popular Dom legend describes how the community came to own this mystical fire. One day, Goddess Parvati misplaced one of her earrings at the ghat. While Lord Shiva looked for the jewel, a Brahmin man found it and pocketed it. When Shiva learnt about this, he sentenced the culprit, and the generations that would follow him, to the lowest caste, for eternity. The man grovelled for forgiveness, leading Shiva to gift the family a boon: an eternal fire that would enable Hindus to receive moksha.

The Doms are believed to be descendants of the man who received Shiva's curse.[1] For generations, only the male members of the community cremate corpses.

Adjacent to the steps that lead into Manikarnika Ghat, there is a huge, partially enclosed space that was built centuries ago with stone slabs. I think of it as the unofficial headquarters of the corpse-burning business. Locally called madi, this room is on a slight elevation, compared to the cremation ground, and provides an undisturbed view of the masaan. From here you can watch the theatre of death slowly unravel before your eyes. Time moves at a sluggish pace. Everything seems drawn-out; everything seems surreal. Yet here, nothing is more real than death.

Within the community, the Doms who are maaliks, bosses, wield authority over the sacred fire. They also oversee the cremation proceedings and recruit poorer Doms—corpse burners like Aakash and Mohan—who directly labour on the ground.

At the headquarters, a Dom maalik and his manager sit cross-legged on a pair of thin cotton mattresses. A few feet away is the Doms' agni, the fire that glows in a shallow pit. It is consistently replenished with dry wood. The maalik's job is to provide this fire to mourning families. Bundles of khar—reed thin and dull gold in hue—lie in a messy heap against the wall. This grass is considered holy. The maalik perfunctorily lights a bouquet of khar with the sacred fire and hands the flaming grass to the primary griever.[2] While performing the last rites, he (or she) will circle the pyre a specified number of times, walking anti-clockwise, before lighting it.

At times when the maalik is not available, the manager or another Dom provides the sacred fire. In his tattered notebook, the manager registers the number of corpses that are cremated at the ghat on a specific date. The notebook changes each year on Diwali, I am told. One of the managers whom I met was not too keen to show the contents of the notebook. Shortcut later told me that written alongside each corpse is the name of the seller who supplied the wood and the corpse burner who built the pyre.

A small shop right outside the madi sells samagri—religious paraphernalia required for cremation, like sandalwood sticks, camphor, raal, ashtagandha, etc. These are packed in airtight plastic bags and made available for purchase along with small cartons of ghee and earthen clay pots. A young man, perhaps eighteen or nineteen years old, sits behind the counter with earphones slung around his neck, playing a game on his cell phone. He seems uninterested in engaging with customers, unless they address him themselves. Similar shops dot the alleyway that leads to Manikarnika Ghat.

In 2022, although the official fee for the fire is fixed at Rs 500, the Dom maaliks can quote a higher fee to their customers, and often do. The bereft families, who at the time are in anguish and trying to cope with the loss of a loved one, are usually not in a position to negotiate and, therefore, almost always agree reluctantly. If the families refuse, the maaliks turn them away.

In a similar vein, the community of wood sellers has control over the wood that is required to build the pyre. They too command a steep price for their timber. There are no Dom-owned wood shops. At Manikarnika Ghat, as well as at Harishchandra Ghat, the corpse burners' and the wood sellers' jobs never mingle; their labour-intensive occupations are sharply divided and caste-bound, and the boundaries between them are almost never crossed.

There are, however, some exceptions.

––––––––––

Sunny Chaudhary stands at a tea stall in a narrow lane that leads to Manikarnika Ghat, wolfing down a kachori, flakes of the crust falling clumsily on his shirt. His legs, 'two matchsticks attached to a torso' according to his friends, are clad in faded jeans, and his black shoes carry traces of mud. Sunny uses the tip of his tongue to wiggle out the remains of the kachori stuck between his tobacco-stained teeth.

We watch a cycle-rickshaw slowly inch its way into the lane. The rickshaw-puller winces as he pushes on the pedal. The uneven ground makes it difficult for him to steer his rickshaw with its passenger. Behind the rickshaw, a trickle of men half-heartedly chant, '*Ram naam satya hai.*'

The cycle-rickshaw's passenger is a slender corpse, bound firmly in white cloth, wreathed in orange marigolds. The deceased was a gaunt, aged man—the only part of his body visible is his face. The corpse has been placed vertically at a slant in the cycle-rickshaw, its feet lodged rigidly into the footrest and its head sticking out awkwardly through the open frame of the vehicle.

Sunny lunges towards the man in the front, who appears to be related to the deceased, but another wood seller, his competitor, beats him at the hustle.

'Sir,' Sunny's competitor says in a raspy voice, crushing his beedi under his slipper, 'you will require wood. Don't worry, I am here.'

'How much will it cost?' the man asks, pulling out money from the pocket of his starched, crisp kurta and handing it to the rickshaw-puller. The wood seller gauges the relative. Most corpses are delivered to Manikarnika Ghat on the shoulders of local men; a cycle-rickshaw delivery is a rare sight. For one, navigating a rickshaw through the overcrowded galis of Banaras is a cumbersome undertaking—the cycle-rickshaw certainly costs more than the physical labour of men on foot. Cars are out of the question since they can neither fit nor navigate through the narrow lanes that lead to the masaan.

Sunny knows that the other wood seller will quote some outrageous number—and that will be his cue to swoop in and offer a better deal. The wood seller is still talking to the relative when Sunny jumps in.

'Sir, sir! We have better wood than his, sir!' he says, disrupting the two men's conversation.

The wood seller frowns and waves his hand dismissively. 'Don't listen to him and waste your time, sir. He's a Dom. He doesn't know anything about selling wood. I'm a Yadav. Come, we'll start the process.'

Sunny mouths a profanity that suggests the wood seller is sexually intimate with his mother. The man in the starched kurta flinches and scowls at Sunny before following the wood seller.

———

There are over a dozen wood shops that flank Manikarnika's lane. Some have boards with neatly painted lettering, which proudly advertise the owner's name—like 'Gupta Ji Lakdi Wale'— informing potential clients of the owner's caste. Each board carries two to three cell phone numbers. Sunny is one of few Doms at Manikarnika Ghat who have managed to pierce the otherwise impervious caste demarcation between corpse burners and wood sellers. He had convinced one of the shop owners to hire him as an employee at his wood shop. This, in practice, is seldom done, but his employer is aware of Sunny's glib tongue and aggressiveness in the field. He is hard-working, intelligent and a canny negotiator. 'The moment I see a client, I can tell how much he wants to pay and how much he can actually afford,' Sunny explains.

Wood sellers are adept readers of body language. By just looking at potential clients—their clothes, their gait, their neatly trimmed fingernails, the air of self-assuredness—the wood sellers can assess a client's position in society and, consequently, their ability to pay. According to Sunny, at Manikarnika Ghat, clients spend anywhere between Rs 2,000 and Rs 60,000 on wood alone. For high-class cremations, the costs tend to be stratospheric. Thousands are spent on using the finest wood, like sandalwood and sweet-smelling dhoop. In the 'package deal', large quantities of clarified butter and other funeral paraphernalia are included. The client is given the option of having multicoloured rangoli designs around the pyre, as well as the freshest flowers to decorate it.

Wood sellers like Sunny are well-versed in manipulating emotions, a negotiation tactic he has learnt through experience. When a client feels uncomfortable paying a high sum, Sunny tries to reason with him. He tells a chief mourner, 'Brother, your father lived for many years, and during that time all the money he made, everything he did, was for your benefit. Now that he is no more, the least you can do to honour him is just give four thousand rupees for his final rites. You are doing this for *him*.'

If the deceased was someone's mother, he might say, 'This is the only way your mata ji will find peace. What are a few extra rupees for good wood? After all, this was the woman who birthed you and lovingly raised you. This is not the time to act miserly. You are doing this for *her*.'

Some of the mourners I spoke to used adjectives like 'insincere' and 'conceited' to describe the men with whom they bargained over the cremation fee and the cost of wood at the ghats. This, however, is the labourers' primary source of income. For them, it is purely business, and a business removed from remorse is the one that thrives. Emotions are an impediment when it comes to financial negotiations.

Interestingly, most Hindus seldom bargain with the Brahmin pandits who are invited to perform sacred rituals at wedding ceremonies, bless newborns and recite mantras during cremations. Their presence on such occasions is deemed necessary according to Hindu customs, and it is on the strength of this indispensability that many mantra-chanting Brahmins charge exorbitant fees. Clients simply do what they can to meet the ask. In his book *Caste Matters*, scholar Dr Suraj Yengde refers to Jyotirao Phule, an important anti-caste social reformer who wrote about 'Bhat-Brahmins' in *Shetkaryacha Asud* (*The Cultivator's Whipcord*, 1881). Phule describes how these Brahmins, who were invited by farmers to officiate certain ceremonies, demanded high-priced food items like chapatti and ghee be served to them. Although these farmers could not afford to feed their own families, they ensured the Brahmins' every need was met in order to please them.[3] Phule, says Yengde, considered Brahmins to be 'freeloaders' who sought to 'extort' the masses.[4]

Competition in the lane is fierce and Sunny's primary competitor has an advantage: his shop is closer to the stone steps that descend into the cremation ground.

Sunny cannot waste time nursing his disappointment. His eyes scour the area. He spots two men who appear lost and confused; they are watching the thick smoke rise high from the pyres and stain a washed-out sky. He hurries over to them and asks, 'You need something, uncle?'

The shorter man, with a freshly shaved head, turns around, scrutinizes Sunny and nods. He and his brother have travelled in a four-wheeler from a small town in Bihar and brought their mother's body to Manikarnika Ghat to be cremated. They are accompanied by a string of shavyatris—about ten male family members.

'Not to worry, uncle,' Sunny assures him immediately. 'You need wood? I'm here to help. I will arrange everything for you. From a Dom's agni to a Dom corpse burner who will place the body on the pyre, the samagri, the wood—total!'

The brothers agree. Sunny clasps his hands behind his back and instructs them to follow him. Although the pair does not appear to be as wealthy as the customer he lost moments ago, he has to make a living.

The brothers and I follow Sunny, who leads us away from the cremation ground and the din of death. We ascend the stone steps and walk past groups of men who are sipping tea, crushing tobacco and smoking beedis. As we make a tight right into another gali—a slight climb—rows of wood shops raise their heads: logs spill out of them like a hundred tongues. Sunny leads us to what looks like a dank cubbyhole.

'We're here. Please come inside,' he says, ushering us in. The men precariously step over smaller logs that lie near the shop's entrance. More logs are piled inside, next to a small seating area. After spiritedly dusting down a frayed, blue couch with his hands, Sunny invites the men to settle down. They politely decline, saying they want to attend to the matter in hand.

In Hindu tradition, it is either the eldest or the youngest son who performs the role of the primary griever. Sunny peers at the brothers: the older one, possibly in his late forties, is dressed in civilian clothing and speaks calmly. The younger one, in his early forties, stands beside him, tongue-tied, in a white dhoti. It is he who will perform the last rites for his mother.

In the shop, amid heaps of pyre wood, is a rusty batkara— an old, bulky iron beast used to weigh the logs. Sunny informs the brothers about the mann, or quantity, of wood that will be required for the cremation, which depends on the size and weight of the corpse.

<hr>

One mann or maund is approximately 37.32 kilograms. If a corpse weighs 35–40 kilograms, 5 mann of wood is sufficient. If a person weighs 40–70 kilograms, then 7 mann of wood is required. Similarly, a person weighing 70–90 kilograms would require 9 mann, and so on. Vendors usually charge Rs 400 for dry wood and Rs 300 for wet wood per mann. If the client is wealthier, the ask rises. In a month, Sunny earned anywhere between Rs 15,000 and Rs 25,000, depending on the client and his haggling expertise.

For those who have the means, it does not matter how much the deceased weighs. They can afford to purchase surplus dry wood for their dead, since the quality and quantity of wood are recognized as symbols of power and abundance. Conversely, the poor are often forced to buy cheap, wet timber, which takes longer to catch fire. Sometimes, to mitigate expenses, two or more corpses from different families are piled on top of each other on a pyre.

The wood from mango, babul, deodar and other trees is used, but not from peepal and banyan trees, since the latter are believed to be the residences of deities, or sometimes, malicious spirits. 'That is why no one cuts or burns them,' Sunny tells me.

Once their mother's corpse has been cremated, the two men return to the same room where they met Sunny earlier.

'*Ao, chacha.* Come, uncle,' beckons Sunny. He is seated on the blue sofa with another client.

I watch the elder brother take the lead. He quietly hands the payment to Sunny. When he is done counting the notes, Sunny appears vexed. 'Give a hundred rupees more,' he says.

'What for?' the elder brother asks. There is an unmistakable note of entitlement in his question—a challenge in his voice.

'Twenty-six hundred rupees was our deal,' Sunny asserts. One of his co-workers quietly moves forward and stands beside him as though offering support. He glares at the brothers as he puts his hands on his waist.

The frown that creased the elder brother's forehead softens. 'Let's agree on twenty-five hundred,' he coaxes Sunny. 'Come on, I'm your brother from Bihar.'

'This is not a joke,' Sunny replies, his voice full of contained aggression. 'I have already given you a discount of two hundred. Give what is owed to me.'

Sunny is no longer the polite, affable man the brothers had met earlier that day. His sentences are terse, his demeanour cold. 'I have to give hisaab, accounts, to my maalik,' he continues. 'Pay up.'

The man flinches. It appears as though the strength to argue has dissipated from his body. He retrieves a sweat-soaked hundred-rupee note from his shirt and reluctantly places it in Sunny's palm. Sunny clenches his fist shut and roughly shoves the money into the pocket of his tight blue jeans.

The brothers turn around and leave, and Sunny returns to his customer, his brow without a crease, his face as charming as before. It is business as usual.

20

A Dom's Duty

ON A SUNNY winter morning in 2015, I meet Bhola's eldest brother, Mohan, in Chand Ghat. He is wearing a pair of olive-green Bermuda shorts and a faded, sleeveless jacket with no vest to cover his belly. Bhola, who is home for the holidays, is sitting next to him on a chattai, a straw mat. Their neighbour Bunty, Shortcut's older brother, a lanky-bodied man with wavy hair, has joined them. Like Mohan, Bunty works as a corpse burner.

The sky is losing light. Wispy clouds make feathery patterns. Cicadas begin to stir. A pair of moths flits across the room, their brown wings scraping against the walls in manic urgency. A 1980s' Bollywood song is playing in a house nearby. Bunty absently whistles the tune.

Mohan fishes out a rolled-up bundle of ten-rupee notes from his pocket and hands a note to one of his other younger brothers. '*Ja, chai la.* Go get tea,' he mumbles.

In Indian households, offering tea is a way of welcoming guests. In a Dom's home, however, it carries connotations that are more profound, rooted in the enduring narrative of untouchability. The gesture serves as a litmus test to discern whether the guest, particularly one from a dominant caste, is willing to drink from their cup and accept them as equals.

Twenty-eight years old, Mohan has seen things he wishes he could unsee. He has an intimidating presence. A reticent man, he isn't the kind who is quick to make eye contact with strangers. He only speaks when he is addressed directly. His neatly trimmed, oil-slicked hair shimmers silver-blue under the white tube light. He seems dour; his lower lip, plump and pink—a blush of cerise—has been dyed by chewing paan with surti for years. There is a small scar near his right eye. His body, darkened by the sun, carries other marks too.

Although Mohan is Bhola's oldest brother, and Kamala Devi's eldest son, he does not look like either of them, nor does he carry their warmth. (In the years that follow, his strained and awkward body language loosens up. He becomes more open with me, offering to exhibit all his irregularly shaped physical scars, like a soldier displaying his wounds like badges of honour.)

I watch Mohan quietly crush tobacco granules in his palm. He wears a taveez—a sacred black amulet—around his thick neck. Mohan has had it since he was fifteen, to ensure that he remains protected from the evil eye. He believes he had a preternatural tendency to invite harmful energies.

When we turn to the subject of cremating corpses, Mohan raises his head slowly. His hard black eyes stare back at me. At the ghat, he says, carefully weighing his words, the blood simmers under their skin. Working in these conditions, even their strong, masculine bodies feel fatigued and weak.

Over the years, I have realized that Mohan's stories are anchored in reality as well as flights of fancy. One wants to believe him, but some things just defy logic. The story of his birth, for instance, is one such blend. He says his father arranged for a procession of dhol-walas, percussionists, on the day he was born, since he was the first male heir after three daughters: *believable*. That his aunts and uncles resented his birth since he was a possible threat to family property: *plausible*. That his relatives poisoned him by offering him a ladoo that made him 'piss blood' till the age of fifteen: *unlikely*.

'Several visits to a witch-doctor and multiple sessions of jadu-tona later, out came a clove from my throat,' he claims. That bewitched clove had been secretly stuffed into the ladoo and fed to him. Thereafter, the witch-doctor fashioned the taveez out of charcoal and bones, and told Mohan never to remove it.

Mohan speaks with a unique drawl, as though his tongue is bound by a string. His voice is often muffled. It isn't because he is an alcoholic—he has not touched liquor since his father, Keshav Chaudhary, passed away in 2011; he wants to set a good precedent for his younger brothers—but because he chews more paans in a day than he can count.

Bunty, who is sitting next to Mohan, now joins the conversation. He talks quickly, one word racing with the other. He has seen terrible things at the masaan too. He has watched stomachs and chests that belonged to 'ladies and gents' brutally burst open. 'Awful things leaked and spilled,' he says. Bunty has cremated corpses of women who had set themselves on fire or had hanged themselves and arrived at the masaan with protruding tongues. He has seen bodies crushed in accidents—their organs mutilated or ripped apart.

'Have you ever seen a skull being broken?'[1] he asks me, his hard eyes searching my face. Before I can respond, he continues, 'How long will we have to bear such sights? The rookies here begin by chewing gum or gutka to stifle their disgust and keep from vomiting. But if you see death over and over again, you will end up doing nasha. Otherwise, you're not human.'

The men speak of feverish dreams, of meeting the dead in the land beyond this, where time is no longer linear but jumps and fluctuates, where the dead breathe and walk. 'When we go to sleep, that's when it really hits us. Only we know the kind of effect it has on our minds,' Bunty says.

One night, around 3 a.m., Mohan saw the woman he had cremated earlier that day. She was sitting next to him, watching him quietly, until she reached out to touch his face with her fingers. From afar, he heard *Ram naam satya hai*. 'The echo of five hundred voices,' he recalls. Mohan woke up red-eyed and drenched in sweat. 'No one was around,' he says. 'I looked outside, into the distance, but there was no sign of her.'

Mohan pauses for a moment and then reiterates, his eyes holding mine: 'We drink to forget *such* things. You won't find anyone in Manikarnika who doesn't do nasha.'

Manikarnika Ghat is not for the weak. It is not for those who turn pale at the sight of burning flesh. Working at the ghat, in the midst of hostile pyres, is akin to the feeling of a thousand tiny needles piercing your skin and settling deep within. Water becomes a haunting thirst. Fire and wind bellow in unison, like the angry litany of wild spirits.

In a day, a Dom cremates three to five lifeless bodies, earning around Rs 150 for each corpse. (As of 2023, the earnings have increased marginally, to about Rs 200–250 per corpse.) A corpse burner may pocket a little extra—'anywhere between a hundred to a thousand rupees' depending on the generosity of mourning families, says Bunty.

To the Doms, death is the everyday—a stabilizing constant, a pragmatic means to an end. 'Have you ever wished more people would die in a day so that you could earn more?' I ask them bluntly. It is an uncomfortable question, one I have been hesitant to put before them until now, but I am curious to know how Dom men—who survive on paltry earnings and whose livelihoods depend not on the living but on the dead—feel about it.

'No, not at all,' Bunty answers almost immediately. 'Who would want anyone else to die?' He carefully hoists himself on his haunches. 'This is our dharma, our duty. We may have a small, insignificant life, but God has sent us here to do his work, to give mukti to others. No matter how many bodies come, no matter how hard it is, we have to keep working. We have to keep liberating each soul. Whoever comes to Manikarnika becomes pure once again.'

When Bunty speaks of 'dharma' and 'mukti', there is a hint of pride in his voice—as though cremating corpses is not a profession consigned to the Doms through the directives of the caste system, but a responsibility voluntarily accepted by his people as the will of God.

In India, the caste system thrives on the possession of social capital. Dominant castes carry immense social capital, while oppressed castes have historically been denied any of it.

The Doms, thus, stress on their symbolic or ritualistic importance, often glorifying their underprivileged work to validate their place in the world. 'Only we can gift the dead moksha,' a Dom man once told me. 'No other caste can. You may be a Kshatriya or a Thakur, but when one of your relatives dies, you will always come to us. You will join your hands and request us; you will ask us to name a price in order to get our fire … Only then will we give it to you. It's a rule that is socially bound and dictated by the gods. For that one day we become higher, superior.'

At the masaan, the maaliks overwork the corpse burners and launch a tirade of insults at will. 'They drink and treat us like filth,' says Bunty, slapping his palm against his wrist for effect. He pauses. 'I don't want to burn murdas, dead bodies, any more,' he admits woefully, even though moments ago he spoke of dharma and mukti. The fire, for him, is too punishing, too wayward, too intense: it has burned him several times. '*Humko vahaan taqleef lagti hai.* It pains me to work there,' he continues. 'I would rather wash ashes and bones in Ganga mayi, Mother Ganga.'

21

Glass, Nails and Gold

IF YOU NEGOTIATE your way through the maze of blazing pyres; side-step the cow dung; untangle the glass-coated kite string caught around your shoe; ignore the territorial indie dogs sniping, snapping and fornicating; and pass a motley crew of shavyatris—the river, in all its grey-blue grandeur, reveals itself. It will draw you in and pull you closer.

Not too far from the bank, a few men bob in the water. These are ash sifters, skilled labourers who work in the shallows for long hours. Bare-chested, with langots tied around their hips, the men immerse themselves waist-deep in the water.

I learnt that the ash sifters also belong to the Dom community. They wash bones and ash all day, performing the back-breaking work of combing through the light-grey remains of the cremation to salvage tiny, shapeless pieces of metals like gold and silver, which they sell for small sums of money. These are the remnants of the ornaments the deceased were wearing that have melted in the heat of the pyre. Mourning family members often do not remove their loved one's jewellery before the last rites, perhaps out of sentimentality or the belief that they might need these items in the afterlife. It could be a pair of silver earrings, a gold ring, gold bangles, a nose ornament or a silver tooth.

After the cremation, the ashes become the property of the Doms. In fact, I was told by one of them that everything—from the ashes to the melted jewellery, from the bamboo frame on which the corpse arrives to any saris or shawls placed on the deceased as gifts from the relatives—belongs to the Doms.

At dawn, when soft orange light slowly suffuses the sky, buckets of water from the Ganges are poured onto the pyres. The roar of the flames is silenced into a slurring hiss.

At the cremation ground, the ash is swept up, gathered and compacted into dense, dark mounds that indent the riverbank. It is this dark waste that the Doms sift through. The competition to pick out pieces of metal in the ash is fierce; the Dom men dash into the water, tearing through the thick layer of surface goo. The men pin their heels in the riverbed to find their grounding.

The ash sifters work tirelessly, dipping in and out of the water. One of them, an older man, sinewy of body, squats to sweep the slurry into a large-mouthed tasla using the base of his palm.[1] Once the vessel is filled to the brim, he walks towards the river with his bony knees bent peculiarly under the weight he is carrying. He inspects the contents of the vessel with great care, as though it is a prize. Waist-deep in the water, the old man dips it ever so slightly and swirls the sludge in the water clockwise and then counter-clockwise, using the momentum of the tasla to his advantage. He runs his fingers through the dark matter: ash, when mixed with water, becomes bulkier. Heavier metals like gold and silver sink to the bottom of the container, while the lighter ones usually drift away into the water.

There are at least ten other men who perform the same task, working in close proximity to the old man. Mohan is part of the working cluster. He tilts his vessel, carefully reading its contents. There is mud and ash, parts of a broken clay pot and the smashed remains of a human skull.

'*Haddi, mitti, rakh—sab hai yahan.* Bone, mud, ash— everything is here,' Mohan says. He fishes out a two-inch piece of bone that is as white as chinaware and holds it up. 'This belonged to someone's foot,' he says.

Boats—packed with pyramids of firewood—are silent spectators of the rigorous work that goes into sieving and cleaning ash. A large, unpiloted, empty boat glides towards the ash sifters. Mohan looks unperturbed; he uses his arm to casually nudge the boat in another direction. Once it veers away, he gets back to work. Fat droplets of water glint in the sunlight and roll off his back. Some get caught in the knotted field of hair on his chest and quietly die out. Mohan runs his hand across his forehead and sighs with exhaustion.

Not everyone can do this job. Those who do it don't actually want to, but have no other option. 'No other caste person can do this,' says Golu, an ash sifter and a resident of Chand Ghat. More importantly, no other caste will be expected to carry out such an arduous and repulsive task, which the Doms are compelled to, in order to survive.

Golu takes a break from work and slips out of the water to talk to me. He wraps a dry, red-coloured gamchha around his body and pulls off his soaking langot. Later, he splays the langot on a moored boat to dry.

'The first time you came here, do you remember how you couldn't bear the heat?' Golu asks. 'You vomited and almost fainted.'

I nod quietly, remembering the sharp ringing in my ears, the tenseness in my body, the smoke filling my lungs and, above all, my desperate wish to hurl my innards onto the ground. It took me two days to convalesce in the comforts of my guest house, unlike Golu or Mohan, who—like Sisyphus pushing his boulder—have to keep returning to the masaan.

'Where can we go?' Golu asks. 'We have to keep coming back here, doing the work. We get used to it. We do what we have to. Earn what we can.'

He and I are sitting on a boat, watching the others work. I glance at his tasla and he offers its contents for inspection. It is his catch for the day. Golu pinches a twisted and shrunken toe ring between his fingers and holds it up for scrutiny, and then coolly throws it back into the tasla. *Clink!* The metal sharply hits the bottom. His other meagre finds include a lone ghungroo—a tiny silver orb that once belonged on an anklet—and what might have once been a copper nose pin. His new-found possessions are covered in blackish-green patina. Anyone else would have thrown the pieces away as junk. But to Golu, they are a meal ticket.

'What will you get for this?' I ask him.

'Two kachoris, one jalebi. That's it,' he replies, wiggling a broken matchstick between his teeth. It had taken him three hours to retrieve these three tiny pieces. Upon sale, he will earn a paltry sum of Rs 30.

Our boat has drifted close to Mohan, who is still working in the water, cradling his tasla. 'We can tell in one glance what is precious and what is muck,' he says, as he picks out a small piece of gravel. 'This,' he says, 'is muck.'

Mohan finds a target, squints his right eye and flings it. It soars in the air for a moment and then lands on the head of another man who is also working in the water.

'Eh, motherfucker!' the man snaps, frowning at first and then quickly breaking into a chuckle.

'He is a friend,' explains Mohan before exchanging a knowing glance with the man and getting back to work.

A few feet away, a wiry boatman with crooked teeth, a smattering of stubble and a receding hairline struggles to pull apart a used bamboo bier. He had picked up the bier from the cremation ground. Once successful, the boatman fixes the bamboo staves into grooves on either side of the bow. He walks to the stern and does the same. The man then fastens the corners of a large, jutelike fabric to the four upright poles. Once secured, the fabric catches the wind, serving as a canopy. Pleased with his handiwork, the boatman extends his hand to his clients, who happily jump on board.

At Manikarnika Ghat, nothing goes to waste. Almost everything is reclaimed from the dead to make a living.

Colloquially, the process of sifting through ash is called 'dhulna', which means 'to wash'. The Dom men do this work on days when it isn't their shift to cremate corpses. When they search for the jewellery left behind on the dead, they do so without any remorse, they say, since they believe it is God's will. One of them told me that it was God's way of mitigating their poverty. Dhulna is honed while working for countless months, even years, in the water. It is an art—a tightly braided relationship involving the dexterity of the ash sifter's fingers, the sharpness of his eyesight and his willingness to brave the petulant weather. The Doms have learnt how to differentiate between bone, ash, gravel, gold, silver and base metals like copper and brass.

For hours, ash sifters pinch their noses and repeatedly immerse themselves in the water, searching for pieces of once-precious ornaments that may have sunk. They resurface a few moments later, slick back their hair and wipe away the sludge that burns their eyes.

In school textbooks and corporate corridors, this work would be written off as 'unskilled labour'. The fact, however, is that dhulna requires being extremely skilled; it is also exhausting and unrewarding.

For a river that is revered for its healing powers and worshipped as a 'mother' by countless Hindus in India, the Ganges is alarmingly polluted. Every day, thousands of God-fearing people of all ages faithfully take a ritualistic dip in the Ganges in the belief that this will cleanse them of all their sins. Devout Hindus travel from afar to take back Gangajal—river water that is considered holy and auspicious. Women dressed in multicoloured saris, with strings of jasmine in their hair, fling garlands upon garlands of marigolds into the river. A few ghats away, local men relieve themselves standing at the river's edge.

Thousands of cremations are held in Banaras each year. Sometimes, partially cremated corpses are tossed into the Ganges in order to make way for more corpses. As a result, not only is the river polluted with disposed ash, but charred human remains float in it too. Certain individuals who have died, like babies or ascetics whose souls are thought to be pure and uncorrupted, are tied to a large stone and immersed in the water.

Heaps of human waste, sewage and industrial filth are also dumped into the river without batting an eyelid. The toxins from the garbage piled on the banks of the river seep into the water. The river carries excessive quantities of metals such as lead, arsenic and mercury, and could lead to many diseases.[2] In 2019, the Uttar Pradesh Pollution Control Board estimated the level of faecal coliform bacteria found in the river, particularly near Banaras, was 22,000 MPN/100 ml. The acceptable limit is 50 MPN/100 ml,[3] thereby making the river highly unfit for drinking. In 2023, it was reported that 'hazardous chemicals' continued to be found in the Ganges, particularly between Banaras and Bihar's Begusarai, which were responsible for causing 'human health problems' and for disturbing the river's 'aquatic ecosystem'.[4]

Golu cups his palm and scoops up some water to drink. Between gulps, he describes his experience of working at the ghat. 'Collect all the ash from all the cremation grounds in India and throw them in the Ganga. Then see what happens. The men will rush in; they will fight and abuse each other, because the person who gets the most ash has a greater chance of getting the gold.'

To reduce the competition, other Dom men throw shards of broken glass, rusted nails and razors into the Ganges, I am told, to make the process more arduous for others. 'There are times when a Dom might accidentally step on glass,' one of them explains. 'Though he might be bleeding, he will continue to work. *Majboori hai*. The man has no choice. If he stops working, he doesn't earn.'

Once out of the water, Mohan sits on the stone steps and splays his legs to exhibit his wounds. On his right leg is a discoloured rectangular patch that has assumed a mustard-green hue; the surface resembles the rubbery texture of cottage cheese. A breach of skin had occurred while he was cremating a corpse; the wound is healing now. There are smaller, darker scars that resemble tiny hooks and some others that mimic the contours of continents unknown.

If a Dom man gets wounded or contracts a disease, a few visits to the doctor alone can eat into his monthly finances. Until he is fit enough to work again, his family suffers. Bhola once explained, 'Mohan works in filth; he works in smoke. If he gets injured, more than half of whatever he may have earned will go into paying off the doctor's bills. If he earns five hundred rupees in a day, three hundred goes to the doctor. We need to go to the doctor so many times that eventually we have to stop.'

Due to health expenses, many are forced to take loans and are burdened by debt.

Another time, while I was talking to Bunty about dhulna, he raised his foot and waved it spiritedly. 'Can you see how big this scar is?' He was sitting cross-legged and lifted his leg to exhibit a sizable injury on his sole that ran from his big toe to the centre of his foot.

'We get many cuts like this that get infected. For twenty days, I wasn't able to work, till my foot healed,' he continued. 'I had to borrow money to make sure there was food in the house.'

'Are you in debt right now?' I asked.

'Definitely,' Bunty replied, smiling self-consciously. 'We are poor. We are always in debt.'

Mohan labours in the water for two to four hours, sometimes, even six hours. 'Whether there is a storm or the Ganga is swollen, we have to work,' he tells me.

In the summer, sifting ash is arduous. Boils erupt all over the body. Due to the strain, there are times when Mohan falls dreadfully ill. 'Even with fever, I tell myself that I have to go out and earn. I feel sick but then I think: how will the household manage if I don't go? So, I push myself,' Mohan says.

He wakes up at four in the morning and leaves his home by five on an empty stomach. 'If we eat in the morning, we cannot work,' he explains. 'How can we work if our stomach is full?'

On a full stomach the workers often feel like retching at the ghat or feel too sluggish to move, and on some days, '*Latrine aane lagti hai*. We have to shit,' Mohan says. All corpse burners, therefore, practise appetite restraint. 'We don't eat,' he continues. 'We only have dinner once we are home.'

At night, Mohan's body aches. He makes slow, fatigued movements. His mother heats kerosene oil and sits down on the floor beside him to massage it into his rounded arms and muscular legs. Using her forefingers, she scoops the warm oil and silently rubs it into his skin, making small concentric circles. A light breeze catches the corner of her sari.

'*Roz kamana, roz khilana*. Mohan earns every day, so that his family can eat every day. It's a hand-to-mouth existence,' one of Mohan's younger brothers says. 'He can't take even a day off. If he doesn't go to work, there will be no food that day. Sometimes, for four-five days, he earns nothing. Only we know how we manage during that time.'

———

Tucked away in one of the circuitous alleyways is a shop where the Dom labourers sell their prized finds. Some days, after spending hours in the river sifting ash, Mohan sits outside the shop, waiting for the owner to assess his hard day's work. The owner, a middle-aged man with a thick moustache, sits hunched, peering into a small steel plate, examining its contents—river sediments mixed with small pieces of gold, silver and base metals, almost invisible to the eye. A pair of black mobile headphones dangles from his neck. Occasionally, he takes personal calls on them, leaving his fingers free to assess what otherwise looks like featureless sand.

A three-hour toil in rain or a five-hour slog under a harsh sky, sifting ash can be as valuable as it can be meaningless. A man can make Rs 10 or Rs 1,000. '*Taqdeer hai*. It's fate,' Mohan says, throwing his hands in the air. More often than not, however, a labourer earns Rs 20–30, just enough to buy a fried snack and a cup of sweet tea.

That day, the rate for 10 grams of gold was Rs 48,000. Mohan's back-breaking work in the river was rewarded with a find of 10 milligrams of gold. The shopkeeper handed him two notes of Rs 20 and that was that.

22

Mohan's New Bride

IN CHAND GHAT, Kamala Devi's eldest son, Mohan, lived on the lowest floor with his wife, Twinkle, while Kamala Devi and three of her other sons occupied the room above and on the terrace. She had fulfilled her duty of marrying off her daughters early. Bhola only visited her during his summer and winter breaks from college.

Twinkle is Mohan's second wife. Neighbours whispered stories about Mohan and his first wife not getting along, of her not toeing the line, of them arguing into the night. One day in 2015, she stormed out of their home in a rage, leaving behind their two-year-old daughter, Imlee, in Kamala Devi's care. The wife's absence indicated an irreparable schism. She refused to return to her husband's home. Sometime later, they received the news that she had died of a terrible disease.

When asked about Mohan's first wife, his family said that she had been unwell for a while. That she was too skinny and too weak, had a series of miscarriages, and complained of headaches that seldom left her. The family said that she had been sullen for quite some time and relied heavily on sughni, a light-brown powder that relaxes the nerves. The intoxicant is popular among married women in the community; they rub their gums and teeth with it at least twice a day. Some say its components include raw tobacco and lime. Even the most hardy women in the community use it as a balm while trying to seek calm in the cacophony of nagging offspring, household chores and spousal demands.

In essence, the fault lay with the first wife. No one revealed anything further. Mohan too refused to speak about his late wife. Over the years, I learnt that Mohan had never cared for her. A dark-complexioned man, he found his wife, who shared the same colouring, unappealing.

Like many other parts of the world, colourism is rampant in India. One might question whether that could cause a marriage to fracture and collapse, but the fact is that colour prejudice is deeply rooted in Indian culture and is a considerable part of our upbringing. New mothers breathe a sigh of relief when their children are born light-skinned, more so in the case of daughters. In conventional Indian households, while a man's marriageability is determined by his annual earnings, a woman's is determined by the colour of her skin. Mothers often forbid their daughters from playing outdoors in the sun, fearing that their skin will darken.

Fairness is an asset: a sought-after currency that often determines a woman's fate—including social likability, career ascent and marriage appeal. In the marriage industry, women with dark complexions are considered less desirable. Fairness creams or 'skin-lightening' products thrive on such insecurities. Adjectives like 'beautiful' and 'fair' are often used interchangeably. A survey conducted in 2018 by the Tata Institute of Social Sciences (TISS) of 1,992 individuals (1,238 women and 746 men in Mumbai) revealed that 59.6 per cent of women and 46.1 per cent of men had been consumers of fairness products.[1] While 31.2 per cent used skin-whitening creams to look 'beautiful', 36.2 per cent used them to look 'fairer' and feel more 'culturally accepted'.

Mohan's first marriage was born out of a certain desperation. One of his older sisters had been unable to find a suitor. Twenty-something and unmarried, the sister had become a community 'relic', having crossed the appropriate marrying age. She had faced rejections from several suitors since her father was unable to provide a substantial dowry. The family was desperate for a match.

When Keshav Chaudhary did find a potential husband for his daughter, the groom's family insisted that they would only agree if their own daughter (who had also faced multiple rejections from suitors) could marry Keshav's son Mohan: an ideal trade. Neither Mohan nor his future bride was consulted before the marriage was fixed. Mohan was now duty-bound, morally obligated to marry someone he did not like, in order to ensure that his sister was no longer ridiculed in the community. The pair's marriage, however, was an awkward alliance, strained from the very beginning.

'As soon as they got married, there were fights. Many fights,' Bhola says recalling that time.

After Keshav's death, Mohan assumed the role of the family head and was its sole earning member at the time. The family felt too indebted to him to interject or end the fights.

'We didn't feel it was right on our part to interfere,' admits Bhola. 'We could not do anything because we were under his control.' At the time, he had also felt beholden to Mohan because while he studied in school, his older brother served as the bulwark between his education and burning corpses. Bhola could not afford to speak up against Mohan. 'In the end, she died in absolute sadness,' Bhola says in an apologetic tone.

Kamala Devi brought up her granddaughter Imlee, single-handedly. Less than a year after his first wife's death, Mohan remarried.

Mohan's new bride, Twinkle, was lighter-skinned, with fuller breasts, a narrow waist and an easy sway in the hips. She had an oval face and a disarming smile.

———

Kamala Devi and Twinkle did not get along. When Twinkle was not around, Kamala Devi called her a 'nikammi', useless. Kamala Devi felt that daughters-in-law were meant to hold their tongues and be reverential towards their in-laws. Twinkle didn't seem to think so. She was a woman governed by intuition and wit. During domestic scuffles, Twinkle's voice climbed higher than her husband's, her tone assertive and controlling. She had learnt early on that a serrated tongue kept unreasonable domestic expectations at bay. Twinkle established her own set of rules. She would not cook for Kamala Devi or her brothers-in-law; they could take care of themselves. However, whenever Kamala Devi was sick and could not do any work herself, Twinkle would step up and offer to help.

When wives spoke about their husbands in the community, they shied away from mentioning their names. They would use phrases like '*humara aadmi*'—my man—or, '*inke papa*'—this one's father—to refer to their husbands. Twinkle, however, boldly took Mohan's name in the presence of other women—as long as there were no elders around.

Twinkle was never meant to be Mohan's bride. As a young girl, she lived a few houses down his lane. A married man by then, Mohan often watched her play outside with the other children, and Twinkle would respectfully call him 'bhaiya', elder brother, every time she spoke to him. Even today, she unconsciously referred to him as 'bhaiya' sometimes instead of using intimate identifiers like 'my man'.

As a teenager, Twinkle had attended Mohan's first wedding. A few years later, at sixteen, she was married off to a man four years older than her. By nineteen, Twinkle had become a widow. Her husband had died due to the excessive consumption of alcohol that caused his organs to fail. Her mother immediately brought Twinkle back home from her in-laws', knowing that she was young and childless and, therefore, eligible to marry again.

Around the same time as Twinkle's return to Chand Ghat in 2015, Mohan's first marriage began to turn drastically sour. A few months into 2016, his first wife passed away, and after a brief, almost unnoticeable, period of mourning, Mohan spent his spare time in wooing Twinkle. Nine years younger than him,

Twinkle found Mohan—a man with a bulbous nose and a rotund stomach—unpalatable to look at.

'You tell me, who would choose this man for a husband?' she quipped once. 'He is so dark and big-bellied. Look, his tummy is falling out. Who would marry him?'

In order to convince Twinkle to marry him, Mohan offered expensive gifts, including 'a diamond locket'. While he managed to impress Twinkle's mother, who was a widow herself, Twinkle maintained her distance and politely declined his generosity.

'If you accept even one gift, men begin to have expectations. Then they put pressure on you to marry them,' she continued.

Twinkle knew her worth. She was intelligent and wanted to pursue further studies instead of mooring herself to domestic life, which she perceived as a dark forest: thick, stifling and impervious. But Mohan would not have it. He concocted damaging lies about Twinkle's whereabouts to her mother.

'I used to tell Twinkle's mother that she shouldn't let her go out so often, because Twinkle was meeting unruly boys instead of studying,' Mohan admitted later, adding that he wanted to make sure Twinkle did not fall in love with some other man.

Mohan justified his meddling as a 'romantic' gesture rather than harassment. He was a self-proclaimed guardian of his community who had all the young girls' best interests at heart.

'You see,' he began one day, trying to defend himself, 'it doesn't matter which house a young girl belongs to. If she is from our community and goes out to have fun, would it look nice? No, it wouldn't.'

Twinkle, who was sitting beside him, snapped back, 'Then you should have been more concerned about the whereabouts of your *own* sisters, not mine.'

Back then, though, Mohan's craftily invented lies were enough to cause storms in Twinkle's house, instigating familial spats that would result in the increasingly stringent curtailment of her freedom to go out in public. Twinkle's mother felt that the anxiety growing within her would only melt away when her daughter—a young widow who sat 'idle' in her house—found a new husband and family to call her own.

Mohan ticked the only two boxes that seemed to matter in a Dom woman's future: '*Achha kamatein the, khilatein the.* He made good money and fed his family well,' Twinkle said, listing her mother's reasoning on her fingers. It wasn't long before Twinkle's mother consented to the match, so that she could move on with her life and focus on marrying off her other girls. And so, Twinkle, who had managed to keep Mohan at bay for a while, had to agree under the pressure.

'I did not have a choice,' Twinkle recalled. Once married, her life was tied to her new husband's whims. She could not go anywhere or do anything without his permission. The only way forward, she concluded, was to change her thinking and accept. She did what most women in her situation do. 'I realized it was best to be accommodating because only then could I live my life. Otherwise, I would be miserable forever.'

When Mohan married Twinkle, Kamala Devi's displeasure was apparent. Kamala Devi had wanted her eldest son to bring home a woman from another Dom basti—one who knew little about their family, was timid and did not have the gall to answer back. But most importantly, she had wanted her son to marry a woman who had not been touched by a man before—and certainly not a widow.

'My mother-in-law did not care that her own son was a widower but she wanted him to choose a woman who had not been married before,' Twinkle said, emphasizing the irony. 'So, she chose not to like me.'

The dislike grew stronger when Twinkle became pregnant. At night and during afternoon naps, Dom wives, even when pregnant, sleep on the floor. The single beds in their small rooms are reserved solely for their husbands. In the initial months of their marriage, Twinkle too was expected to roll out a thin mat on the floor and lie down on it at night while Mohan slept soundlessly, well-insulated on a sturdy wooden bed. During winters, the crippling cold would flow from the ground and sink into Twinkle's back, settling deep into her spine. Her body ached in protest. Her calves swelled and her toes felt gnarly. Sometimes, Twinkle imagined a centipede crawling its way into her ear canal. Eventually, she had had enough. One day, during her pregnancy, Twinkle told Mohan that if he wanted a healthy child, he would have to make some changes in their house.

The next night, Mohan slept on the floor.

It is unusual for a husband to accommodate a wife's request. Women in the community are regarded as dispensable: 'People in the community think that a wife is the lowest of the low,' Bhola once said.

Mohan had never let his first wife sleep on the bed. It was unthinkable. Yet for Twinkle, he was willing to forgo the luxury. Kamala Devi did not appreciate her son's descent—neither to the floor, nor in his marriage. Or the fact that he had given in to Twinkle's 'demands' so easily. It signalled her daughter-in-law's unfathomable hold over him, which irked her. Straitlaced Kamala Devi, who had worshipped her late husband and remained at his feet till he drew his last breath, felt deeply affronted that Twinkle—a prickly, irreverent young girl—dared to rise above a stifling tradition and expected to be spared.

'It doesn't look nice that your husband sleeps on the floor while you snore like a princess on the bed,' she reprimanded her daughter-in-law one day. Twinkle gave a curt reply to her mother-in-law and their exchange exploded into a tussle of words. Both would later be placated by Mohan.

'To tell you the truth, it wasn't just my mother-in-law who didn't like the fact that I slept on the bed,' Twinkle said. 'No one liked it.'

In 2019, Twinkle gave birth to her first child and Mohan's second daughter. 'I will have one more child after this and then no more,' she promised herself then. Twinkle knew she was different from other women. She was educated, and a thinker; she could persuade Mohan to be content with three children, which included Imlee.

23

The Great Makeover

BY JULY 2019, the anatomy of Banaras had begun to change. The city's landscape, particularly near the ghats, was being transformed: some of its charming (though heavily crowded), two-foot-wide alleyways that meandered and led to the river were being demolished. The state government, with Prime Minister Narendra Modi's blessings, had decided to give the revered Kashi Vishwanath temple, and the area surrounding it, a 'facelift'. Centuries-old ancestral homes were razed to the ground. Small temples that had dotted the area were allegedly torn down.[1] Libraries—some that had proudly stood their ground since the 1800s, like the Carmichael Library—were destroyed in the blink of an eye. While a few larger decrepit temples were spared, the residences and structures surrounding them were reduced to rubble.

Once a jagged skyline of tightly packed buildings, Lahori Tola, for instance, had been turned into a sorry sight of debris

174

and shattered wood. Dark-skinned cows flicked their tails as they surveyed the wreckage, dawdling awkwardly over mounds of dirt and rubble, licking water from muddy puddles. A few locals, including saffron-clothed priests with mobile phones in hand, scurried across the levelled area to reach their destinations.

In a corner, a two-storeyed house with blue-framed windows stood gloomily; a part of it had been knocked down. Two unchaperoned children threw stones into the window of the abandoned house. Each throw measured their aim and agility. While at it, one of them tripped over a broken cement slab and scraped his bony knee. A stranger passing by called out to them: 'Aye, boys! Move away from there. You will fall and break your heads! Run off or I'll personally come and beat you up.' The kids half-heartedly flung the stones one last time, before walking away sulkily.

In the distance, workers who were employed under the Kashi Vishwanath Corridor project swung their hammers into the facades of the buildings that remained. One of the men perfunctorily kicked away the shattered pieces with his feet to make way for a fresh batch of fragments that skittered down. The sky, as though mimicking the desolate ground below, appeared robbed of colour, marked occasionally by splashes of black, fluttering crows.

Bhola and I stood amidst the rubble, watching the proceedings. He was quiet for a few moments before volunteering geographical insight. 'There were small galis that ran through this neighbourhood. The rest were all mostly homes,' he said, gesturing at the vacant space around us. 'Now, everything has been broken down; everything is bare.'

I pointed at a few temples that remained. 'What about them?'

'Some temples that you see here were, in fact, retrieved from homes that were demolished,' he replied. 'At least twenty or thirty temples, I think, have been discovered till now. All of them were hidden within residential walls,' he said.

'Why are the homes being demolished?' I asked him.

'When the men finally clear out everything from here and make a wide path, you will be able to see Ganga ji directly from the Kashi Vishwanath temple.'

In 2017, BJP's saffron-clad monk, Yogi Adityanath, became Uttar Pradesh's chief minister. The following year, in 2018, Adityanath's government announced the commencement of the 'Kashi Vishwanath Dham', a beautification project of the temple, considered to be the abode of Lord Shiva. Among the many things envisioned for the temple's facelift, it was decided that a 50-foot-wide corridor would be built connecting the temple to the sacred waters of the Ganges.[2] The temple complex itself would be state-of-the-art, with newly installed ramps, lifts, toilets, lockers and escalators. It would have everything, from a museum to a multipurpose auditorium, a tourist facilitation centre, a food court, a communal kitchen, as well as a Mumukshu Bhavan, where those who might want to spend their final days in Banaras could come and stay.[3] This was part of the BJP's 'grand vision', one that aligned with Prime Minister Modi's pledge made after his return from Japan in 2014: to transform Banaras into a world-class smart city like Kyoto.[4] The Kashi Vishwanath Corridor would go on to be touted as Prime Minister Modi's 'dream project'.

Sprawled over 5 lakh square feet, the Corridor was Uttar Pradesh's most ambitious project yet, and received a whopping investment of Rs 800 crore. The cost of the first phase of construction would amount to Rs 339 crore.[5] Yogi Adityanath stated that the project was a 'rejuvenation of Indian pride'.[6]

The behemoth project would sweep across the areas neighbouring the temple, razing homes, labyrinthine lanes, old libraries and shops—anything that came in God's way—to the ground in order to clear a 400-metre-long passage that would allow devotees to walk hassle-free from the temple gates to the banks of the holy Ganges and take a ritualistic dip in the river.[7] Supporters claimed that this way Lord Shiva could directly see the flowing Ganges.

Not everyone was on board with the government's vision, though. There was resistance and resentment. Many locals claimed that the charm of the city, in particular its ancient structures, its smaller monuments and temples, its numerous lanes and by-lanes, was being destroyed. Senior journalist Padampati Sharma, whose 175-year-old home was on the list of homes that needed to be evacuated, took to Facebook to voice his displeasure. 'The government is once again conspiring to decimate Kashi's old cultural heritage,' he wrote in Hindi.[8]

Other residents expressed discontent,[9] and filed petitions;[10] many took to the roads to protest with placards and black bands, claiming that under the garb of modernization, the city's heritage was being destroyed.[11] A 10-kilometre protest walk from Assi Ghat to Adi Keshav Ghat was organized by those opposing the Corridor project.[12] Nothing worked, though; the excavators and the backhoe loaders kept coming. A representative of the Varanasi Development Authority would proudly say that, after all these years, it had taken serious 'political will' to finally bring the project to life.[13]

Simultaneously, there was a cleanliness drive initiated in Banaras, where locals employed by the Varanasi Nagar Nigam (Varanasi Municipal Corporation) picked up garbage from the ghats, including Manikarnika Ghat. One of them, Meena, who worked alongside her husband to collect garbage from the area near Manikarnika Ghat, said that she began work at 7 a.m. each day. The garbage was discarded at a location beyond Rajghat. While working through the muck on the ghats, Meena, who wore a flimsy, pale-green jacket over her sari to identify herself as a safai karamchari, wore no gloves.

'There are more than a hundred people who are currently employed to clean up the ghats,' she said. 'I am a poor woman who earlier sat at home. With this cleanliness project, I now have an opportunity to earn. A lot of good work is happening. This area is visibly cleaner now,' she said.

For decades, the approach to the city's most famous temple was cramped in between tiny shops, low-rise residential buildings and narrow, filthy galis, making it difficult for hundreds of pilgrims to reach it each day. Barefoot devotees formed serpentine queues in the lanes leading to the temple, causing problems for other residents running errands, motorists, passers-by and tourists.

In 1916, when Mahatma Gandhi visited Banaras, he was aghast by the congested, maze-like lanes that led to the Kashi Vishwanath temple complex, and the bungling, slapdash manner in which the houses around it had been constructed. 'Is not this great temple a reflection of our own character?' he asked during a speech he gave at Banaras Hindu University. 'Is it right that the lanes of our sacred temple should be as dirty as they are? The houses round about are built anyhow. The lanes are tortuous and narrow. If even our temples are not models of roominess and cleanliness, what can our self-government be?'[14]

———

On 8 March 2019, Prime Minister Narendra Modi laid the foundation stone of the Kashi Vishwanath Temple Corridor project, marking the beginning of the construction process. In his speech, he thanked the residents of Banaras for giving up their 'invaluable properties' and laying them as offerings at the feet of Baba Bholenath, or Lord Shiva. He called their sacrifice the 'greatest daan' to the god. Bhole Baba, he said, had been 'cramped' all this while and was suffocating within the temple walls. 'It's a good thing,' the Prime Minister stated with certainty, 'that Bhole Baba kindled a consciousness within me and was able to make this dream come true.'[15]

There were residents in Banaras who imbibed, and subsequently echoed, what he said. Prashant Kumar, one of the locals I spoke to, who proudly bore an inked 'Om' on his forearm, and whose forefathers had all been born in the city, deemed the Prime Minister to be equivalent to a radiant deity. '*Woh toh sakshaat devta lagtey hain.* He appears to be God himself,' he said with a glint in his eyes. 'One can tell he is no ordinary human being. His face is always glowing. No other politician can carry the aura that Modi's stature carries.'

To 'liberate' Bhole Baba, however, families had to be uprooted. Small shops that sold flowers, saris, sweets, paan and sundry items were dislodged, taking away several livelihoods. The overall government approval allowed for the demolition of over 300 buildings and structures to pave a way for an uncongested, slick boulevard dedicated to God and his devotees.[16] The Corridor would bring a certain order and salubriousness to the city's blueprint, otherwise defined by the chaotic cluster of buildings.

By April 2019, about 230 homes had reportedly been destroyed.[17] While some locals felt pressured to move, others believed it was their 'divine duty' to relocate, so that their residences could make way for the Corridor. The government promised a monetary compensation to homeowners. The highest compensation the administration offered, however, was reportedly Rs 10 lakh.[18]

———

On a rainy day in 2019, Lakshaya sat in Dolly's home, flipping through videos on his phone. A lone tungsten light bulb threw an unflattering yellow cast on his face. He wanted to show me videos of himself working out at the local gym. Bhola sat next to him, cradling Dolly's youngest in his lap, who nibbled on a biscuit.

Lakshaya, working as a tourist guide and scrimping money to fund his wedding to Komal, seemed excited about the grand temple's renovation. An eighteenth-century temple now equipped with modern facilities, cleaner surroundings and increased accessibility would surely boost religious tourism, he thought. And an increase in the number of pilgrims in the city would mean a fatter wallet for him.

There was just one problem: his regular route to the mandir was disrupted. Chand Ghat residents could earlier walk to the temple by cutting through several galis. With the galis now being demolished, they had to take the longer way, which took twice as much time. Still, Lakshaya seemed unfazed when I spoke to him. 'Right now, we are experiencing a bit of difficulty. But once the Corridor is ready, this problem will also end,' he said, ruffling his hair.

'Will Chand Ghat also be demolished?' I asked.

Lakshaya took a deep breath. 'They're saying that the plan to break down Chand Ghat has been cancelled,' he replied. 'But let's see what happens. If it breaks, it will be good for us, I guess. We will be able to make a better home elsewhere.' Lakshaya's family had official documents for their home, which meant that they would be entitled to some monetary compensation.

Bhola was quiet, though. His family did not have the required documents for their house, even though they had been living there for generations. In the months that followed, the stress of possibly losing their home would age Bhola quickly, triggering an early receding hairline. It would also spur him to scrounge, save and ask friends for loans to purchase a small plot of land on the outskirts of the city.

'Where will residents like you, who don't have official papers for their homes, go?' I asked Bhola.

'We will have to see if they [the government] will make some arrangements for us,' he replied glumly. 'If not, then I don't know where we will go.'

Bhola's concerns were not unfounded. In April 2019, a Dalit settlement tucked between Lalita Ghat and Manikarnika Ghat had been torn down since it was situated in the plot earmarked for the Kashi Vishwanath Corridor project. The Dalits who had been displaced—some whose occupations were directly linked to Manikarnika Ghat—were forced to move away from the city. The homeowners claimed that they had not been given satisfactory compensation.[19]

'What is happening is illegal,' an elderly Dom told me later that day. 'It's not good work. Kashi has many galis. Lord Shiva resides in all of them. It's the galis that have made Banaras famous. You walk into one and get out from another. What Modi ji is doing is not good for Hindu samaaj. Banaras is no longer the same. It will die,' he said, disheartened.

The views of the younger generation of Doms aligned more with Lakshaya's. Balram Chaudhary, who worked as a corpse burner, felt that the Corridor would boost tourism in the city. *Kashi galiyon ka sheher hai.* Kashi is a city of alleys. If the alleys are being broken down, it's for development. If something is being destroyed, something is also improving. What is being done is good for our tourism. Those who have a problem with it are leaving the city. Some people are not bothered by it much. I agree that the old Kashi's map is being spoiled, but at the same time a new map is being made.'

———

The next day, Bhola and I visited Lahori Tola again. Bhola was silent for a large part of our walk.

A solitary motel stood at the periphery, beyond the ruins. A tube light at its entrance flickered hesitantly. For the time being, Priya Guest House had been spared since it was not part of the expansive swathe of land marked to be cleared to make way for the Corridor.

Curious, we walked inside the guest house. Prashant Kumar who had worked there since it began its operations in 1994, told us that before the Corridor project commenced, their guest house was thriving, always overflowing with travellers. However, since April 2019, their business had become 'thapp', collapsed, he said.

'We have just been sitting here without work. We come to the guest house, spend the hours we have to and then go back home. I do feel that Banaras's legacy has ended. This area itself, Lahori Tola, is no longer the same. Now they call it "Corridor" instead,' Kumar told me dismally. He paused, shrugged his shoulders and continued unconvincingly, 'I suppose it is for the good. Whatever is being broken now will be good for our future. More tourists will visit our city—there will be accessibility for handicapped persons at the temple as well. Right now, we might be facing difficulties, but the future looks promising.'

'Do you feel disheartened that the lanes are being destroyed?' I asked him.

'No, I have no grief,' he replied almost immediately. 'It's good what is being done. Change has to come and should come. Earlier, the galis were dirty. People stuffed plastic bags with garbage and threw them on the ground from the windows of their homes. The pilgrims walked in the same filth to do darshan at the temple. They would first bathe in the Ganga and then walk barefoot towards the temple, sometimes accidentally stepping on the discarded garbage or cow shit. Now it's all clean. So, from that viewpoint, I feel what is happening is good.'

Kumar, however, was uncertain whether Priya Guest House would survive the demolition brigade. 'I'm not sure whether we will remain. One can only hope that we will.'

Bhola and I stepped out of the guest house back onto the grounds. In the distance, among the newly discovered temples that speckled the land, a solitary shed stood out like a sore thumb. Bhola noticed my curiosity and instinctively began inching towards it. 'Come this way,' he gestured, knowing that I would follow him. He lowered his voice like a magician about to present a great reveal. 'There is a mandir within.'

Even in broad daylight, the makeshift shed did not hold much light. Two narrow plinths ran parallelly within, which were being used as temporary walkways. If you did not tread carefully, you could easily plummet into a gaping space below. A Shiva lingam rested underground, surrounded by pale blue walls.

'They say this is a part of Neelkanth Mahadev temple,' Bhola informed me as we carefully peered down. 'No one knew there was a mandir below. It was only when the officials began breaking the structure of the house that they realized there was a hidden mandir here.'

The Archaeological Survey of India (ASI) authorities would later announce that as of 2019, forty-three 'old temples' had been discovered, dating back to the eighteenth and nineteenth centuries, which were earlier hidden among myriad residential buildings. These needed to be documented, preserved and subsequently restored.[20] By 2021, seventy-eight temples would be reportedly found during the construction process.[21]

24

City of Death

IN 2020, THE coronavirus outbreak hit the country with no relief in sight. On the evening of 24 March, Prime Minister Narendra Modi announced an immediate twenty-one-day lockdown to 'break the chain of infection'.[1] No one had expected it; no one was ready for it. In the months that followed, more restrictions were imposed and countless lives were lost. By November 2020, however, the scare had slowly begun to dissipate. Restrictions were eased but with strict COVID-19 guidelines in place. Schools and temples began opening up,[2] and wedding celebrations resumed.[3] A sense of achievement reverberated throughout the country, as though it had finally won the war on COVID-19.

Little did anyone realize that this was just the lull before the storm.

In March 2021, the second wave of COVID-19 rushed in, setting the ghats in Banaras ablaze. Endless rows of pyres glowed

185

with topaz fervour long into the night. A thick layer of smoke, like a sprawling grey shroud, blanketed the cremation ground. The dead waited in queues and crowded the ghats. The once towering columns of pyre wood were reduced to meagre piles. Dom labourers numbly hauled the bodies and built tombs of straw and timber around them.

The World Health Organization published guidelines that stated that death-care workers who handled the burial or cremation of diseased bodies should wear personal protective equipment (PPE) like gloves, and that once the funerary task was complete, they should wash their hands with soap.[4] In India, the Ministry of Home Affairs issued public protocols and directives for 'COVID-appropriate behaviour' in order to manage and contain COVID-19. These included 'observance of social distancing in crowded places', wearing face masks and ensuring personal hand hygiene.[5] The corpse burners, however, worked tirelessly without masks and refused to wear the protective paraphernalia; it would be a hindrance rather than a safety precaution, they said. The heat was unbearable; the gloves would cling to their skin, or worse, would swiftly melt. Moreover, there was a deluge of corpses; most of the labourers were burning multiple bodies at once. None of them had the time to catch their breath or wash their hands.

By 8 April 2021, Uttar Pradesh had reported 8,490 fresh cases of coronavirus in just twenty-four hours.[6] Banaras, among other cities, observed night curfew. On 17 April, India 'registered the biggest daily spike', reporting over 2 lakh COVID-19 cases for the third consecutive day.[7] The caseload had swollen to more than 1.45 crore.[8]

Over the next few months, the horror would only escalate. In the blink of an eye, pharmacies ran out of vital medicines.

The sick crammed the hospitals, but there were no beds. In the searing heat of April, they waited outside health centres—in personal vehicles and ambulances, on stretchers, on benches, on the ground—many hooked to oxygen cylinders, hoping to be admitted.[9]

While the country's health infrastructure was flatlining, politicians and ministers remained determined to campaign for assembly elections, holding rallies and roadshows, while unabashedly overlooking the social distancing directives issued by the ministry itself.[10] A few days after making their public appearance, senior leaders including Uttar Pradesh's chief minister tested positive.[11] The virus was indiscriminate and unstoppable.

Soon, another pressing crisis reared its head: hospitals began running out of oxygen cylinders. As the number of available medical oxygen cylinders precipitously dropped, countless patients lost their lives.[12] Family members frantically conveyed sick relatives from one hospital to another, only to be refused admission due to inadequate oxygen supply.[13] Suddenly, oxygen had become 'more precious than gold',[14] one reporter noted while sharing a video of a large O2 tanker zipping through the city under police protection.

In the midst of all the chaos, the black market thrived. Swindlers hoarded and sold cylinders at ludicrous prices: some were sold at Rs 90,000 a unit.[15] The number of scammers surged too; desperate customers were duped into buying fire extinguishers that were painted and sold as oxygen cylinders.[16] The situation was dire: reports surfaced of police in Uttar Pradesh allegedly 'snatching' an oxygen cylinder from a poor family. A viral video of a young man outside a hospital in Agra pleading with the cops not to 'confiscate' his cylinder, which he needed to save his mother's life, made headlines. A few hours after the incident occurred, his mother passed away. The cops, of course, refuted all claims and called the video fake, but it was reported that the cylinder was given to a VIP.[17]

By the end of April 2021, *The Hindu* reported that 'India had become the first country in the world to report over 4 lakh new cases in a single day', and more than 3,000 deaths on the same day.[18]

———

Uttar Pradesh was struggling. While officials of the country's most populous state insisted that the situation was under control, it was reportedly spiralling. Some newspapers argued that the number of deaths that were stated by the government did not tally with the actual number of cremations taking place in certain cities like Lucknow.[19] Based on the on-ground data collected from graveyards and cremation sites, The Wire, a digital news website, claimed that at least half of the deaths caused by COVID-19 in Uttar Pradesh during the second wave had not been registered in the state's official records at all.[20]

Never in a hundred years had Banaras experienced such a nightmare. Locals admitted to news channels that they had never seen such dreadful sights. '*Zindagi mein hum logon ne itni bhayanak sthiti nahi dekhi thi. Dead body gintey-gintey hum log thak gaye hain.* I have never witnessed such a frightful situation in my life. We've become tired counting the number of dead bodies here,' a mourner confessed to a reporter.[21] People waited six to seven hours for their turn to cremate their loved ones.

As fires raged across the ghats, the corpse burners became increasingly overwhelmed. One of them claimed that they were cremating nearly seven hundred bodies a day. Soon, the men who were used to the morass of death became afraid of it. Many retreated into their homes and latched their doors, refusing to work. The cremation ground managers, who worked directly under the maaliks and oversaw the corpse burners' work, went door to door, pulling the labourers out by their collars, telling them to man up and not shirk their 'duty'. But the burning ghats, believed to be the gateway to heaven for the deceased, had transformed into dizzying pits of hell for its workers.

While the privileged could take refuge within the comfort of their homes, the Dom men were expected to step out and carry on their work, around the clock.

This is how things have always been done. Historically, during natural disasters like earthquakes that razed homes to the ground and tsunamis that tore through cities, the dominant castes were the first to receive aid and protection, while the Dalits were the last to be thought of. More often than not, they were expected, instead, to risk their lives and take on the dangerous, potentially fatal, jobs.

During the 1896 bubonic plague, for instance, innumerable 'low-caste' labourers were put to work to get rid of the feverish rats that scrambled through the Indian cities. The *Report on the Bubonic Plague in Bombay* (1896–97) noted that 'at the time when the plague was at its height, it was not possible to obtain high-caste coolies to carry out the necessary measures'.[22] As a result, hundreds of native coolies (indentured labourers in British India) belonging to oppressed castes were sent on cleansing and disinfecting operations to countless villages. They were tasked with burning the infected bedding and clothes of the diseased persons, disposing and torching garbage, and lime-washing homes.[23]

Major W.B. Bannerman, a military surgeon who worked in the Indian Medical Service in the nineteenth century, observed that 'the handling of rats, dead of plague, seem[ed] attended with danger'. He noted one instance where twenty coolies in Bombay were employed to 'remove the bodies and clean' a warehouse full of rats. Shortly after, twelve of the coolies were infected by the disease.[24]

When the 2004 tsunami took thousands of lives, the oppressed castes were at the forefront, picking up animal carcasses and unearthing human corpses from the debris for a pitiable sum and a meal per day. Initially, they weren't even provided with appropriate safety gear.[25] Among those affected by the catastrophe, Dalits were the last to receive support and rehabilitation during the relief efforts. They were deprived of access to food, water, bedding and clothes, and faced discrimination while sharing emergency shelters.[26] Similarly, in the aftermath of Cyclone Gaja in Tamil Nadu in 2018, it was reported that Dalits experienced systemic pushback during the relief processes and were among the last to be considered for rehabilitation schemes.[27]

―――――

The months of March and April 2021 were terrifying. One of the managers, Shankar Chaudhary, in his early forties, informed me, 'COVID bodies were cremated strictly at Harishchandra Ghat.' He was wearing ordinary clothes, a baseball cap, and slippers. Shankar had been working at Manikarnika Ghat for the last twenty years and had witnessed the pandemic's massive death toll with his own eyes. He noted, 'Only non-infected bodies were allowed in Manikarnika. But if a few infected ones did slip in, one wouldn't know.'

Despite seeing countless corpses rolling in, the manager speculated that the pandemic had its roots in fiction. It was all 'a made-up noise,' he said; a noise that he insisted had been invented by those in power for an ulterior gain yet unknown to him. 'A few months ago, things were normal,' Shankar said. 'Now suddenly all this has started again? Naa!' He clicked his tongue. 'Something doesn't seem right.'

A pyre sputtered behind him. He slipped off his cap and wiped the sweat off his forehead. 'We and our labourers have been working day and night at the masaan and nothing has happened to any one of us.' The Doms believed that serving at the feet of Lord Shiva made them invincible; even if the pandemic was real, they had nothing to fear. 'Besides, 90 per cent of Dom men drink alcohol,' Shankar mentioned offhandedly, 'and alcohol keeps corona away.'

The manager wasn't the only one who thought that COVID-19 was a myth. Many Doms shared his belief. *'Itna dara rahe hain corona se.* They are scaring us so much with this corona news,' Mohan said one day in a tone that barely suppressed ridicule. He belonged to a handful of Doms still working at the ghat in March and April 2021, during the peak of the pandemic. Over a short yet difficult span of two months, Mohan proudly claimed that he himself had cremated 'hundreds of corpses daily'.

'Did I get corona?' he asked, his piercing black eyes examining my face. 'No!' he said, answering his own question. 'Wouldn't I have died by now?' he asked again. I remained quiet.

Although Harishchandra Ghat had been officially designated as the burning ground for the cremation of COVID-19 corpses, Mohan's account was different. He said that he had cremated infected bodies at Manikarnika Ghat.[28]

'Regardless of who died—someone's father, someone's son, someone's mother—no one was touching those bodies. We were the ones picking them up one by one and placing them on the pyres,' he said, thumping his chest. 'There were so many bodies that all the firewood was used up.'

The situation had become alarming. People were throwing their parents' bodies and running away, Sunny, the wood seller, claimed. Bodies were being burned in heaps. 'If a body was burning, the corpse burners threw more wood and dumped another body over it,' he recalled. The long-drawn funerary rituals that promised a safe route to heaven now seemed inconsequential.

Since Mohan was one of the few Dom men who continued to work at Manikarnika Ghat during the pandemic, he claimed that mourners were offering him Rs 2,000–3,000 to cremate their loved ones. 'Brother, please do this for us,' they would plead with him, and Mohan would do it without flinching. '*Uss samay koi dar nahin tha.* At that time, I felt no fear,' he said with arrogant confidence. 'I didn't even wash my hands!'

The state government declared that wearing masks was mandatory and anyone caught without one would be fined Rs 1,000, while repeat offenders would have to pay Rs 10,000.[29] The government also appealed to people to remain indoors and maintain a distance of 6 feet in public spaces. The Doms did not wear masks. 'We Doms don't scare off that easily,' Mohan said. 'Nothing happens to us.'

Mohan was not infected by the disease, even though he spent hours in the mouth of death. This made him fearless and cocksure. There was sureness in his stride. Once, when he was returning from Manikarnika Ghat after work, four masked policemen stood in his way. One of them gruffly manhandled him, inquiring why he wasn't wearing a mask. Mohan replied calmly, 'I am on my way back from burning corona's dead.' The officers shuddered and immediately took a step back. 'Should I be on my way then?' Mohan asked. The men in khaki parted, clicking their fingers dismissively to shoo him away.

———

Despite the Prime Minister's ambitious nationwide vaccination drive, Mohan did not believe in the vaccine. He, along with the rest of the Doms, refused to be vaccinated. '*Arre, itna body jala diya hum log, toh bhi humko nahi hua.* Arre, I have burned so many bodies and I still haven't got it,' he told me at the time. 'We all have to die someday; either we die today or tomorrow. Whatever happens, will happen.'

By May 2021, vaccines against COVID-19 were available for each Indian citizen who was eighteen years or older.[30] Everyone in the neighbourhood, however, was as sceptical as Mohan. Rumours floated that the first dose made a person sicker rather than making them healthier. The women—including Kamala Devi, who had given birth to nine children—feared the needle. When one of her younger sons, Raja, was told by his employer at the sari shop that he had to get himself vaccinated if he wanted to work, Kamala Devi forbade the boy. No one had fallen sick in the community till now, she told him hotly, but the injection would definitely make him ill, if not kill him. Raja sneakily visited a government hospital to have the dose administered without Kamala Devi's knowledge. He was done sitting at home. He was ready to go to work and start earning as soon as possible.

Although Lakshaya also held the same view as the other Doms, upon Komal's insistence, he too had booked a slot at the government hospital to be vaccinated.

———

In the midst of mass hysteria and panic, exploitation was rife. The maaliks became cold-blooded. Dom labourers claimed that the maaliks refused to allow mourning families to place a corpse on the pyre if they could not pay an exorbitant sum— sometimes as high as Rs 20,000. The number of priests, once very visible around Manikarnika Ghat, had dwindled. Those who were available, charged a high fee for their services as well. This was the case in not just Banaras; prices were spiking across the country. The demand for and cost of samagri like ghee, honey and camphor, as well as firewood, bamboo sticks and earthen pots, had risen astronomically.[31]

The wood sellers' business flourished. Sunny was able to buy 680 square feet of land on the outskirts of the city with the money he earned during the pandemic.

'Young kids who worked at the ghat made huge amounts of money,' Mohan said. 'They were the daring ones.'

Mohan also profited. Over a period of two months, Twinkle said, her husband had earned at least Rs 60,000, if not more. Gifts were bought for the family: clothes for the children and jewellery for Twinkle. Mohan bought things for the house too: a television with a set-top box and a spanking new refrigerator with a plastic sheen. The fridge was transported from the shop to Mohan's home on a rickety wheelbarrow that moved slowly through the neighbourhood, allowing everyone to take notice. His daughters routinely played with the refrigerator: opening and closing the door, trying to lick the cold air, giggling happily until Mohan yelled at them and sent them scurrying.

A refrigerator is a status symbol in Chand Ghat. It is a big deal. Not everyone has one. It was something Mohan's father and grandfather had only dreamed of. Mohan was the first in his large family, and was second or third in his community, to own a fully functioning fridge. Mohan bought sweets and shared it within his community to celebrate the occasion.

According to the National Family Health Survey (NFHS 2019–2021), only 37.9 per cent of the population owns a refrigerator in India.[32] Among the Scheduled Castes, it was reported in 2018 that only one-fifth owned them.[33] Twinkle stored milk and water in the refrigerator, happy to make the switch from the clay pots that easily cracked and were often infested with ants. She proudly offered cold water to anyone who visited her home.

The resentment of her neighbours, however, was palpable. Some, she recalled, were frustrated enough to scheme behind her back. 'Sometimes, people cut our electricity cables'—electricity that everyone in the community procures illegally—'they fidget with them or slash them,' she said. 'We have a fridge, a television, a machine that pumps water from the ground: all of that eats power. There is a lot of jealousy here. In our community, all of us are so envious of each other that we cannot stand to see anyone succeeding. If someone makes a little extra or buys new jewellery, people start wishing that person ill.'

Before the pandemic's second wave hit the country, Kamala Devi spent her afternoons lying on the cement floor in her house on hot summer days, undisturbed by her boys, who were either busy at work or hanging around on the streets. An elderly woman now, she would slip off her blouse, wrap her translucent sari around her bare breasts and turn the fan on full speed. The only person around was Mohan's eldest child, young Imlee, who would return home from school and help her grandmother with household chores.

When Kamala Devi fell asleep, eight-year-old Imlee would sneakily whip out the smartphone she had 'borrowed' from one of her younger uncles and browse online. If anyone asked, she told them she was playing Candy Crush, when, in fact, she was watching YouTube videos—many of which were do-it-yourself make-up demos posted by young urban women. Bewitched, Imlee studied their every move: how they tilted their head and pouted for the camera. She would put the phone camera on selfie mode and lift her narrow chin to pose in a similar fashion, mimicking the women in the videos. She watched herself as she raised her brows, tucked her straw-dry hair behind her ears and gingerly ran her fingers across her protruding collarbone. With one click, she captured this imagined and preferred version of herself in time. When her stepmother, Twinkle, called out to her, she would stow the phone away and rush down.

Once the lockdown was imposed, however, Imlee's family members were crammed together in the house. All the time. Imlee no longer had access to her uncles' mobile phones—her only portal to the other world, one that existed parallel to hers, but now seemed further away and out of reach. Her uncles spent most of their time on their phones; they had nothing else to do, nowhere else to be. The housework increased, and since Imlee could no longer go to school, she had no choice but to help Twinkle at home.

Everything from small paan shops to sari stores was shuttered; the number of pilgrims and backpackers flooding the city had already dwindled; rows of empty boats bobbed silently on the water; and schools locked their gates. The freedom to move was restricted once again.

Though Imlee's two uncles had temporarily become jobless— they were employed at a sari shop (the owner knew of their background)—her father's work had exponentially increased. In the afternoons, she watched Mohan return home from pulling an all-nighter at the cremation ground. Her stepmother carefully took his clothes and washed them outside the house using washing powder, even though their room had an attached bathroom. Twinkle made sure Mohan bathed and scrubbed his body clean with soap before he stepped inside the house. On days when he was exhausted, he cribbed about Twinkle being a hygiene witch. Twinkle would snap at him, 'You are out there exposing yourself and then coming home. If something happens to you, you will put all of us at risk.'

Imlee was tired of having her family members in the house all together at once. It was stifling. She wanted to play outside without the fear of the masked stranger in khaki who visited Chand Ghat daily, corralling everyone, threatening to smack those who were 'loitering' outside. This was a lockdown and everyone had to observe quarantine in their homes. He walked through the gali, waving his baton, mouthing Hindi expletives. Imlee would watch his bushy brows dance above the mask he wore, animated in anger. Whenever he arrived, everyone pelted inside their homes. As families huddled together like anxious chickens in a coop, the Doms wondered how all this was for their 'own good', like the man claimed.

The blanket draconian rule imposed by the government instructed families to quarantine within their homes and step out only for essential goods and emergency services. This seemed to favour only the privileged. In areas with poor sanitation and in neighbourhoods where each family had eight to nine members living under one roof, it was unimaginably repressive.

As soon as the officer left Chand Ghat, however, young boys would spill out of their homes—half their bodies over the threshold, the other half inside, in case they had to quickly withdraw. Eventually, once they were certain the coast was clear, they went back to chatting with each other or pushing their noses into the screens of their mobile phones. The girls were held back by their mothers. The less time they stood under the sun, the lighter their skin would remain. Besides, the older women always needed an extra set of hands to help with the never-ending household chores.

By May 2021, newspapers began reporting that there was a massive shortage of wood to build funeral pyres and it had become immensely expensive.[34] People were resorting to various ways of disposing bodies. In some areas, corpses were tossed into water bodies from bridges,[35] while in regions like Prayagraj and Unnao, mass shallow graves were discovered. Abject poverty and desperation forced many families to bury diseased corpses in the sand, on the banks of the Ganges.[36]

On 10 May, as the sun mounted the sky, a peculiar object surfaced in the Ganges, in Bihar's Buxar district. In Chausa village's Mahadev Ghat, two fishermen, a father and son, on their morning fishing round spotted a ghoulish, bloated body bobbing down the river, along the current. A few feet away, they noticed more unidentified corpses drifting directionless.[37] In the distance, a wild dog had begun gnawing at the flesh of a corpse that had washed ashore.

At the peak of summer, reports emerged of partially cremated bodies dotting the Ganges between Uttar Pradesh and Bihar.[38] In Chausa itself, some alleged that corpses were being 'thrown' directly into the river.[39] The sacred river, considered pure, was now putrid. The floating bodies were an eyesore: a disconcerting sight that immediately made national news. Investigations revealed that a precipitous rise in deaths, combined with the unavailability of firewood and lack of cremation space for disease-stricken corpses, had forced people from the border districts and villages to get rid of the bodies by dumping them into the Ganges.

Corpses that were hurriedly buried in shallow sand graves on the banks of the river, were either washed into the river or feasted upon by vultures and dogs. Locals feared that these were corpses of COVID-19 patients discarded unceremoniously by families.[40] Concerns arose about the transmission of the disease through water. Communities that lived near the river were completely dependent on it for drinking, bathing and irrigation. Could they become infected too?

———•—————•———

It May 2021, Lakshaya sipped a glass of sweet, watered-down lassi, which Dolly had made for him in the early afternoon. He sat on the threshold of her home, watching the news on his mobile phone. One video claimed that fifty-two half-burnt bodies had been recovered from Ballia,[41] a city situated 140 kilometres east of Banaras in Uttar Pradesh. '*Sab halla hai.* All this is just noise,' he mumbled, scrolling down to another video. This one showed censored clips of abandoned bodies floating downstream in the Ganges at Buxar, Bihar, where seventy-one corpses had reportedly been fished out.[42] He sighed and slid his phone back into the pocket of his jeans.

Lakshaya refused to believe anything that was being reported during the pandemic. News channels, in his opinion, were there to distract people from the ground reality. Stories about corpses piling up at the cremation ghats in Banaras because the firewood had not been replenished, may have been true in April but Lakshaya insisted that by late May, the number of corpses had become a mere trickle. There were 'about twenty or twenty-five bodies' arriving at Harishchandra Ghat in a day, even fewer at Manikarnika Ghat, and there was plenty of firewood around, he said. 'The news is saying that there is no space in Manikarnika Ghat, not enough wood or that people have to stand in long queues for three-four hours to get bodies cremated. Nothing like that is true right now,' he said. Lakshaya said that the city had transformed into a ghost town. It had buckled under the lockdown.

Shortcut would later corroborate this. 'The market is quiet. Policemen are running after everyone with sticks. If we walk on the streets without a mask, they hit us and fine us one hundred rupees,' he told me on the phone. He added that although there had been countless corpses turning up at the cremation grounds a week before the lockdown, since it was imposed however, there were hardly any. '*Lockdown ki vajah se lashein kum aaney lagi hain. Abhi bhi lashein aa rahi hain, lekin pehle se kum.* Due to the lockdown, fewer dead bodies are arriving. They are still coming but not as many as before.'

The surge of corpses may have reduced in Banaras's cremation grounds, but this seemed to coincide eerily with the dumping of the dead bodies in the Ganges.[43]

Lakshaya gulped down the lassi and decided to take his motorbike for a spin. Life and work had come to a standstill. He wanted to visit Harishchandra Ghat to see what was really happening there. If the cops stopped him, he could always invent an essential chore he could not put off. He rode through the city's narrow galis, once swollen with crowds travelling on foot, in cars, in rickshaws, but now deserted and forlorn. Barring the sporadic appearance of a few strangers—usually men—out on errands of their own, Lakshaya saw no one. Nobody raised an eyebrow as he zipped by.

When he arrived at Harishchandra Ghat, an ambulance was reversing into a corner. Two men stood behind the vehicle, directing the driver to steer the rear wheels towards the left. A cleaning lady in a sari swept the ground with her broom. A rooster crowed nearby. Another man watched the scene while he tore open a gutka packet and funnelled its contents into his mouth. The otherwise silent afternoon was rent by the desperate wails of a woman who had just lost her husband.

Later, Lakshaya would describe the entire scene as nothing out of the ordinary: '*Sab normal tha.* Everything was normal. *Hum logon ko kuch ajeeb nahi lagta, kyunki hum log humesha yehi dekhte hain. Aadat si ho gayi hai.* To us, nothing seems strange because we've been seeing this all our lives. We are used to it.'

From the ambulance, a man dressed in a white PPE uniform, with a face shield strapped to his forehead, jumped out. 'What a day,' he said to a stranger standing near him. Then he walked across the street and exhaled. 'I'm taking this off here,' he told someone else as a perfunctory courtesy, before unzipping his PPE suit. The man peeled down the top portion of the suit, grabbed a white gamchha and wiped the sweat off his face, before tying it around his head like a bandana. He rolled down his suit, pulled it off, bundled it up roughly and casually cast it aside.

This incident wasn't an anomaly. Thousands of masks and PPEs were being indiscriminately discarded on roadsides and at crematoriums. Medical experts warned that these unattended medical castaways could be the 'biggest potential carriers of coronavirus', and had the potential to spread the virus by harming at least ten people in one go, who, in turn, could affect hundreds more.[44] The World Health Organization noted that the virus also spread 'via indirect contact—when droplets attach to surfaces like the inside of a PPE suit'.[45] In a Delhi crematorium, PPE suits used by relatives of those who died due to COVID-19 were dumped recklessly among unattended garbage.[46]

Between June 2020 and May 2021, the Central Pollution Control Board stated that the country had 'produced 45,308 tonnes of COVID-19 biomedical waste', which needed to be incinerated immediately.[47]

25

The Electric Crematorium

THE MODERN-DAY CREMATORIUM at Harishchandra Ghat, which had been neglected for over three decades by Hindus who visited Varanasi to cremate their dead by using wood and fire, was in 2021, suddenly in dire demand. But it could not cope with the alarming number of infected corpses that arrived at its doorstep every day.

Banaras's sole electric crematorium was inaugurated in 1989. For several decades prior, particularly in the 1970s and early 1980s, the Doms had fiercely stalled its construction. They feared that the modern-day crematorium's services would blight their only source of survival. Devout locals backed the Doms' fight. At the forefront of the resistance was Dom Raja Kailash Chandra

Chaudhary, who wielded symbolic clout and was vehement in protecting his family's claim over the 'burning ghats'.

He declared that the presence of the electric crematorium in the holy city would tamper with the faith of the Hindu masses.[1] For many years, due to Kailash Chaudhary's stance, the electric crematorium project was delayed. After his death in 1985,[2] however, the government speedily launched the Ganga Action Plan, which was geared towards mitigating the pollution in the river, and under this plan the electric crematorium at Harishchandra Ghat was successfully set up.[3]

The electric crematorium was positioned as a solution not only to keep the Ganges clean, but also to diminish the degree of air pollution caused by open-air pyres and to extensively reduce the usage of wood. It was easy on the pocket—in 2012, the electric crematorium cremated bodies at the subsidized rate of Rs 500 per corpse—while the cost of traditional cremation was upwards of Rs 4,000.[4] The modern crematorium was also time-conscious: it took forty-five minutes to do the work, while the waiting period for a body to cremate fully with wood and fire was over three hours. In a nutshell: the new crematorium was cheaper, quicker, safer and environment ally friendly.

Despite its many positives, the electric crematorium failed to run successfully. Many believed that a non-wooden cremation, one that was not held at the sacred river's edge, would not provide absolute salvation. And so, corpses continued to be laid out and cremated on traditional pyres.

For years, then, the electric crematorium was only fired up when unclaimed corpses were found on the streets by the police or when the poor could not afford to buy the expensive samagri and wood. They would have their loved ones cremated at the electric crematorium out of desperation, not choice. The first time I visited the electric crematorium in 2015, I learnt that as few as three to five bodies were cremated on a daily basis there. To encourage more people to use the electric crematorium, the service was made free. However, that did not do much to boost its popularity either.

I also learnt that to pacify the Doms, the crematorium authorities agreed to hand over the ashes obtained after cremating each corpse to the community, allowing the Doms to use the ashes for 'dhulna'.

———

In 2015, in the middle of winter, Santosh Chaudhary wasn't expecting visitors. At the decrepit electric crematorium, Santosh worked as its chief operator. The crematorium was within a building that stood at a height, next to the traditional cremation ground at Harishchandra Ghat.

On the day of our meeting, Santosh, a wiry man in his late twenties, was standing in front of a glassless window, in a cotton shirt and a blue sweater that hung loosely over his shoulders. His hands were clasped at the back as he solemnly looked 'out of it'. The window framed the regal bluish-grey river, flowing and alive—a stark contrast to the eerie stillness of the crematorium. Natural light lit the interiors. The room was sparse, inhabited by twin giant furnaces that occupied a large portion of the space. One of the Dom children once described the furnaces as 'flesh-eating' machines that swallowed bodies wholly. The air in the electric crematorium was still and quiet, occasionally disturbed by the cooing of pigeons: a stray flutter here, a one-legged perch there.

Santosh told me that when the corpses were delivered, it was his job to keep a diligent record. In a single-lined notebook, he wrote, in Hindi, the deceased's name, age, city's name or village, and so on.

'As an operator, I ensure that I maintain the file and see that the documentation is fine. I have to make sure that all the documents are there, and at the end, I open the gate [of the electric chamber] while another Dom assists me,' he explained. The corpses were laid on a lift table—an iron tongue that resembled a gurney—and the bodies were then wheeled into the mouth of the cremation pit. 'We get at most five bodies a day,' Santosh informed me. 'Not more than that.'

Santosh, who belongs to the Dom community, holds a Master's in English. Through a special quota for Scheduled Castes/Scheduled Tribes, he studied at the Banaras Hindu University (BHU), considered to be one of the finest institutions in the city. After graduation, he worked as a tuition teacher for a while, before securing a full-time job at the crematorium. Despite his education, the only job Santosh managed to acquire involved dealing with corpses. 'For now, this job is good, but I'd like to do much more,' he said in an aspirational tone. 'I'm currently preparing for my Master's in Political Science. I want to become a professor at a government college.'

Santosh comes from a family of maaliks. While his four brothers, who live in the Dom colony near Harishchandra Ghat, had studied, they had decided to carry the family tradition forward as maaliks. Santosh had dreamed of becoming much more, he told me. As the only one in his family who desired a profession that strayed from tradition, he studied and received a Master's degree.

'My brothers sometimes make five thousand rupees a day, while I make that much in a month,' he said dryly. It was a price he paid, he said, to do something different. Yet, Santosh, who felt that his presence at the crematorium was vital, said that unlike at the burning ghats, where a day's earning was dependent on the number of corpses that arrived there, working at the electric crematorium offered a steady income and a cooler, less frantic surrounding.

Could his job, however, be given to anyone else who was perhaps as educated as him but came from a different caste, I asked.

The question seemed to offend him. 'You see,' he said, challengingly, 'we might be able to work the camera that you are holding once we learn how to use it. But no upper caste man or woman, including *you*, would ever want to touch a dead body, let alone do our job.'

Santosh narrowed his eyes. 'This is my birth right!' he continued, enunciating the word 'birth' with discernible pride. 'Only *I* and those in my community can burn corpses. We are the Doms.' His voice resounded through the crematorium.

It is the caste system, however, that continues to ensure that only the Doms handle the dead. No 'upper-caste' Hindu will be willing to perform the task of burning corpses, even if the said work has been 'glorified' for centuries as the only way of 'providing moksha'.

Santosh took a deep breath and assessed the vacant crematorium and its morbid calmness. As its chief operator, he wished more corpses were cremated there so that the crematorium's purpose was fulfilled. 'If one body burns here, at least one tree is saved,' he said.

'Would you be content with having your own body cremated at the electric crematorium?' I asked him squarely.

Santosh clicked his tongue in disagreement. 'When I die, my body will be burned using wood,' he answered. He seems to have no desire to put on a charade for me. 'This is what I want and so do my family members. My body has to go the traditional way. It's one's thinking. I am working here at the electric crematorium, but I would want my body to be cremated on land. If one tree is cut down because of me, it's fine. Sadly, this is the way everyone thinks.'

When I returned in 2019, I found that the electric crematorium—*bijli ghar*, as it was locally called in Hindi—had been renovated and turned into a gas-powered crematorium, with CNG being supplied by the Gas Authority of India Limited (GAIL).

———

In some perverse way, Santosh's wish for the crematorium to become gravely in demand came true during the peak of the pandemic. Santosh had left his job long before that—sometime between 2016 and 2017—making it difficult to track him down.

In October 2021, I met Vicky Chaudhary, the man who was working there. During the pandemic, he had witnessed the chaos that had ensued at the gas-powered crematorium.

'*Chaubison ghante hum kaam kar rahe the.* We were working twenty-four hours a day,' he said, speaking about the endless queues of corpses that lay outside awaiting their turn, and the twin furnaces that worked night and day to reduce COVID-stricken bodies to ash. The crematorium could cremate only thirty to forty corpses in a day, he told me, and the cremations were done free of cost.

Manually at the ghat below, however, Dom labourers were frantically building pyres to cremate 'three hundred to four hundred bodies' on a daily basis. The bodies, covered in 'plastic bags', were brought in ambulances and the labourers at the ghat poured 'lots of petrol' on the bags that encased the corpses, Vicky said, so that the synthetic caught fire quickly. At the gas crematorium above, however, none of that was required. All the while that Vicky worked directly with the COVID bodies, he didn't wear any protective gear. Like any other Dom labourer whom I spoke to then, he too parroted an overarching belief that boasted of some superhuman invincibility that benefited him: '*Baba hamaare hain na.*[5] *Sab baba bharose. Dar nahin tha.* Lord Shiva is with us. Everything is in his hands. There was no fear.'

What is significant to note is that like Santosh, Vicky is a Dom too. Turns out, this job is solely reserved for individuals that belong to his caste.

'People believe that if they are cremated by the hands of a Dom, they will receive mukti, liberation,' Vicky explained. '*Toh raja ho ya fakir ho, aakhir mein Chaudhary ji ke pair pakarna hi pakarna hai.* Whether it's a prince or a pauper, in the end everyone has to fall at the Chaudharys' feet. We are not just any Chaudharys,' he rambled, barely catching a breath after the delivery of each sentence. 'We are the Chaudharys of the ghat. We offer mukti. We are not like the sweepers.' The last remark held a touch of snobbery.

Post the pandemic, however, the pollution-free, smoke-free gas crematorium has no takers once again. It obviously cannot compete with the long-held parampara, tradition, of burning a corpse on a wooden pyre on the banks of the Ganges.

26

The Pandemic's Casualties: Shortcut and Bhola

THE PANDEMIC HAD left several casualties in its wake, including Shortcut's future.

Among the Dom boys, Shortcut (like Bhola) was one of the few who had continued his studies in school. The pandemic turned his future completely upside-down. When the lockdown was imposed, Shortcut was in the middle of taking his twelfth standard Board exams. However, in April 2020, he was compelled to return to Chand Ghat and prepare for his exams from there.

Despite having things to keep him busy all day, a certain kind of hollowness engulfed him. One after another, things seemed to be going awry. His basti was nothing like the hostel he had left behind. The constant din of high-pitched clamour all around rattled him. It made it difficult for him to focus on anything.

But his discontent ran deeper, the cause of which was elsewhere.

Soon after his return to Chand Ghat, he had received a phone call from a known number with an unknown voice.

'You seem to be an intelligent boy,' the voice said cryptically.

It was his girlfriend's aunt. Shortcut had been seeing one of his classmates from school. On the phone, the aunt, with clinical detachment, informed him that she was aware of their relationship. She had slyly listened to a recording of the two of them speaking to each other on her niece's cell phone, where the girl had broached the subject of marriage. 'What the two of you are doing is wrong,' Shortcut remembered the aunt cautioning him. He was instructed to leave her niece alone, and Shortcut acquiesced.

When Shortcut recounted this episode, he did so with bewildering calm. 'When I called it off, my girlfriend told me that she would wait for me,' he said. 'Besides, she likes to argue. At school, she fought with everyone and barely had any friends. If I married her, she would have had to stay in my mahaul, where her demands would be overlooked. Would she have quarrelled with everyone in my community then?'

It seemed as though these were excuses or justifications for why he felt he had no future with the girl. The truth, however, stared him squarely in the face. 'Her aunt is extremely wealthy,' he admitted. 'She is a doctor. They are Yadavs. Where am I and where is she? What could I have done?'

The break-up was one of the many things that left Shortcut disenchanted with life.

Bhola's life was also thrown out of gear by the pandemic. When it descended upon the country in 2020, Bhola was in his third year of college and had been visiting his family for a few days. During the lockdown, he was forced to stay on in Banaras. His drive to study, however, did not wane. He was relieved when his college announced that classes would be held online.

But Chand Ghat did not offer the peace Bhola needed. He tried everything. At home, he wore headphones and worked on his laptop, only to have his nieces prance and screech about in the background. The internet connectivity was faulty too. Next, he tried sitting on a neighbour's terrace, but the intense sun overheated his laptop. From the terrace, Bhola watched as Shortcut, sitting on the threshold of his home, resentfully tossed away his textbook, failing to find the focus he once could easily muster in his dormitory.

'I won't be able to survive here anymore now. Nor will Shortcut,' Bhola told me on the phone once.

By May 2020, Bhola was desperately scouting for a room away from Chand Ghat. He needed a space that championed quietude and was uncluttered. A basic desk, a chair, a tube light and strong Wi-Fi connectivity was all he needed. Eventually, he found what he was looking for. He approached Shortcut with the idea of co-renting the study space. Shortcut agreed; he decided to study for his exams from there.

As the days passed, however, Shortcut found himself dithering. The grim circumstances of living at home and watching his parents struggle with funds each day saddened him. At school, Shortcut had blissfully forgotten the life he had left behind: the smallness of his home, the long stretches of darkness when there was no electricity and the heat it left behind. He had even forgotten the worrying small, pus-filled boils on his mother's legs that refused to heal or disappear.

Living for months in Chand Ghat, though, had once again brought him face to face with a reality that he had tried to smother all his school life. It made him come to terms with a disquieting truth: he needed to stop underlining the words printed on the cream-coloured paper of his textbooks and start earning so that— in addition to addressing other household responsibilities—he could take his mother to the doctor.

Unlike Bhola, Shortcut did not have the backing of four brothers. Bhola's brothers had somehow managed to earn enough to pull through the financial strain cast by the lockdown. Shortcut, however, had just one brother, who wanted to look after his children first before troubling himself with his parents. It was then that Shortcut grasped with a haunting certitude that education was never meant to be his.

Disheartened by an uncertain future, he stopped caring about his studies. He did not perform well in his exams and failed his twelfth standard Boards.

When the lockdown eased slightly, a dejected Shortcut spent the first few months taking on menial odd jobs until a friend offered him work as a part-time electrician. He accepted, assuring himself that he would pick up the necessary skills as he went along and perhaps, in a couple of years, he would get a job in a city like Delhi or Pune. Then he would be able to send a portion of his earnings back to his parents.

'*Mujhey yeh basti nahin chaahiye.* I don't want to be in this ghetto,' he told me plainly.

At the time, though, he was stuck here. He could not run away.

Each time Bhola made a breakthrough in his plan to leave Chand Ghat, a powerful, invisible energy reeled him back to Banaras, ensuring that he remained anchored to his neighbourhood. For instance, only a year after he began studying in Cholapur, his father passed away. When Bhola returned to Chand Ghat to attend Keshav Chaudhary's last rites, a sense of foreboding sank deep within his chest. He was almost certain that his father's untimely death meant that he would have to quit school and work with corpses. Not only had he lost a parent, but he was about to lose hope too. At that time, however, Mohan assured his brother that he could return to Cholapur and continue his education. And so, Bhola resumed his schooling, away from the caste-ridden, stifling life at the ghats.

This time, however, it was COVID-19 that was keeping him lodged in Chand Ghat. He felt like everything he had worked towards had suddenly been flipped on its head. Throughout Bhola's growing-up years, caste had been an all-encompassing reality. It had colonized his thoughts, defined his existence, intruded his dreams. But when he was at university in Ludhiana, for a brief moment, Bhola had felt its presence wane; no one there knew about his roots.

In Chand Ghat, though, things were different. Once, while buying goods at the grocery store, Bhola's forearm had accidentally brushed against that of the man beside him. The man scowled and immediately distanced himself. Bhola felt the blood rush to his cheeks, and the trauma that had blighted him for years returned. He was convinced that the stranger's behaviour was dictated by the knowledge that Bhola was a Dom, rather than nervousness about catching the virus. Bhola wondered whether he would ever be recognized for his worth and not just as the son of a corpse burner. He had wanted to flee Banaras at once.

In his spare time, he actively searched online for potential jobs outside the city. Staying in his community had been stifling, but the chance to truly escape only arrived towards the end of March 2021. An educational consultant company based in Chennai reached out, informing him that he had been selected for a sales internship beginning 1 April. The company expected him to join immediately.

A strange lightness lifted his spirits—until the iron-clad anxiety settled in again. April was less than a week away and a train journey from Banaras to Chennai would take a few days. Bhola made a quick decision. He dug into his savings, borrowed money from his wealthy college friends and requested one of them to book a flight for him to Chennai. He would do everything in his power to leave Chand Ghat. This was not an opportunity he was willing to let go.

<hr />

When Bhola arrived at the airport, he spent a few moments taking in the building: its expansive size, the gleaming, freshly mopped floors. He took in the bustle of travellers passing security and the languid movements of the security staff, the airlines personnel—dressed in crisp, colourful uniforms and wearing masks—standing behind the ticket counters. From the corner of his eye, he noticed a stray pigeon fluttering across the lobby in a panicked hurry.

When Bhola checked in, he smiled. He read his name on the digital boarding pass over and over in delight. This was real. He was going to fly for the first time in a few hours. Who would have thought that a boy from Chand Ghat, who had cried sitting near the Ganges while watching an eagle soar, would be flying one day too? He was giddy like a young boy.

'It was like a dream come true,' he admitted a few days later. 'My family doesn't know what the feeling is like. Nor does anyone else in my community. Even I had never thought that I would fly in a plane.'

To ensure that he wouldn't miss his flight, Bhola had reached the airport three hours prior to departure. In all the excitement, he had forgotten to eat breakfast. A small café inside the airport was serving snacks. Bhola walked up to it and gaped at the prices. At his university, Bhola had never even bought a vegetarian sandwich that sold at the campus canteen for Rs 15. It was too expensive for him. At the airport café, however, he reluctantly paid Rs 150 for a similar sandwich and ate it. 'I was starving,' he said. 'What else could I do?'

Inside the plane, he settled in the window seat. Bhola heard the loud thrumming of the engine and clutched the armrests. When the flight took off, he squeezed his eyes shut and leaned back stiffly. Each time Bhola mustered the courage to look outside, he shifted nervously and closed his eyes again. The woman seated beside him looked at Bhola's awkwardly squirming body with a mix of curiosity and annoyance. 'She must have wondered how a grown man could be so fearful,' he said. 'But I am afraid even of sitting on swings! Each time the swing goes up, I feel terrified looking down,' he confessed, chuckling embarrassedly.

Eventually, the plane stabilized and Bhola's breathing returned to normal. He wished his mother was flying with him; he wanted to share this experience with her. He pulled out his smartphone and began taking photographs and videos of the clear blue sky and cotton clouds. When the plane began to descend, Bhola's ears felt stuffy and clogged. He could hardly hear anything or anyone. Dread gripped him again: was he turning deaf?

Earlier that morning, Kamala Devi had cried her eyes out. She had repeatedly warned Bhola not to take the flight. 'What if something happens to you?' she had asked, panicked. Had his mother been right? Bhola thought. When the plane hit the tarmac and the doors were unlocked, his ears popped open and he finally felt at ease.

In Chennai, Bhola rented a room with two boys where he stayed as a paying guest. On 1 April 2021, he joined the internship programme. It took him a month to settle in the new city but he embraced his hard-earned freedom. When he received his first salary—Rs 15,000—he felt that all his years of tireless hard work had paid off.

A few months later, however, the invisible tug that always pulled Bhola back to his home would return. He would be forced to leave for Banaras again.

***

In August, a few months after Bhola's departure, Kamala Devi fell terribly ill. She began having strange, incomprehensible fits: muscles twitching like a broken wind-up doll; eyes turning terrifyingly opaque; and a side of her face and her limbs stiffening up. The first time this happened, Kamala Devi collapsed in her house. She was alone at the time. Her granddaughter Imlee found her lying in an ungainly position with her eyes closed and legs apart. Her sons, once notified, hauled her in a wheelbarrow to a nearby hospital. There, they were informed that Kamala Devi had lung cancer that had spread to the brain, triggering the erratic seizures.

'No one thought that she would survive that day,' Shortcut said, recounting the incident. Kamala Devi stayed in the ICU for four days. 'Her condition was so bad that we felt she must have fought hard with God to live.'

Across the country, Bhola packed his bags to take the first train out of Chennai. For the sake of his mother, he had decided to work from Chand Ghat for as long as he could. Once again, he found himself in his mahaul, back where he had started.

27

The Way Things Have Always Been Done

By NOVEMBER 2021, there is a taut roundness to Twinkle's belly, a recognizable tightness in her blouses, a new language in her gait and a pronounced curve in her back. The hemline of her sari has become discernibly higher so that when she walks, her feet—with red nail paint and silver bichhiyas, toe rings—are visible. Twinkle is seven months pregnant with her second, and Mohan's third, child.

When I meet Twinkle, she is sitting in Kamala Devi's terrace kitchen on a patri, a low wooden stool about four inches high, and slicing vegetables. The cement floor is her chopping board. Her sari is hitched up and tucked between her thighs to ensure it doesn't come in her way. Outside, from the windows of other homes, plumes of grey smoke rise and twist like wispy beards of old men—a sign that the afternoon meals are being prepared. It is eleven in the morning.

Mohan's younger sibling, Mitthoo sits beside her. She offers little assistance to her sister-in-law, merely watching as a full-bellied Twinkle sets the rice to boil. Mitthoo lives three doors down the alley. She is visiting her mother since Kamala Devi has not been keeping well. Although Twinkle dislikes Kamala Devi, a sense of familial solidarity possesses her whenever her mother-in-law is sick, and she willingly takes over the responsibility of household chores.

Twinkle places the pressure cooker on the stove. She is cooking arhar dal, or pigeon-pea lentils, mixed with turmeric, salt, chillies and garlic. The stove is connected to a gas cylinder by a pipe. Ever since a number of galis were razed for the Corridor project, making the route to Manikarnika Ghat longer, procuring firewood from the pyres had become difficult. By 2020, housewives had no choice but to warm up to the idea of having gas cylinders in their homes, even though elders like Kamala Devi feared that their settlement would explode along with the cylinders. Not all homes opted for gas cylinders, but Twinkle was grateful when theirs did so. Earlier, the children brought home wet pyre wood from the ghat, which was known to be an uncooperative cooking fuel that took a while to ignite. Vicious, thick smoke would rise and spread, before settling deep inside the lungs of the women who busily slapped rolled-out dough onto the tawa.[1] It took a few months, but Kamala Devi eventually got used to the newfangled, non-sooty way of kitchen life.

A raven-hued taveez, the size of a small pebble, is tied around Twinkle's right arm with a thick black thread. This is a common practice; people believe the amulet, made by tightly knotting asafoetida and garlic cloves into a ball, will protect the child in the womb. Due to extreme poverty and undernourishment, pregnant women rely on superstition to ensure the safety and health of their unborn child. Once the baby is born, however, the taveez is removed from the mother's arm during her first bath, usually eight to twelve days after giving birth. Twinkle does not know why this tradition is followed, but relays that it is an uncomfortable and peculiar experience. The days immediately after the birth involve multiple rituals, including worshipping the household deities, like Phoolmati Mata, and other goddesses like Sitala Devi (who is believed to cure small pox), as well as a gifting ceremony for the mother. New mothers are allowed ten to fourteen days of rest, I am told, before they are expected to resume household chores.

The rice water bubbles. Twinkle lowers the heat and begins making onion paste in the mortar. I ask Twinkle if she will have a third child, after birthing her second. She says that she has no such intentions. Mitthoo smiles politely, in a manner where one considers somebody delusional. Then, Mitthoo says, '*Woh kehtein hain ki jab tak zindagi hai, bacchey hotey hi rahen.* Our husbands say that till the time we are alive, we should keep producing children.'

Twinkle chimes in, 'It all depends upon the man who has the money to feed.' She scoops the thick, creamy onion paste with her fingers and dumps it into the kadhai. The oil in the pot sizzles. Twinkle turns to me. '*Humare husbands humey maante hain, aur maarte bhi hain.* Our husbands worship us and hit us too. The decision to have children rests entirely with the husband, not his wife,' she says. 'If the husband has the financial ability to feed ten children, then he will expect his wife to produce ten children.' She jabs at the paste with a flat ladle and moves it around, ensuring the paste does not stick. 'Personally, I feel it is better to have a smaller family. We live in such a small house. There is no place to keep anything or have more people in it.'

If new brides do not birth children within the first year of their marriage, scornful gossip brews within the community. People almost always hold the woman responsible, assuming the fault lies in her womb. 'They say, "What kind of a woman is she? She can't even produce children,"' says Twinkle, stirring the paste again.

Mitthoo looks around absently. Then she informs, rather quietly, that she has been collecting information from social workers who visit their homes to make them aware of the possibilities for birth control. At twenty-five, Mitthoo is already a mother of four. Her husband is keen that she has more. 'He wants to have six children at least!' She laughs to mask her anxiety. To ensure that does not happen, Mitthoo has been considering having her fallopian tubes tied. She is fully aware, however, that the community does not believe in contraceptives and believes abortions and other related procedures to be sacrilege.

Twinkle brings her stool closer to me and lowers her voice: 'Mitthoo's husband tells her, "Why do you need to get the operation when I am the one feeding the children and taking care of them?"'

Mitthoo nods dismally. She carefully picks up the discarded garlic skins that lie scattered on the ground like forlorn petals. Her husband has denied her any choice, she says. He feels that since she is living in his care, she has 'no haq—no right' to protest. 'Your job is to make food, take care of the family and look after the children,' he told her once. 'That's it!' Spawning children is a way of tethering a woman to the house. Motherhood ensures a woman's mind is no longer swayed by other desires—the babies' demands alone fill up her days.

—•—

For the longest time, particularly when Kamala Devi's hair was still black, giving birth at the hospital was considered terrifying and strange. Women in the community feared being under the cold gaze of strangers who wielded sharp tools in brightly lit rooms. They preferred giving birth in the comfort of their own homes, under the trusted supervision of their friendly dai, a local midwife. Umbilical cords were cut with razor blades or the jagged edge of a broken clay teacup. Upon her mother's reassurance, Mitthoo had delivered her own babies at home through natural birth. Mitthoo says that the midwife gave her an anti-tetanus injection as a precautionary measure.

When it was Twinkle's turn, however, she vetoed staying at home. After aggressive insistence on her part, she had a caesarean for her first child at a government hospital. Kamala Devi failed to understand what the fuss was all about. 'Back in my day, I managed to pop all nine children out of me at home with the help of a dai,' she had stated proudly. 'I did not need any hospital assistance.'

But some of the younger women in the community, like Twinkle, have increasingly been wanting to give birth in hospitals, opting for C-sections. Twinkle has been advised by her doctor to have a maximum of three caesarean deliveries, after which further caesareans may cause complications; but having only three children is considered absurd in many Dom families.

—•—

In the community, there are certain niyams, rules—rooted in tradition, and echoed and dispensed by elders—to be followed only by women. This includes the symbols of matrimony. A married woman's hair must always be neatly parted and streaked with orange sindoor. Her eyebrows must be bridged by a crimson bindi, her nose pierced, bangles at her wrists, anklets on her feet and her toes adorned by traditional bichhiyas, or toe rings.

Bangles are a symbol of fertility. If a married woman happens to serve water to a guest, especially an elder, and if her wrists are bare, she is reprimanded. 'They will say, "Wear something!" since our wrists look very "lonely-lonely,"' says Mitthoo. 'It's a strange tradition, but we have adjusted to it. This is the way things have always been done.'

Married Dom women don't wear a mangalsutra. 'It doesn't have much fashion, nor does it have any value in our community,' Mitthoo explains. For them, bichhiyas are a sign of their wedded status. Bichhiyas are worn by many married Hindu women across India, regardless of their caste or economic status. They are usually fitted on the second toe, as it is believed that the rings provide a soft pressure that ensures the health of the wearer's uterus and aids in conception.

The toe rings that graced Twinkle's and Mitthoo's feet are chunky and elaborate. I wonder whether the metal pinched their skin, scraping against it when they labour at home or sit cross-legged. The women assure me that they have grown accustomed to it, but there are also tales of swollen toes pinched by the rings, of the metal snagging on saris and making inconvenient holes in the fabric.

From the terrace window, we hear the sharp screech of a metal latch being dragged into place. My eyes trace the source of the sound and land on a woman with a deep blue wrapping—a 'chaddar'—gracefully draped over her head. The netted fabric, an addition to her sari's pallu, obscures her face completely. The woman stands obediently outside the doorway, waiting for her husband to lock their house. When he is done, she walks off with him, her anklets tinkling, the heels of her pumps smacking against the ground: *tuck-tuck-tuck*. Under the chaddar, the woman no longer appears human, but a shapeless, decorative figure—with no identity of her own—gliding through the alley.

Each time a married woman in the community has to step outside her neighbourhood, she must cloak herself in the net-like drapery that covers her head and flows onto her shoulders. Twinkle clicks her tongue in disgust. 'We don't like it,' she tells me, as she slits open a bhindi, scoops out its sticky insides and stuffs the belly with an ochre masala of turmeric, cumin and rai. 'Whenever we go out, we put on so much make-up, but all of that is hidden under that ugly chaddar. But we only step out when it's really needed; otherwise, we don't leave Chand Ghat.'

Women don't have the liberty to step out on their own. Once, when I was visiting Chand Ghat, I had seen Mitthoo burrowed deep inside her home, flattening a ball of roti dough between her palms in the darkness. There was a power cut that afternoon. The only light filling her one-room home poured in from the doorway. The heat from the lit stove sank deep into her skin; her back was dotted with pimples. Her sari blouse was damp and her hair was dishevelled. The air inside was oppressive, stuffy.

Mitthoo was making around fifteen rotis for her family, each about 8 inches in diameter. She used a folded cloth to turn the roti clockwise on the tawa. The tawa wobbled slightly on the stove; orange sparks flickered for a few moments, then died. Her husband sat outside under the open grey sky, pulling on a beedi and plotting a night of adventure with his neighbour. I asked Mitthoo if she could step outside for a stroll later. '*Abhi order nahi hai*. Right now, I don't have the permission,' she said bleakly.

'If I want to go somewhere, I need to take his permission. If he says I can't go, I won't. I will sulk but I will listen to him,' she continued. 'I haven't stepped outside Chand Ghat without my husband ever.'

Mitthoo is not permitted to inquire about her husband's whereabouts either. It would spawn a futile argument. 'If I dare ask my husband where he went, he'll snap, "Who are you to ask?" he will say. "What I do outside our house or where I go, is not your concern. You are getting everything you need, aren't you? So sit down and be quiet,"' she said at the time.

On the terrace kitchen, Twinkle has finished cooking. She transfers the rice into a wide-mouthed plate and uses a steel glass to scrape and collect the obstinate grains stuck inside the cooking container. Then she takes water from the steel vessel that rests near the other utensils to wash the dishes. Twinkle uses a toothbrush against the pressure cooker's lid to scuff out the pale-yellow lentil remnants. By the time she is done, the cookware is gleaming.

Suddenly, my cell phone rings. Mitthoo stares at it as I cancel the call. 'You know, my husband refuses to give me his phone,'

Mitthoo whispers. 'If I ask, he gets suspicious and wonders whom I might want to speak to. In our community, if girls are seen talking on a mobile phone, people have all sorts of questions. "What is she doing? Who is she speaking to?"'

In Chand Ghat, girls and married women don't own a phone. They may borrow it from their brothers, husbands or sons to occasionally talk to their relatives. Boys as young as twelve or thirteen years old, however, strut about the neighbourhood brandishing their shiny phones. They pass their time playing Hindi songs and awkwardly posing in front of different backgrounds to take selfies.

Similar restrictions are placed on young girls and married women in other regions across India. In 2021, a member of the Uttar Pradesh State Women Commission stated that girls should be forbidden from using cell phones, since it allowed them to converse with boys, which could result in elopements and subsequent rapes. She recommended that girls who were given cell phones needed to be monitored by their parents and insisted that any crimes against women were due to the 'carelessness' of mothers.[2] Many families, particularly those living in rural and semi-urban areas, share the belief that women using cell phones is taboo.[3]

In Chand Ghat, children prance around, weaving in and out of homes and lanes, stirring up dust. Unattended by adults, they scamper about—their high-pitched shrieks echoing in the alleyways. Twinkle's toddler, Mohani, scurries up to the terrace kitchen and disturbs her mother, who is busy making a plate for Mohan—a large heap of white rice drowned in piping hot dal, the colour of marigolds. Twinkle clutches her child by the elbow and draws her closer to wipe her nose. 'She has just returned from playing,' Twinkle tells me.

While Mohani plays freely now, when she grows taller, older, fuller, her movements will be curbed. By the age of twelve or thirteen, girls are discouraged from visiting other homes, even those in their own immediate neighbourhood. They are cautioned to be on their best behaviour, which includes not interacting with the mohalla boys. If they do, they are written off as characterless—a label difficult to peel away.

Girls in the community are taught to become experts in scouring the cookware, peeling potatoes, pounding garlic, picking out rice husks, making rotis that are perfectly circular, darning clothes and taking care of younger siblings. It's home-schooling for a supposedly happy conjugal life.

Adolescent girls in the community are groomed to wear salwar-kameez, with their dupattas neatly pinned to their shoulders and their hair braided. They cannot wear kurtas that settle tightly on their hips or are sleeveless. If young women step out of their homes without a dupatta across their chests, they are thought to be promiscuous. Married women in the community can only wear saris. Jeans are considered inappropriate.[4]

If you visit Chand Ghat in the morning, you will find women within the four walls of their homes, breastfeeding their newborns, cooking, bathing or sweeping the floor with bristled brooms while their glass bangles clink in unison. Most homes have a small-sized bathroom consisting of an Indian-style toilet. In some, a wall partition separates the bathroom from their bedroom in their 9-by-9-foot homes. In others, a poorly lit bathroom is built outside, and the entry is covered with a thick, jute like fabric or a decrepit wooden board for privacy.

Inevitably, women find it challenging to bathe—the wandering eyes of neighbourhood voyeurs are in plenty. Aakash's open terrace, for instance, is lower than Bhola's, whose house is adjacent to his. Aakash's sisters must take extra care while bathing on their terrace, since it offers an uninterrupted view. Some women tie their petticoats tightly under their armpits and then lather soap, while others bathe wearing saris, unwilling to undress at all to protect their dignity. When they are done, they go inside their bedrooms to change into dry clothes.

28

Describing a Ghost

In 2021, FIVE years have passed since Dolly's husband died. His name is rarely mentioned in the community now—it is as if he had never existed. Sekond Lal is a spectral being floating aimlessly in people's memories, appearing at the forefront only when someone asks about him.

'I am about five feet tall. Sekond Lal was slightly taller than me,' Aakash says, sucking in his left cheek and chewing gutka fiercely. He has a day off from the pari. He is wearing a white dhoti and a half-sleeved undershirt. His eyes are jumpy and his fingers fidgety. When he speaks, his body exhibits slight tremors; the continuous use of gutka and alcohol over the years has begun to serrate his nerves. '*Shareer se motey the.* Physically, he was fat.'

A majority of men in Chand Ghat are wire-thin: overworked and subsisting mostly on nicotine and alcohol. 'Fat' is commonly used as an adjective to describe a well-built man who has a few spare kilos. 'Sekond Lal's skin was sanvala, copper-toned,' Aakash continues. 'His cheeks were full and physique was "fit-phat". Health wise, everything was good.'

Whenever Dolly speaks of Sekond Lal, it is with immense love and fondness. He was gentle and kind, caring and considerate, she says. Her memories of him are invaluable gifts that she hopes to pass on orally to her youngest, who will never know her father. And it is in these moments that her eyes well up.

Once, while visiting Dolly, I asked her to describe her husband. Twinkle, who was walking past the house and was within earshot, saw me and took an immediate detour. She entered Dolly's home and sat comfortably on the ground beside her.

'He was handsome,' Twinkle said, coolly cutting off Dolly before she could reply to my question. 'Ve-rrr-y good-looking.' She rolled the word 'very' off her tongue slowly, allowing its emphasis to linger. 'Dolly didn't look too great standing next to him.'

'Dolly is beautiful,' I interjected.

'No,' Twinkle insisted. 'He was better looking than her. He was fair and healthy. Next to him, Dolly looked like a stick.'

Dolly stared at the ground, pretending as though she had not heard a word. It encouraged Twinkle to reiterate, 'He looked great.'

'He worshipped her,' I reasoned.

'Like my own husband loves me,' Twinkle replied competitively.

Dolly sat quietly in the corner of her room with her head bowed, listening to our conversation. There was no electricity at her home that day. Light poured in from the window and the open doorway. Dolly's eyes did not move; her body was still.

'Don't you have a photo of him to show?' Twinkle asked Dolly.

The young widow lifted her head, nodded and smiled limply. She said that she had been wanting to frame a photograph of her late husband for a while, but hadn't been able to do so. Money was scarce. Dolly nudged her eldest son, who was lying next to her, to bring his father's photographs. He was busy playing Candy Crush on his cell phone but got up almost instantly on his mother's request and burrowed in the back of the room to retrieve a yellow plastic bag. When he returned, he plopped himself on the bedsheet beside us and overturned the bag, dumping a stack of glossy photos onto it.

'Careful!' Dolly gasped. The photos were all she had left of her husband.

In one of the photographs, Sekond Lal was wearing a green-and-black check shirt with white pants, looking vacantly into the distance. He had a full head of wavy black hair, neatly parted to the left, and a moustache. The photo was taken at a local studio, possibly a few days after they got married, against the backdrop of a pink bedsheet. On his forehead was a crimson tilak. Dolly sat beside him in a parrot-green sari, her face framed by a red chaddar embroidered with gold motifs. She was smiling brightly, her eyes closed, her red lips slightly parted.

In another, Sekond Lal's face was streaked in colours of purple and deep green. It was taken in a summer month, during Holi. He was wearing a red dhoti. His arm was resting on his wife's shoulder. Dolly was dressed plainly in a blueish-grey sari; sindoor streaked her parted hair. She was wearing a golden nose ring, a thin necklace and dangling earrings. There was a hint of a smile on her face, as though just moments ago Sekond Lal had whispered something romantic into her ear.

These photographs, with their glossy surface and flimsy bodies, were taken using a traditional film camera long before cell phone photography blew up and transformed the world. For Dolly, these photographs were what she could hold carefully in her hands and look at whenever she wanted. They were precious. Dolly carefully gathered them and returned them to the plastic bag; they were the only tangible evidence of her late husband's existence.

The studio visit and that Holi celebration were now mere recollections for her—brief, finite snatches of a time long gone.

Dolly is now just biding time; she has accepted two absolutes: the clawing certainty of her husband's absence and the stifling permanence of grief.

She spends her days working the shop, tending to her children, washing their soiled clothes, cooking meals, eating less so that they can have more. Some days she will eat twenty paans to curb her hunger. Although it has been years since her husband's death, she still cannot bring herself to sleep on his bed. It is now used by her eldest son, and sometimes by Lakshaya.

Earlier, when her television was still functional, she would flip it on when she wanted to unwind—a small box that rested on a cluttered shelf above the bed. Dolly would sit cross-legged on the floor to watch it.

'I don't turn the television on nowadays,' she tells me in a weary voice when I ask about it.

Twinkle, who is visiting, smirks and says cuttingly, '*Paisa nahin hai na cable ke liye, iss liye.* She doesn't have the money to pay for cable, that's why.' She does not try to conceal her condescension by feigning niceness.

Twinkle's contempt for Dolly stems from a certain insecurity that only made itself apparent when she flung snide remarks at the other woman. Perhaps it is because Dolly had married someone with 'smart looks' and a charming personality, while Twinkle had been forced to marry a man, the very thought of whom made her toes curl. The only thing she appreciates is how smitten Mohan is by her. He finds her sharp tongue endearing, her repartee thrilling. It keeps him on his toes—entranced and interested.

It is in front of Dolly and other women less fortunate than herself that Twinkle enjoys parading her small wins the most. She routinely mentions how Mohan displays affection. She describes, for instance, how one winter, he playfully held her by her wrists and dragged her to get her ears pierced. Twinkle had already had her ears pierced once before, but Mohan was adamant that she should get two more holes in each ear. Then, he went and bought two sets of gold earrings.

'My husband expects me to be decked from head to toe,' Twinkle says, beaming. 'He feels that if you are a woman, you should be dressed in gold and silver, nothing less,' she adds, her eyes darting in Dolly's direction, whose ears have pieces of broken twigs for earrings.

Twinkle's misery seems to be salved when she puts others down. Her tongue has the slant of privilege. She is known to speak her mind and when she does, it is with a sense of entitlement, one born from the assurance of being married to a man who is doing well for himself in the community.

Simply put, Twinkle feels she is better than Dolly; after all, her husband is still alive.

29

A Death Remembered

THAT OCTOBER MORNING in 2016, the neighbourhood was in disarray. The community tap was coughing up water in glum spurts, a neighbour's goat was bleating and flies were buzzing over rotting piles of garbage. A sickly, sweet odour from the garbage laced the air. The garbage collector—who allegedly belonged to a caste even lower than the Doms—had not yet arrived.

Dolly, who was staying over at her mother's home that day, felt weighed down by a sense of unease. She described it as an inexplicable heaviness: a sinking, gnawing feeling in the pit of her stomach that slowly crawled its way up her spine and induced a perplexing pain. She had shooed the feeling away determinedly and thought nothing more of it.

Outside, in the narrow lane, she watched Sekond Lal exchange a few words with their neighbour Gopi. She watched him laugh and slap Gopi's back in jest. The lanky-bodied neighbour guffawed and nodded animatedly, but there was something disingenuous about his reaction. Something about Gopi's body language seemed unusual.

Sekond Lal had been on duty at the cremation ground, burning corpses one after another, but had been called back to Chand Ghat at the behest of Gopi, whose family was among the maaliks at Manikarnika Ghat. The two men were making plans for a night of revelry in Ramnagar. For about a month leading up to Dussehra, the Doms abstained from drinking or consuming meat. For days after Dussehra, however, the men gathered to celebrate, drink and eat. Sekond Lal and Gopi planned to do just that. Shortcut's older brother, Bunty, would join them too.

Years later, when Dolly recounts the night of Sekond Lal's death, we are sitting in her home. She has just undergone surgery to remove kidney stones. Her mother and maternal grandfather are visiting for a few days, to help out while she recovers. Dolly is weak, but she vividly recalls what she had experienced that night.

On 16 October 2016, Sekond Lal combed his hair and wore his best shirt. Dolly and Sekond Lal were staying at her parents' home for a few days. It was around four or five in the evening, Dolly says, that Sekond Lal got ready to leave for the fair in Ramnagar. By that time, Gopi had arrived at the house and was waiting outside the door. There was some small talk and laughter between the two. In the middle of a repartee of crude jokes, Gopi looked directly at Dolly and made an unprovoked, unsettling statement.

'Look,' he said, 'I'm taking your husband now. But I won't bring him back.'

There was an uncomfortable silence in the air, an unintended pause, before Sekond Lal slapped Gopi's back and chortled, writing it off as a grim joke. Dolly's body stiffened. She did not laugh. Gopi's words seemed like a downright threat; in hindsight, she says, it was a blatant confession.

Before leaving, Sekond Lal turned to Dolly, lifted her chin and asked her indulgently, 'Tell me, what should I bring back home for you? What will you eat?'

Dolly looked at him with fear in her eyes. 'I don't want anything,' she said. 'Please don't go.'

Sekond Lal went anyway.

This memory weighs heavily in her heart, like a long-drawn sigh lodged in her chest. She has played that moment in her head over and over again. Her poignant request to her husband, 'Please don't go', is full of pathos and longing. If only she had been sterner with him. If only she had repeated herself multiple times: *Please don't go. Don't go. Please don't.* If only she had taken her husband's hand and pleaded. Would he have listened? Would things be different?

The cyclical pattern of regret—the could-have-should-have-would-have—leaves behind a shrilling disquiet in the body. One never recovers from it, but as the years slip from one to the next, the disquiet becomes less trilling, less haunting, more distant. It becomes lighter, more manageable. Yet, even today, Dolly tears up at the thought of what might have been, had Sekond Lal stayed behind.

That evening, before he left, Sekond Lal had soothed Dolly's concerns with a balm full of promises: he would return home by ten, and the next day he would begin whitewashing their own home (with limestone powder and water) in preparation for Diwali—something Dolly had been after him to do. Dolly merely nodded and said nothing. She watched her husband leave.

Dolly's mother helped her prepare dinner. Geeta still remembers what they had cooked: stuffed aubergine roasted in mustard oil, spiced dal and steamed rice. But the food would be left untouched. Dolly refused to eat until her husband returned. She waited patiently, saying she would eat only after she had served him.

At night, the sky became an unending stretch of darkness speckled with stars. Dolly climbed to the first floor and slipped into Lakshaya's room. Every now and then, she would look out of the window, hoping to see some sign of movement in the alley below, to see Sekond Lal returning, riding pillion on Gopi's motorcycle, half-drunk and loud, slurring profanities into the air.

Yet, hours went by and there was no sign of him.

Around 11 p.m., Dolly grabbed Lakshaya's mobile phone and started making calls. Sekond Lal had left his phone behind that day, so Dolly called Gopi. The phone rang, but no one answered. She called Bunty next. When his phone repeatedly went unanswered as well, the manner of her tapping the redial button became frantic. She called Gopi again. Finally, Gopi picked up; he sounded hassled. When Dolly demanded to speak to Sekond Lal, he told her that her husband was busy and hung up.

Dolly paced the length of Lakshaya's room. At 2 a.m., a frazzled but hawk-eyed Dolly peered out again; she had heard a loud rattling. A neighbour was kick-starting his motorbike below. 'Where are you off to so late in the night, brother?' Dolly asked him.

The man looked up and answered: 'Has no one informed you? Your husband has been in an accident. Why are you still at home? Head to Rajghat bridge.'

Dolly, who at the time still did not know the enormity of the accident, felt the sharp, gnawing anxiety return to her body. Her heart pounding, she hurried downstairs to tell her mother, who gasped and then composed herself before announcing the news in the house. Lakshaya and his father rushed out and headed to Rajghat bridge.

'*Uss waqt, kisi ne yeh nahi bataya ki woh khatam ho gaye the.* At that time, no one told me that my husband had died,' Dolly recounts.

'That ... he had died by falling off the bridge?' I ask.

Dolly's maternal grandfather, who is also in the room with us, answers. 'He did not fall,' he corrects me. 'That was all a show.'

When I later speak to Lakshaya about this incident, he too narrates what he saw that fateful night. When he reached the bridge, Sekond Lal was lying on the side of the railway track on which he had fallen. He says that some people must have picked up the body and placed it on the side. Lakshaya, and a few others, placed the body on a stretcher, into the waiting ambulance, and took it to the nearby hospital. Bunty appeared to have broken his leg and Gopi his arm, Lakshaya says, so the police at the scene sent them to the hospital as well.

Dolly and Geeta arrived directly at the hospital. The family milled around, desperately waiting for news. Eventually they were told that all three men—Sekond Lal, Gopi and Bunty—had fallen off the Rajghat bridge. The bridge was a double-decker: its upper deck was reserved for vehicular traffic, while trains rumbled underneath, through the lower deck's tunnel-like shell. Sekond Lal's body was found on the railway track, near one end of the bridge. The men had been riding on one bike, without helmets, at a dangerous speed. Sekond Lal had died on the spot; Gopi and Bunty had miraculously survived.

Sekond Lal's body was brought into the corridor on a stretcher. The family rushed towards it.

Geeta says that Sekond Lal looked as though he was peacefully sleeping, '*Par woh ek dum khatam ho gaye the.* But he was completely finished.'

Upon seeing Sekond Lal's lifeless body, Dolly fainted and fell to the ground. The police told her family that Sekond Lal had been riding the motorbike under the influence of alcohol. The family was surprised, but, overcome with grief, they did not say anything at the time. 'He did not know how to ride a bike,' Geeta reveals. Then, she recounts their theory: 'We feel that Gopi and Bunty cleverly laid down his body on the tracks, hoping that the train would run him over. That way, the two wouldn't be accused of anything. But, you see, that day, no train came. From there, the police took his body to the hospital.'

Geeta's statement that Sekond Lal did not know how to ride a bike would be confirmed at different times by both Lakshaya and Shortcut. In fact, Shortcut would say that even Bunty, his elder brother, did not know how to ride a motorbike. Only Gopi did.

The day after the accident, Gopi and Bunty were quickly discharged from the hospital with their supposedly deep wounds wrapped in plaster. '*Banavati patti.* Fake bandages,' Dolly's maternal grandfather says with a huff.

During our conversation, Lakshaya says that the post-mortem report stated that Sekond Lal had died 'due to a severe wound on the head'. According to him, it was a cover-up of what actually happened.

Geeta shares a murkier detail. The police told the family that they had found alcohol bottles in Sekond Lal's pockets. Geeta believes that the bottles were deliberately planted to defame him.

At the hospital, the bottles were still in her son-in-law's pants. She swears that they were intact.

'How could the bottles not break if Sekond Lal had fallen from a height?' she asks aloud.

'They fed the cops and the doctors a lot of money to suppress the case and close it,' Dolly's grandfather insists. 'They must have told the doctors to write a report that said that Sekond Lal was the one riding the bike under the influence of alcohol, which caused the accident.'

Bhola, who has only heard about the events of that night, doubts it was a mere accident. '*In log aapas mein kuch to kiye honge. They must have got together and done something …*' he tells me another day.

Shortcut, on the other hand, had only seen Sekond Lal's body at the hospital from a distance, covered with a white cloth, the day after the incident. He believes it was an accident. 'Why would they do it?' he asks. 'They were related to each other; they grew up together. There was no animosity between them.' He makes a comparison to prove his point: 'It's like Bhola and me—we have grown up together. Would I kill Bhola?'

Members of the community narrate different versions of the events that night. Each depends on whom you speak to and where their sympathies lie. There isn't a homogenous, overarching consensus. Some iterations are peculiar; some are not. Some memories are hazy, some are lucid, some hardly make sense, some ring eerily true. Some members of the community believe that it was a drinking party gone dangerously awry, while others speculate it to be a cold-blooded murder and a shoddy cover-up.

30

Aakash's Version

In 1887, the Rajghat bridge opened to the general public. A formidable iron structure spanning the Ganges, the bridge has twin pathways that run one on top of the other. The lower section is for trains, while the upper one is reserved for cars, auto rickshaws and motorbikes. When it was built, the bridge was christened 'Dufferin Bridge', in sycophantic reverence for the former Viceroy and Governor-General of India, Lord Dufferin (1884–88 in office).

The Dufferin Bridge was a part of the herculean imperial railway project in India led by Lord Dalhousie, Governor-General of India from 1848 to 1856. Much of the material that was needed to build the bridge—emblematic of the state-of-the-art Victorian engineering in the 1880s—had to be imported from Britain. Enormous brick pillars were erected and embedded at least 100 feet deep into the riverbed.[1]

In 1948, a year after India won its independence, the bridge was renamed 'Malaviya Bridge' in memory of Madan Mohan Malaviya, scholar, politician and founder of Banaras Hindu University. Today, the bridge is commonly known as the 'Rajghat bridge' due to its proximity to the eponymous area, Rajghat.

The bridge had a complex, dark beginning. Reportedly, there were nineteen documented fatal accidents while the bridge was being built,[2] but the undocumented number was probably far higher. The construction of the bridge faced immense resistance from the locals, who felt that this heavy iron symbol of modernity—an ugly, structural blemish—would disrupt the sacredness and beauty of Mother Ganges.[3] As a result, they never welcomed it with open arms. Although the bridge is much in favour today, some locals say it is cursed. There have been a number of accidents on the bridge, and reportedly, some people have also jumped from it to end their lives.[4]

Every once in a while, as one casually smoothens the fold of a newspaper, a report mentioning the collapse of a bridge or a vehicle dropping off the edge due to a missing railing somewhere in the country, might catch one's eye. In 2017, the Ministry of Road Transport and Highways recognized that over 6,500 bridges on Indian highways were in 'distressed condition'.[5] In Uttar Pradesh alone, it was assessed that at least 226 bridges were in terrible form and needed immediate care.[6]

On 15 October 2016, the Rajghat bridge made national headlines. Over 1 lakh people had gathered to participate in a spiritual procession that had been organized by the Jai Gurudev Dharma Pracharak Sanstha. The organizers had taken permission for 3,000 devotees. However, scores of people had joined the procession en route to Domri village, which involved crossing the Rajghat bridge.

The bridge was teeming with devotees who waved white flags and shouted slogans.[7] Mini-trucks with followers perched on the vehicles' roofs made their way through the crowded passageway.[8] Suddenly, someone shouted that the bridge was on the brink of collapse. Considering that the structure was over a century old, this seemed extremely plausible. The announcement triggered mass hysteria, resulting in an unexpected stampede. Chaos and panic led to the death of at least twenty-five devotees that day,[9] leaving several others grievously injured. It was later discovered that the stampede had occurred due to a rumour; the bridge had never been in any danger.

The stampede occurred at 1.30 p.m. on 15 October—a day before Sekond Lal's accident.[10] In 2016, 268 road accidents were reported in Banaras, in which 154 people died.[11]

Sekond Lal's death was a mere blip.

———

'All three fell from the bike,' says Aakash. He is wearing a cotton vest with a thin white cloth tied around his waist. A gamchha rests on his shoulder.

We are sitting in a sequestered part of Chand Ghat tucked behind the main alleyway, which is filled with the boisterous hurrahs of boys playing cricket and the shrieks of their toddler siblings waddling about, demanding to play with them. Strangely, though, this place has a peaceful, levelled quietness. It is a spot seldom frequented by the locals. Occasionally, wraithlike young men who are up to no good come here to pass the time. The place is surrounded by green stubble and marked by an edge that sloppily falls off to mimic a cliff. From a distance, the edge visually underlines the Ganges; its water appears serpentine under the afternoon sun.

A few feet away from the brink, stone slabs that have fallen into disuse and are stacked haphazardly together, serve as our makeshift seating arrangement. Large ants in shiny black armour, soldier in and out of the crevices. He swipes his red gamchha to displace the crawling formation, then turns to me to speak animatedly.

When they fell, he says, Gopi broke his collarbone and hurt the left side of his upper body. Bunty's right foot got caught in the 'gutter' of the railway track. A jutting iron rod 'went in from one side and came out the other. But these two guys, Bunty and Gopi, survived the fall.'

Aakash was supposed to join Sekond Lal, Gopi and Bunty and party that night. However, hours before they left, Aakash had taken ill and bowed out of the plan.

For a man who was not physically present when the incident took place, Aakash is remarkably detail-oriented. 'When Sekond Lal fell, the impact was so immense that it resulted in his chest collapsing,' he says, pressing his hand to his chest and forcefully pushing it inwards. 'That's how he died.'

'All three fell. All three hit the track with force,' I repeat. 'Then how did only Sekond Lal not survive the fall?'

'He was heavier,' Aakash reasons. 'That is why he died.'

'That doesn't make sense,' I insist.

Aakash tweaks his response. 'Sekond Lal fell directly onto the railway track's gutter. That's how his chest caved in completely.'

Which suggests that Sekond Lal fell flat on his stomach, face down.

'Bunty fell on the other side of the railway line,' Aakash continues. 'But the bone of his foot got wedged between the tracks. Both Bunty and Gopi fell on ground carpeted by rubble. Gopi fell on his left side—that's why that side of his body was injured,' he says, 'while Sekond Lal's body lay splayed on the ground.'

'What about the alcohol bottles found in Sekond Lal's pants?' I ask. 'Logically, the glass bottles should have smashed upon impact.'

Aakash has a ready answer. 'The bottles were made of plastic.'

Even then, I want to point out, the bottles should have been damaged in some way.

It appears as though Aakash has the sequence of the events well-articulated in his mind. Of course, there are certain details that seemed to defy reason. For one, it is odd that Bunty's and Gopi's dangerous descent was cushioned in some way, while Sekond Lal plummeted face down, hit his chest and died.

Aakash then reveals something more peculiar: '*Aur bike tika tha wahan par, gira nahi.* And the bike stayed up there; it did not fall.'

'Stayed where?' I ask.

The bike had not spiralled downwards into the darkness with the men, he clarifies; it had remained on the bridge. Aakash had noticed it the next morning when he arrived at the site of the accident with the others. 'The bike was still hanging there'— suspended in mid-air, lodged in the broken remains of the bridge's protective barrier, he says—the last witness to the events of that night.

Aakash chuckles as he describes the scene, surprised by the bike's acrobatic efficacy. It seems almost macabre in a way. When he narrates what happened to Sekond Lal, a childhood friend, no grief engulfs him. One might reason that many years have passed since, or that a man who has spent a lifetime observing the stillness of flesh, a man whose senses have been blunted as an occupational necessity, will be cold and emotionally removed while talking about a friend's passing.

Left to the imagination, one can visualize a high-speed bike losing its bearings, skidding towards the edge of the bridge in sheer ferocity and getting entangled in its structural anatomy, before flinging its passengers into absolute darkness.

What does not make sense, however, is Gopi's chilling warning to Dolly.

'That he had said in *comedy*,' Aakash reasons with a keenness to defend Gopi. 'Who knew that this would become a reality?'

The day after the accident, once Gopi was discharged from the hospital, Aakash helped him attend Sekond Lal's funeral in the evening. Bunty could not make it due to his broken foot.

31

What Twinkle and Mohan Said

ONE NOVEMBER AFTERNOON in 2021, Mohan is sitting on the ground, twisting the nimble spine of a pigeon feather between his fingers. Sunlight filters in through the window. Twinkle, sitting next to him, takes the feather from his hand, halves the slender bone and scrapes the tip against the ground to sharpen it before returning it to her husband. Mohan inserts the stick deep into his ear to scratch it. Outside, the sounds of kids whooshing through the alley has simmered down. Mothers have reined them into their homes to eat the afternoon meal. The narrow gali, a quasi-playground, is eerily quiet.

'There was an accident,' Twinkle says, pushing her back into the wall and running her fingers over her glass bangles as she describes what happened that night in October 2016. 'It was only later that we learnt that it was something more than that,' she alleges. Her tone—which should have been rooted in speculation, since neither she nor her husband was present at the bridge—doesn't have even a hint of uncertainty.

Mohan clutches his slipper by its ribs, lifts it high above his head and then releases it. 'If three people fell from a height,' he says as the slipper falls on the ground with a loud *thwack*, 'then how is it that *one* man died and these other guys merely broke their arms and legs?'

Both Twinkle and Mohan rubbish the police's claims that Sekond Lal had been riding the bike. Gopi, they say, had the reputation for riding bikes at a dangerously high speed. The pair is convinced—through an unchallenged assumption—that it was Gopi who was riding the bike, Sekond Lal was in the middle and Bunty sat behind him.

'So, how is it,' Mohan asks incredulously, 'that the man sitting in the middle dies and the other two survive?'

'Whenever there is danger or an accident,' Twinkle adds, 'the ones who are seated at the front and the back are more likely to get seriously hurt.'

Mohan nods. 'There must have been something,' he speculates, lowering his voice. 'Some issue due to which there was friction between them.'

So far, the husband-wife account had steered clear of what Aakash had suggested earlier. But Mohan reveals one detail that somewhat aligns with Aakash's version: Sekond Lal's body had a gash on the upper left chest. Mohan had noticed the injury when he visited the post-mortem building with a few other men from the community.

The wound was over his heart, he says, hovering his forefinger over his own chest. Mohan had also noticed Gopi and Bunty bearing small wounds, which were 'quickly concealed' in huge plasters later that night. He corroborates that Gopi and Bunty were discharged from hospital the next day.

'Now tell me,' he says suggestively, 'if Sekond Lal fell from a terrible height, how was it that he wasn't hurt anywhere else on his body, only on his chest?' Mohan wipes the corners of his mouth and slowly leans forward. He repeats his earlier question, as though it were a riddle on the precipice of being unravelled: 'How was it that only he died and no one else?'

'The way I see it,' he continues after a pause, 'someone hit him with a rock, and got slightly hurt in turn. There must have been a fight, a scuffle … something.'

'Did you see the bike?' I ask.

Yes, he grunts.

'Where did you see it?'

'It was on the bridge. Nothing was wrong with the motorcycle,' he says. Mohan means that it wasn't wrecked or mangled in a way that a vehicle should be if it was involved in a crash. 'Only, it wasn't working. We received a call at two in the morning, after which we immediately rushed to the site of the accident. Then an ambulance came, picked up the body, took it to the hospital, where they sent it for the post-mortem. The doctor said that Sekond Lal had died two hours earlier.'

Mohan gives a pointed stare, as though he is exhausted watching me struggle to connect the dots. There was definitely foul play, he alleges.

'How can you be sure?' I voice my doubt.

Twinkle raises her brows. 'Over time, the truth unravels. Slowly, slowly we learnt what had happened.'

If that was the case, why didn't anyone probe further into the matter?

'We couldn't even if we wanted to,' Mohan claims, since Dolly didn't have any fight in her. As a woman who had just lost her husband, whose children had become fatherless in the course of one night; as a woman who was emotionally broken, Dolly lacked the stamina to initiate and push through a criminal investigation. At the time, she had other, more pressing concerns: How would she cope in the aftermath of losing a loving husband? How would she handle her in-laws? How would she feed her children?

'If the wife is not ready, what will an outsider do fighting on her behalf?' Twinkle asks. 'Dolly didn't have the brains at the time. She wasn't half as clever as she is today.'

32

The Last Photograph

A DAY AFTER SEKOND Lal's accident in 2016, a pithy report about the incident appeared in a local Hindi newspaper. The headline read: *Party kar laut rahe bike sawar teen yuvak Rajghat pul se neeche gire: ek ki maut, do ki halat gambhir.* Three young men returning from a night of revelry fell off the Rajghat bridge: one dead, two are seriously injured.

The report described how, on the night of 16 October 2016, the men on a bike lost their balance and fell off the bridge onto the railway track below. According to the newspaper, Sekond Lal's father told the reporter that some eyewitnesses had alerted the police. When the police arrived at the scene, they immediately took Gopi and Bunty to a nearby hospital, while Sekond Lal was driven to another hospital that was twenty minutes from the bridge. He was administered medical care there, but he passed away. Next to the report was a photograph of Sekond Lal, printed in greyscale. It was clear that it was taken on the night of his

253

death. The image framed his face and, partially, his shoulders. His eyes were closed and his hair was tousled. His cheeks appeared swollen and round, and his lips were pinched shut. A line ran across his right cheek, close to his eye, as though an injury caused by a sharp object, perhaps a knife, had been medically sewn into submission and forced to withhold a secret.

Except for the scar, there were no stray wounds on his face. His face was intact, not smashed, which meant that Aakash's account of Sekond Lal falling face down could be challenged. In the newspaper photograph, Sekond Lal certainly did not look like a man who had dropped from a dangerous height and whose body had landed hard, belly down, on the railway tracks.

For years, Dolly would keep this newspaper clipping cached away. It carried the last photograph of her husband. This fragile piece of paper was a stark reminder of her permanent loss. A marker of time: the day her life overturned.

Years later, Bhola describes to me how, for days after Sekond Lal's death, strange cries pierced the nights. Gopi and Bunty had begun experiencing bouts of night terror, he says. They would wake up screaming, flailing their arms in sudden panic. The men spoke of spectral forms. 'They were so scared, they were behaving like mad men,' Bhola recalls. 'They'd scream, "Help! Help! He is coming to kill us!" It was as though Dolly's husband was haunting them. Everyone in our community knows about this.'

Lakshaya too remembers his neighbours' manic episodes. The men lived in chronic fear for at least two or three weeks. Eventually, their families consulted a folk healer to rid Gopi and

Bunty of the menace that was bothering them. It was only after these consultations, Lakshaya says, that their nerves calmed and their dreams ceased to be hostile.

When I ask Bunty's younger brother Shortcut about the supposed nightmares, he immediately shoots down the story. 'Nothing like that happened,' he insists.

However, he does say that his aunt Saroj, Sekond Lal's mother, was inconsolable after his death. Shortcut describes her screaming, pointing accusatory fingers at the two men who had survived. Grief-stricken yet livid, she told them, 'How were you driving the bike? You survived and my child died? You should have been hurt as well ...'

When she was presented with the choice of filing a case against Gopi and her nephew Bunty, though, she hesitated. Although the wounds were raw, what was paramount to Saroj, Shortcut explains, was the present, the now, and the relationships that were still alive. If Bunty was put behind bars, the damage would be irreversible. It would set off an avalanche of schisms: her relationship with her older brother (Bunty's father) and his family would shatter completely; her brother would be criticized by the community for having fathered a murderer; and Bunty's own life would be ruined. What would happen to his wife and children?

Saroj had watched Bunty grow up. As a child, he would visit her home and gobble up the food she cooked. Bunty was like a son to her, Shortcut says. Saroj convinced herself of his innocence; she told herself that Sekond Lal's death was nothing more than an ill-fated accident, '*sanjog ki baat*'. As far as she was concerned, her son was gone and nothing could undo that. And so, she backtracked. She cautioned Dolly against taking any legal action as well.

'That's why Dolly was so upset,' Shortcut clarifies.

Shortcut believes in his brother's innocence too. He feels that it was Gopi's bad company that had led their lives to take a tragic turn. 'It's like when you are grinding wheat and a gnat flies in and gets ground up with the grains, it ruins the quality of the flour.'

He seems bothered by the gossip traded by community people who considered themselves amateur sleuths. 'Everyone says that Bunty and Gopi killed him. But my brother says, "Why would I? What angst did I have against him?"' Shortcut continues. 'Whether they actually committed a crime or not—God is the only witness.'

33

What Dolly Believed

For days after Sekond Lal's death, everything was a blur for Dolly. '*Kya hua, kya nahi hua—kuch humko khayal nahi.* What happened, what didn't happen—I have no idea,' she tells me later. Whatever had taken her husband's life seemed to have snatched the light from her eyes as well. She stopped eating. Sleep evaded her. Her face was tear-stained and forlorn. Dolly could not believe her husband was dead. There had been times in the past when her husband had unnecessarily hurled himself into manly brawls on drunken nights at Manikarnika Ghat. But it did not matter to her if he returned home with a swollen lip, a battered jaw or clothes whose seams had been ripped apart—what mattered was that he always came back to her. Now, she sat at the threshold of her parents' home, waiting for hours, hoping for her husband's return: 'Like a dog,' she says of herself.

Her mother, Geeta, did not know what to do. She wanted her daughter to soak her hair in oil and tame its tangled frizz with a toothed comb, but Dolly always left her hair in an unmanageable lump. Geeta wanted Dolly to scrub her face, line her eyes with kohl and wear earrings, but Dolly would tilt her head and look at her mother with glazed eyes. 'For whom?' she would ask vacantly. 'For whom should I look nice?'

'*Ek dum pagal ki tareh rehti thi*. She was living like an absolute mad woman,' Geeta says.

Other family members expressed concern too, including Dolly's maternal grandfather. 'Normally, people wash their faces, brush their teeth, clean their ears,' he says plaintively. 'She stopped doing all of that completely.'

A few days after her husband's death, Dolly had wanted to raise an alarm and barrel her way into the police station to file a report against Gopi and Bunty, she says, but her mother-in-law stopped her. 'If you accuse Bunty, I will rip apart your maternal home,' Saroj had allegedly threatened.

Dolly's eyes well up as she recalls the incident. 'Bunty was more precious to her than her own son. *Isliye majboori mein kuch nahin kiya.* That's why, out of helplessness, I did not do anything,' she says. According to Dolly, Sekond Lal's obvious worship of Dolly had left his mother embittered.

———

In 2019, even though some years have passed since his death, a strange disquiet continues to linger in Dolly's body. It makes its presence known whenever she speaks of Sekond Lal's death or of those who she believes are his murderers. The disquiet manifests in the form of dry grunts, a widening of her eyes and incessant name-calling. Tired and alone, Dolly is consumed by feelings of anger, sadness, betrayal and vengeance. She slings accusations at Gopi and Bunty routinely, and at times, she issues roaring threats. 'I say this: Those who have murdered my husband—the way they have stolen my youth, the same way their own youth will be ruined.'

She keeps anyone who supports Gopi and Bunty's version of the story at a barbed distance. Aakash is kept at bay too. His regular visits to her home have become fewer. Whenever he is around, Dolly's shoulders stiffen.

Once, they broke into an argument: Dolly was shouting hysterically, adamant that Gopi and Bunty had been lying all along about their injuries; Aakash sat in a corner of the room, trying to remain calm, shaking his head in disagreement.

'No, no. Why would I lie to you?' he insisted. 'I personally went to the hospital and saw both of them.'

'I don't care!' she said, flailing her hands. 'My heart would only believe you if those two had died along with my husband.'

'But I know they got hurt,' he reasoned calmly. '*Kiska-kiska haddi toota hai, hum jaantey hain, dekhein hain.* Who broke which bones … I know because I saw.'

Dolly studied Aakash's face. Then she looked away, mumbling something about men changing their stories once they were paid.

Aakash lowered his head. 'That is a lie,' he said, seemingly affronted. His voice remained in control and low. 'I'm not fighting with you. I eat with my own hard-earned money. God knows this.' There was a pause, a moment when Aakash's lungs expanded to inhale more air. 'But for your sake,' he continued, as he tried to defend the men who were not there, 'let's assume that Sekond Lal was killed in cold blood; suppose they did lay him down on the railway tracks. Would Gopi and Bunty break their own bones? Can that ever happen?'

Dolly hit back. 'Yes, it can! Tell me, why did they not let me speak to my husband when I called? At least they could have let me talk to him.'

Aakash remained quiet.

'And,' she continued, 'it was only my husband whose trousers had alcohol bottles? Couldn't it be that after killing him, someone placed the bottles in his pants?'

'It could,' Aakash replied monotonously. 'But none of us were there to see it.'

Dolly shrugged and looked away. She no longer trusted 'these men' who purveyed 'half-truths and half-lies' as per convenience. Of course, Aakash would defend Gopi, and be his ally. Aakash was Gopi's best friend.

That was the end of their conversation.

Dolly could speculate, theorize and accuse all she wanted; she could listen to varying accounts and imagine different scenarios, but the truth would remain elusive. The only truth that remained uncontested was that Sekond Lal's story had ended years ago. That was the reality. She had to move on.

34

Don't Worry, Kid

DOLLY CARRIES WITH her a discomfiting feeling of being unwanted. There has been a pattern of rejections throughout her life: her parents' desperation to palm her off to any man; having a line of suitors reduce to a trickle; the look of disdain worn by her in-laws who had hoped that she would come to their home with bags stuffed with money.

The only person who seemed to have ever *wanted* her was Sekond Lal. For his grand gesture, she would learn to be accommodating. And so, Dolly chose to ignore the fact that Sekond Lal's home was remarkably smaller than her parents' and smiled quietly as her husband looked at her with affection.

Sekond Lal did what he could to make his wife comfortable. When Dolly did not feel like cooking, he would buy platefuls of chhole-kulche from the market and bring them home. Every New Year's Eve, he brought home a chocolate cake layered with white cream and cherries: Dolly's favourite.

261

'We were enough, you know?' Dolly says. 'We would laugh, cry and share our pain. Now who do I have?'

Within months of their wedding, Sekond Lal suggested to Dolly that they should have a kitchen separate from his mother's. That way, Saroj would not hassle her. And so, the families split up. This is common within the community. Although sons live with their wives and children, and continue to share the same home with their parents, meals are cooked separately.

To make Dolly feel more at ease, Sekond Lal began taking her out more. They would stroll along the ghats, visit local fairs, go out shopping and attend weddings. The first few times Dolly stepped out into the city, cloaked by a chaddar that impaired her vision, she intuitively grabbed Sekond Lal's hand. Fast-moving traffic and pealing horns startled her. Sekond Lal would tighten his grip over her hand with a smile, and say reassuringly, '*Chinta matt kar, bachchi.* Don't worry, kid.'

Years after Sekond Lal's death, Dolly no longer fears the wide stretch of dusty roads or the mechanical shrieks of the vehicles. She needs no one to escort her for long distances. Dolly purchases packets over packets of namkeen, chips, beedis, gutka and detergent soaps from wholesale markets for her own shop. Her eldest son, a teenager, accompanies her to share the load, and to ensure that his mother eschews the community's spite for a lone woman on foot.

———

Anxiety and restlessness have made a home in her body. At night, Dolly lies awake, staring into the darkness. She mourns her past, thinking about what her life was like once: the saris with delicate prints that her husband bought for her, his glances of affection, the small packs of glittering bindis, the songs that danced on his tongue, the boxes of coloured bangles he gifted her.

Life in Chand Ghat is stifling and isolating. Like most women in her community, Dolly has learnt to bottle her emotions and set them aside. She seldom speaks about the shadow that loomed over her head, but her slow, wilted movements say it all. There is no one with whom she can share her grief, no one to counsel her. Occasionally, Dolly converses with her neighbours, but mostly about electricity and water. No one has the time to lend an ear otherwise. Everyone is battling their own problems.

The pandemic had worryingly weakened the sales of her shop. So, when things slowly begin to circle back to normalcy in early 2022, Dolly turns her insomnia into a springboard. She keeps her shop open late into the night to cater to the nocturnal needs of customers. When the stores shutter in the main market around 8 or 9 p.m., Chand Ghat residents flit to her home store till 2 or 3 a.m. These customers, who usually play cards or gamble, buy packets of masala peanuts and bhujia from her shop, and pick up beedis, as well as plastic cups from which they drink alcohol. Around 5 a.m., Dolly wakes up again and cooks chhole-kulche in bulk, which she sells to Chand Ghat residents at Rs 10 a plate for breakfast.

Once a woman who seldom thought about finances, she now hustles fiercely. Her mind is constantly working, imagining new ways to draw in more customers. Dolly wants to save money and purchase a second-hand refrigerator in which she can store cold drinks, bottled water and ice, so that more customers are drawn to her shop, particularly during the dehydrating months of summer.

When numbers do not make sense, she requests her son to look at the accounts. Dolly uses everything sparingly: even when she pours mustard oil into the pan to cook for her children, it is done with measured care to ensure that the bottle of oil lasts longer.

'Dolly has become very smart now,' Bhola notes. 'If other housewives cooked the way she does, their household expenses would reduce immediately.'

Shortcut has also observed a change. 'If you owe her even a rupee as a customer, she will remind you about it every day until you pay her back,' he says. He was taken by surprise one evening when Dolly coldly extended her palm and demanded the money he owed her. Her calm voice had transformed into something bitingly vicious. Shortcut hastily tossed the rupee in her direction and disappeared, swearing never to speak to her again.

He claims that it wasn't her ask that irked him but her manner, as though he was a petty thief. It is lost on him that Dolly is a woman and he is a man, that she is a widow responsible for bringing up five children, while he is unattached. Dolly has to depend on the paltry earnings she makes at her shop to feed her family. To her, even that one rupee is precious.

Since she opened her shop, Dolly has spent her days battling ridicule and freeloaders. She has been compelled to become prickly, adopt a no-nonsense demeanour and a harsh tongue, because she has learnt that only then will the world take her seriously.

35

Komal's Mehndi

ON A SULTRY day in April 2022, Chanchal, Lakshaya's bhabhi, sister-in-law, draws the pallu of her sari over her head, takes her youngest son by the hand and begins towing him along. His pointy shoes with wiry black laces scrape against the scalding road as she drags his tiny body. The child groans. Chanchal instructs her older sons to stick close to their father, Ajay, who is walking ahead of them in search of an autorickshaw. Ajay's cousin's wife, Munni, accompanies them, trying to keep pace with Chanchal. Her body is swathed in a nylon sari, and her head and face are covered with a bright pink chaddar.

I walk beside them. The group is keenly aware of my presence. Like me, Komal's younger brother, Aman, is hitching a ride with them as well. We are on our way to attend Komal's mehndi, a special ceremony where elaborate designs are drawn on the bride's hands, arms, legs and feet with henna, as part of her beautification ritual for the wedding. It is commonly believed that the darker the stain of the henna on the bride's hands, the deeper is her husband-to-be's love for her. Women from both families join in the celebrations and get elaborate henna designs drawn on their palms.

Traditionally, the mehndi is held a day before the wedding at the bride's home. Komal's mehndi, however, is being hosted at the home of Lakshaya's maternal aunt. The house is on the rural outskirts of Banaras, over an hour's travel from Chand Ghat. A wedding in Chand Ghat, at the groom's own residence, is impossible. Were any celebrations and rituals held in Chand Ghat, the Yadavs in the neighbourhood, I am told, would be intolerant.

'They would have tried to stop the wedding somehow,' Bhola says later. 'They might have instigated violence or lied to the police that the girl was marrying against her will. They would do anything to throw Lakshaya in prison, even if it meant filing false charges. The thing is, the Yadavs have known Komal since she was a child. Even though she no longer lives there, they still care about whom she marries and what community she marries into.'

This is why Lakshaya has decided to have the wedding at a location that is far away. The neighbourhood where Lakshaya's maternal aunt lives is unaware of Komal's caste.

In fact, a month before the wedding ceremony, the couple visited a nearby court, got officially married and registered their marriage. This was done to avoid any external obstacles in the future.

＊

Our party of eight climbs into the autorickshaw. Chanchal, Munni and I sit in the back, squished in with Chanchal's two young boys and a large red suitcase; the men sat in front with Chanchal's eldest son, flanking the driver. The red suitcase, brought by Komal's brother, is stuffed with her trousseau: saris, sandals, bags and make-up. At every sharp turn, the overloaded autorickshaw screeches and teeters to one side. The driver does not seem hassled in the least; this is his every day.

In the middle of the journey, Ajay halts the autorickshaw at a paan shop and gets off. He will come later, he says. He wants to have a smoke, drink tea and have a paan. In his place, his younger cousin Suresh joins us—the two must have co-ordinated the place of meeting on their cell phones. Suresh smiles at us, fixes the gamchha tied around his head, sits next to the driver and instructs him to carry on. I watch Munni lift the chaddar that was covering her face.

I am curious. 'Why is it that you lifted your chaddar now and not earlier?' I ask.

'Chanchal's husband isn't in the rickshaw anymore,' she answers meekly. 'Now my husband is here.'

I look at her blankly. 'What does that mean?'

'We have to keep our faces hidden in front of men who are not our husbands,' she explains.

'What about Komal's brother? He can see your face right now.'

'Yes,' she replies. 'He is younger than me. Out of respect, we have to remain veiled in front of men from our caste who are older than us.'

I looked pointedly at the autorickshaw driver, who looked visibly older. 'What about him?' I ask.

'He doesn't belong to our caste, so it doesn't matter,' she says, adjusting her pallu.

Chanchal and Munni are dressed in shimmering saris and net chaddars. Their glossy hair is combed and coiled into a bun, lips flushed red with colour, eyes lined neatly with kohl and feet strapped in high-heeled footwear. The men, though, sit indifferently in loose pants and dirt-smeared shirts that cling to their sweaty backs. It seems as though they have come directly from working in the sun.

'It's not like we don't tell our men to dress up,' Chanchal explains as she gets off the rickshaw and walks towards the house. 'But they say they don't want to get ready. They don't listen to us.'

For the women, any opportunity to step out of their homes is an opportunity to dress up, to wear make-up—a break from the monotony of their homebound lives. They are rarely allowed to go out anywhere, so they make the most of these outings. Most Dom men, however, find such ventures to be tedious affairs. Slumped under the weight of everyday labour and making ends meet, getting ready to go somewhere is the last thing on their minds. For the evening ceremony, however, Ajay and Suresh would change into fresh shirts.

The house is a two-storey brick building, freshly painted in baby blue. It stands near a mango tree. Strings of lights run down from the terrace to the ground. At dusk, the lights glimmer, and if there is a rush of wind, the strings rustle and sway; from a distance, it looks like a dance of fireflies. Outside, children chase one another, their tiny feet raising plumes of dust. A few women peek from the balcony, their faces hidden behind their veils. The house bustles with noise and activity. The women in the family have gathered to chat in a room on the first floor, while their children run in and out of doorways. The men have been allocated a separate room on the ground floor.

Ajay, who has joined us by then, enters the room upstairs to deposit his wife. She quietly settles on the floor with her pallu over her head, next to her husband's mother. Ajay props himself on the bed. He lets out a deep sigh and stretches. Married women sit on the floor, not the bed, especially if there is a man around. The women barely give Ajay a second glance. They busy themselves in exchanging news, admiring jewellery, smiling knowingly, talking excitedly. The air is ripe with energy.

Dolly arrived a day earlier to help with organizing things and assist in household chores. One of the young girls brings out plastic glasses from the kitchen along with a large bottle of cold drink, and hands them to her. Dolly unscrews the cap of the bottle and pours the sugary, lemony drink into the glasses. She promptly hands a glass to Ajay and another to Suresh. Men must be served first.

The women are dressed in all their finery. They sparkle in jewels and are swathed in heavily spangled saris. Dolly, however, wears a pale-blue sari with a broad border, her small breasts cocooned in a plain white cotton blouse. Lost in thought, she sits mostly in silence. There is nothing in her appearance or expression to indicate that she is at her younger brother's wedding. No bindi graces her forehead, no necklace calls attention to her throat, no jhumkas dangle from her ears. The only colour on her face is the orange stain of betel juice on her lips.

Chanchal takes note of her sister-in-law's barren attire more than anyone else. When she stands up, she walks with a conscious sway that allows everyone in the room to notice her bejewelled waistband, which sits snugly on her hips. There is confidence in her walk, reinforced by the knowledge of having a husband who earns well and showers her with gifts.

Dolly cranes her neck and watches her sister-in-law's grandstanding. There are no signs of bitterness on her face. Rather, her eyes speak of emptiness, an unutterable lack. Her brother Ajay is earning, but he never gifts her anything.

Dolly's new sister-in-law, Komal, arrives in the afternoon, when the cool morning breeze has taken leave—late for her own mehndi. Komal was delayed at the salon where she had gone for her facial and make-up. At the house, surrounded by women from her husband's family (Lakshaya and Komal are legally married already), Komal exhibits a kind of shyness that his family finds endearing.

She is dressed in a jade-green sharara with pink blossoms embroidered on the fabric. It is paired with a kurti with an empire waistline. Everyone comments on how beautiful she looks, how graceful she is, how the fabric's colour complements her fair, unblemished skin.

When I ask, she answers gleefully, 'Lakshaya bought this for me.'

Out of respect for the elders, Komal has covered her head with a light, gauzy dupatta, which keeps slipping off under the fan. Lakshaya notices that Komal is uncomfortable—constantly managing the dupatta is keeping her awkwardly distracted.

'Take it off and keep it aside,' he tells her softly. She looks at him, stunned. 'It's okay,' he said reassuringly. 'You need to be comfortable.'

Komal nods and pulls the dupatta away from her shoulders. Lakshaya's aunt opens her mouth to say something and then clamps it shut; her eyes dart around uneasily. The other women remain quiet, as though nothing has happened.

Komal wipes her moist hand against her knee and offers it to the lady who will apply her mehndi. The lady pipes dark green squiggles of henna onto Komal's palm and writes 'Lakshaya ki dulhan'—Lakshaya's bride—nestling the words within the intricate design. After almost an hour, Komal coughs slightly: her throat is dry. Lakshaya, seated nearby on a plastic chair, springs up and offers her a bottle of water. Komal's hands are occupied, so he holds the bottle for her and watches as she takes bird-like sips from it.

Sometime later she murmurs that her legs have begun to feel numb—Komal has been sitting crossed-legged on the floor for far too long. Lakshaya looks at her lovingly. 'Sit on the bed,' he tells her. Komal hesitates. She has to be careful. She is the new bahu, the new daughter-in-law of the house. If she were to sit on the bed, it might be considered extremely brazen of her, as though she is trying to assert some kind of superiority. But Lakshaya insists. Komal quietly obeys. Sitting on the bed, she watches the lady roll up the sharara and pin it so that she can begin decorating her feet with henna.

By the end of the day, Komal's energy has waned and she rests her back limply against the wall. Lakshaya, who has been sitting beside her, pulls her near and holds her in a gentle embrace. She places her head on his shoulder and the two sit quietly, as one, watching the family members whir around them, preparing for the remaining functions. It is an unusual sight.

In most Dom households, women rarely sit so close, so intimately with their husbands, displaying affection: it would embarrass those around them or make them uncomfortable. But Lakshaya has earned a certain respect, a stature within his extended family that allows him to behave in the manner he wants, without anyone daring to raise an eyebrow or question him. For one, he has independently funded the entire wedding. The grind has been tough. He borrowed a portion of the funds from well-wishers, but not once did he expect Komal's family to chip in. Aman, her brother admits, '*Usne humse shaadi ke liye ek paisa nahi manga, na toh dahej manga.* He didn't ask us for a penny for the wedding, nor did he ask for a dowry.'

36

The Haldi and Wedding Ceremonies

THE NEXT DAY, we return to the wedding house for the haldi ceremony. Komal, in her bright yellow salwar-kameez, greets her female friends excitedly and pulls them into the 'ladies' room', filled with the other women of the house. Lakshaya wants to spend time with Komal, and so he enters as well and takes a seat.

The room is painted bubblegum pink. Like most Dom houses, a bed stands high and runs across the width of a wall. The rest of the space is sparse, with no furniture, allowing the women to squat, sprawl and stretch their legs out on the floor. The high ceiling is pockmarked with large hooks from which plastic bags stuffed with clothes and other necessities have been hung. This is a clever storage technique. Narrow niches have been carved into the wall, where the suitcases of those staying the night are kept. On one of the shelves rests a small rectangular mirror that is occasionally circulated within the room by the women, who take turns to shape their brows, decorate their foreheads with studded bindis and colour their lips.

Lakshaya's aunt is giving a four-month-old baby boy an oil massage. The baby lies on his back on the warm summer floor, kicking in the air. Small bubbles form at his mouth as he makes throaty, gurgling noises. Lakshaya's aunt straightens the baby's legs and massages the oil into his soft skin. Her fleshy arms wobble with every determined rub. 'If you extend the legs and rub oil on them, like so, the baby will grow taller,' she coaches Komal, who is sitting next to her, listening attentively. Komal is deeply aware of being watched by the other women in the room, including Dolly, who distractedly unknots a black plastic bag filled with market-bought tea and pours it into rust-coloured clay cups.

The aunt's tutoring is part of the rites of passage—wisdom imparted by older women to the young, circulated only among their sex. It is expected of Komal that she will bear a child soon after the wedding, and so, she needs to be prepared. 'If no one teaches you this, how will you learn?' the aunt asks rhetorically. Dolly nods in agreement as she brings the cup close to her mouth and takes a small sip of the tea.

Lakshaya, who is the only man in the room at the time, does not pay attention to the home-parenting skills being imparted. No one is bothered by his lack of interest. He is not expected to look after the baby; it is not his job. 'Take notes,' he whispers teasingly to Komal before dialling a number on his phone to arrange for large slabs of ice, so that cold water will be available for the guests attending the wedding later.

Earlier in the day, Lakshaya had caked his face with a thick layer of saffron-and-sandalwood paste, squeezed from a tube that promised 'long-lasting, skin-whitening' results. His skin had darkened over the last few months, he tells me, due to his work. Lakshaya still has the now dried yellowy paste on his face. It has cracked and hardened around the tip of his nose. The children in the room giggle, calling him a 'funny' ghost.

Komal smiles slightly. It is an attempt to mask a grief that suddenly overwhelms her. In the heaving thicket of Lakshaya's relatives, she feels alone. If only her mother were around, then it would not be Lakshaya's aunt imparting parenting wisdom but her own nurturer, her own blood.

Her mother's absence from the wedding celebrations has left Komal bereft. No one from her side, except her younger brother and three close friends, is attending her wedding.

The day Komal gave her mother the news of her wedding, her mother told her, 'I will give you my blessing. *Magar tumhari shaadi mein hum khade nahi ho payenge.* But I will not be able to stand beside you at your wedding.'

Komal felt her throat tighten. Her father had abandoned the family. Now her mother was refusing to be present on her wedding day. 'Why are you talking like this, Mummy?' Komal asked.

The news of an inter-caste marriage would upset Komal's maternal uncles, her mother reasoned, and she feared their wrath. Komal remembers her mother pleading: 'I have a family. I have brothers and a sister. Tomorrow if they ask me, "Which caste did you get your daughter married into?" what will I tell them? The truth? They will cut all ties with me. Once you are married, you will go live with your new family. You will stay with your aadmi, your man. But I have to stay here. They are my brothers.'

For the sake of appearances, Komal's mother had decided not to attend the wedding rituals. A maternal sacrifice to avoid familial banishment. Society would interpret her absence from the celebrations as her opposition towards the marriage, and Komal's uncles would not sever their ties with their sister, believing that she was 'against' the alliance after all. She would be able to preserve her relationship with them, even though her daughter would no longer be welcome into their homes.

'Does it pain you when you think about your uncles?' I ask her.

'What kind of pain are you talking about?' Komal retorts.

When her father abandoned them in Chand Ghat, her uncles were nowhere to be seen. 'Did they send money to support my mother so that she could pay rent or buy food? Did they send a hundred rupees each month to fund my education? When my father left my mother, who took her in? No one. Did they call to ask how we were? No,' Komal says. 'In the last few years, has any one of them offered even a single rupee to us? It was my mother who worked hard and made sure we survived. She did it on her own.' Yet, Komal's mother, a single woman, is desperate for the support of her brothers, the only male protection she can count on for now.

Komal's uncles lived with a convenient indifference. They did not care if their sister's children had no clothes on their backs or food in their bellies. They fretted only when matters affected them directly. Their niece marrying a 'low-caste' Chaudhary would threaten their standing in social circles, something they had carefully safeguarded for generations. The expected response from their side would be to cease all contact. 'If they don't want to talk to me, it doesn't matter,' Komal says. She knows that even if she broke up with Lakshaya to gain her uncles' approval, they would simply pat her on her back and then send her packing. 'If I choose my uncles over Lakshaya, it would be the worst decision of my life.'

Her love for her mother, however, remains strong. Komal agrees that the position she had put her mother in was a difficult one. 'My father doesn't talk to me, so he doesn't know that I am getting married,' Komal says. 'If my mother comes to the wedding, she'll be standing alone against society. That would not be nice. If she doesn't, at least my uncles will still talk to her.'

——————

The baby coos and Komal's face relaxes—she is back in the present. She giggles when he wraps his fingers around her thumb. Her eyes speak of sadness, but also of hope. Over the years, as Komal matured, she has taught herself not to fear what hasn't happened yet or slip into a past that might rip a fulfilling present at the seams. This is the life she has chosen: marriage to a man who does not belong to her community, but belongs wholly to her. She will accept the consequences willingly. Even though her mother will not attend the ceremony, Komal has her blessing, and that is just as good.

She watches one of Lakshaya's sisters, Gauri untangle her three-year-old daughter's hair with a plastic comb. The child stands with her back to her mother. Gauri tugs at her daughter's hair, parting it into three sections and twisting each into a taut braid. The girl hums a tune and absentmindedly flicks a fly from her slender arm. Her mahogany-hued skin has the suppleness and sheen of butter. The girl's large, clear eyes follow the winged insect as it whizzes away.

The power goes out just then and the aunt hands the baby to Gauri. He is Gauri's second child. She cradles the baby boy in her lap uncertainly.

'My daughter resembles my husband,' Gauri says, looking at me. She seems painfully conscious of the disparity in the complexion of her children. 'My son takes after me,' she says proudly. 'He is gora, white.' Then, in an attempt to lighten the mood, she adds, 'People say that my son is from Russia and my daughter is from Africa.' The other women respond by giggling and clapping their hands together. She turns to Komal and says in an assuring tone, 'You don't have to worry. Your kids will be fair!'

The aunt returns, plonks herself down on the floor and takes the baby from the mother again. Gauri gets up and fetches the hand mirror. From her purse, she retrieves a doll-sized bottle of liquid paint to draw a bindi on her forehead. 'When I had no kids, I had so much free time on my hands,' she says with a sigh. 'I could do my make-up easily.'

The aunt snaps, 'God has given you children. Be grateful. What will you do when you have six more?'

'Then I will certainly faint. I won't be able to eat or sleep,' Gauri replies.

Komal smiles uneasily. Children are not her concern at the moment; getting on with the ceremony is. It is 1.30 p.m. and the haldi ceremony is yet to begin. Komal is feeling drained. For the last few days, she has been handing out smiles to anyone and everyone she meets—Lakshaya's aunts and uncles, his friends, people who are truly strangers. There has been too much talk, too much waiting.

The electricity has not yet returned. Komal drums her fingertips on her knees impatiently. Her friend Barkha flips on the torch on her phone. Komal's face glows in the silver stream of light. She looks at Barkha, who nods knowingly. 'This is taking too long. I am going to find out what is causing the delay,' Barkha whispers and springs up.

'No, no,' Komal pleads discreetly, grabbing her friend by her kurti. She does not wish to stir any kind of drama. 'Don't say a word,' she cautions. 'Otherwise, the groom's family will say that the new daughter-in-law is cribbing already.' Komal wants to protect her image, that of a young, gracious bride. She does not want to cause any kind of sourness that might ruin her special day.

Time, however, is slipping by. Komal has been wearing her bright yellow salwar-kameez since six in the morning. Beads of sweat have begun to crawl down her back and settle in her armpits. She wants to rip away the heat by pouring ice cold water over her body. But all she can do was wait.

Dolly watches Komal and Barkha whispering, and wonders how different Komal's life is from hers. Komal has close friends to call her own, but Dolly struggles to cultivate friendships. The only relationships she can trust are the ones she has birthed. She has no one other than her children to rely on. Dolly plans to wed her three girls one after another, the eldest in the next seven-odd years, and delay her sons' weddings for as long as she can. It is a strategic plan: Dolly wants her two sons to worship her, to earn and take care of her until they eventually marry, become more concerned with their wives and children, and forget all about their mother.

After the wedding, Lakshaya and Komal will move into a new house, one that is away from the ghats, away from the Chaudharys and the Yadavs. This is one of the few times that a groom from their community has chosen not to return to his parents' home with his wife. Dolly has not seen her own brother's new apartment, but Komal's closest friends have. She feels a discomfiting pang, realizing how distant she and Lakshaya are. She wishes Lakshaya would stay at their parents' house, so that their bond could be strengthened. Besides, daughters-in-law are supposed to take care of the chores of the house and provide relief to the daughters of the house.

'I have done enough slavery,' Dolly says out loud. 'I need some luxury in my life now. Komal should live with us so that she can make rotis and feed us with her own hands.' Everyone laughs—as does Dolly, but only she knows how much she means it. Dolly would have liked it if Komal had lived at their home in Chand Ghat and taken some pressure off her. Komal has a lightness to her, a calming aura that makes Dolly feel accepted, loved—a sense of sisterhood that she rarely finds with Ajay's wife.

Komal, however, cannot wait to move into the new apartment that Lakshaya had determinedly sought out to rent, where they will live together. Lakshaya is prepared to do anything to safeguard their marriage. For now, ensuring that Komal never returns to Chand Ghat as his wife is enough.

'You know the kind of mahaul I live in: no private space for bathing, no privacy while going to the bathroom, no proper kitchens. At least the flat I am renting has an attached bathroom and a functional kitchen,' he tells me.

There are other factors too that have influenced his decision. Lakshaya says that in Chand Ghat, Komal will be placed under a microscope; her movements will be minutely scrutinized. His people will expect Komal, a married woman, to wear a sari, even though she is more comfortable in salwar-kameez and sometimes wears a T-shirt over jeans. They will gossip if the newly married couple does not have a child immediately. If, after marriage, Komal wants to work and offer tutoring services to schoolchildren, people might call her 'selfish' for not putting her family first.

Lakshaya wants Komal to live life on her terms.

While they wait for the haldi ceremony to begin, Lakshaya, seated on the high bed, swings his legs. Komal is sitting on the floor near him. Not knowing what to do with her time, she begins playing with his feet. Lakshaya gasps and draws his feet up. 'Don't touch them,' he tells her. When she reaches for his feet again, Lakshaya scowls. Komal rolls her eyes. 'Look at my nalayak pati, useless husband,' she whispers to me. 'All men want their wives to touch their feet and this one doesn't.'

———

A hired cameraman has been brought into the ladies' room to document the ceremony. The women—Lakshaya's older sisters and mother—line up in their finery, veils in place, jewellery gleaming. They stand stiffly, close to each other, as though tied together by an invisible rope. None of them are smiling. They stare blankly at the camera, far too conscious of the strange man before them.

Lakshaya joins them and pulls Komal into the frame. Komal places her dupatta over her head and stands coyly with her head bowed, her gaze glued to the floor. Lakshaya smiles at the camera, his arm wrapped around Komal's shoulders. Barkha, who is standing in a corner watching them, giggles. 'Why are you holding on to her so tightly?' she teases. 'Komal can't run away now. It's too late.' The other women laugh at that.

It is 4 p.m. when drumbeats—loud and sharp—began ripping through the unmarked gali outside the house. A quartet of barrel-chested percussionists with thick moustaches strike wooden sticks on large, circular drums that hang from their necks. Young boys and girls gather around and begin clapping their hands and dancing to the beat of the drums. 'Nagara!' Barkha squeals. She runs through the house's narrow hallway and hurries outside. She throws her hands in the air and joins the dancing. Lakshaya and Komal emerge too. One of the girls drags Lakshaya in. He awkwardly tries to mimic her movements. Embarrassed by his clumsy sway, he breaks out of the circle and grabs Komal's hand. She shrieks as he brings her to the centre to dance and her girlfriends surround her. Komal closes her eyes to forget the world and moves her waist from side to side. As she dances, her dupatta slips from her head. Lakshaya catches it midway and promptly throws it over her face. Young brides cannot risk showing their faces to strange men, including percussionists. The veil is necessary.

Neighbours have emerged from their homes with folded arms and perplexed expressions. Some stand at their doors, others watch from their terraces. A few boys pull out their mobile phones to take videos. A toddler in a pink frock and tiny pigtails sucks on an ice lolly, observing the scene quietly.

During the haldi ceremony, freshly ground turmeric is mixed with oil to make a golden-yellow paste that is rubbed onto the bodies of both the bride and the groom. After the ceremony, when it is time for the bride and groom to bathe, tradition decrees that the groom must bathe first. The bathing water used to cleanse him is carefully collected in a pot by a male family member. This water is called 'varr ka paani' or 'groom's water'. During the bath, only the immediate male family members are allowed near the groom for the fear that outsiders might cast dark spells on the water.

The bride waits for the varr ka paani to be delivered by the groom's relative, which is then sprinkled on her. The water 'purifies' the bride, readying her for the upcoming nuptials. '*Ladki pavitra ho jati hai.* The woman is cleansed,' an elder explains. Young girls are brought up to believe that varr ka paani has special properties.

'They say that the bride's face blossoms once she washes her face with it,' Komal says.

More importantly, the Doms believe that a woman's kunwarapan, her maidenhood, ends once the varr ka paani is sprinkled on her. In other words, the water unites the bride and groom spiritually before they unify physically.

———

A few hours before the wedding, Lakshaya had told his bride to sneak out onto the balcony to watch him climb the wedding mare in the gali below. From a distance, Komal secretly observes Lakshaya, dressed in a fitted maroon sherwani, carefully mount the decorated animal. His face is hidden behind a veil of white flowers, a sehra, attached to his pagri, turban. Lakshaya sits on the mare quietly, clutching his teenage nephew who is sitting in front of him, and then watches Gauri plop her three-year-old daughter onto the mare's crowded back. Other women from his family huddle coyly around him, their lavishly bordered pallus drawn over their heads, offering glimpses of only their chins.

The narrow, dark gali with no streetlights heaves with family and friends, dholak-walas and onlookers. The only source of light is the one on the groom: he is spotlighted by an eager video assistant. The wedding party crawls through the gali, led by men who dance at the forefront of the procession to the deafening beats of the drums. The younger men pull out their cell phones to capture the moment.

A short while later, the wedding party reaches a well-lit open ground. The area has been transformed into an enclosed private space with temporary walls built on all sides using cloth and metal rods. Inside, red carpets have been rolled out to cover a balding lawn, and overhead, a blue-and-yellow canopy has been secured into place. At one end, there is a stage with a plush red sofa where the bride and groom will sit once the wedding rituals are over. In a corner, an assortment of dishes like noodles, puris, dal, rice, kachori and gulab jamuns have been laid out for the guests.

When Komal walks into the compound, everyone gasps. She is wearing a deep red lehenga-choli, which Lakshaya picked out for her. Red bangles are stacked all the way to her elbows and her glittering scarlet dupatta is pinned to the high mound of her hair. Large gold-plated earrings dangle from her lobes and necklaces cover her throat. Komal's eyes sparkle as the cameraman photographs her. When she takes her place next to Lakshaya at the wedding mandap, both of them smile at each other. As the priest chants mantras, the couple completes the seven pheras, and then Lakshaya fills the parting in her hair with sindoor.

After the ceremony, Komal walks up to the stage and stands with Lakshaya before all their guests. She is given an aarti plate with a lit diya on it. As Komal waves the plate in a circular motion five times in front of Lakshaya's face, one of his friends playfully shouts, 'Arre, arre, go easy. You'll burn his face!' Everyone laughs.

When Lakshaya places a garland of flowers around Komal's neck, the crowd cheers. '*Har Har Mahadev!* Everywhere Shiva!' they chant, their blessings reverberating around the compound. Komal reciprocates by placing a similar garland on Lakshaya. As she kneels to touch his feet, he stopped her midway. Holding her by her arms, Lakshaya looks into her eyes and promises: 'I will never let you bow to anyone. Not me. Not anyone else. I will hold your hand and we will walk together as equals. If you want, you can hug me.'

One of Komal's friends takes a photograph of them with her phone camera and post it on her social media. Beneath the post, she writes, '*Bachpan ka pyaar safal ho gaya.* Childhood love has won.'

⁘

The next day, to evade the blaring horns of street traffic and the thick nuisance of flies, Shortcut and I slip into a lassi shop. We sit on wooden benches, cradling shallow terracotta cups in our hands, tucking plastic spoons into pistachio-sprinkled sweet curd. Around us, locals chat among themselves; scooters whiz past outside; a man peddles half a dozen goats on a wheelbarrow, bound together into one unit by thick twine.

Shortcut is wearing the same clothes from the night before: a deep blue shirt with tiny silver dots and jeans, bought specifically for the wedding and worn again today to make use of them completely before handing them to his mother to wash. What stood out at the wedding for him, he says, was a change in the demographic of guests: there were boys from dominant castes—mostly Lakshaya's colleagues from his line of work as a tourist guide.

'Usually only Chaudharys attend our weddings. Only people from our caste, no one else. But this time, people from the other castes came,' he says. '*Khushi mehsoos hoti hai ki un logon ka soch-vichar badh raha hai.* I feel happy that their way of thinking is progressing.'

37

Clumps of Hair

IN APRIL 2022, Twinkle describes the change in Mohan's behaviour in simple terms: his affection has become 'much less' and his beatings 'far more'. He shies away from attending social gatherings like weddings—outings that are a much-needed respite for his wife. Once, when she fought with him, he reluctantly gave her permission to go with her mother. His own absence from such social occasions, however, makes Twinkle the subject of mean-spirited chatter among the other guests.

There seems to be a darkness that has been shadowing Mohan. Some weeks ago, an acquaintance alerted the family that he had spotted an unconscious, possibly inebriated, Mohan in a belly-up sprawl at the corner of a road. An embarrassed Bhola had to locate him and bring him home on a neighbour's motorbike. Something was bothering her husband, Twinkle notes, causing him to go back on his promise of staying off alcohol.

Mohan's behavioural change, Twinkle imagines, is symptomatic of a greater discontent. Over the last few months, his attitude towards her has become more abrasive. In January 2022, she gave birth to their second daughter, who was fondly called 'Babu' or 'Sugi', a female parrot, at home. Mohan now has three daughters to take care of. Twinkle believes that it is the birth of another girl that has left him feeling glum and disenchanted. Perhaps this is what has caused a punishing rift in their relationship. It is the only answer that Twinkle—who cannot understand this change in a man who was once so desperately in love with her—can arrive at.

The earlier years were so much better. When she gave birth to Mohani, her husband had given her his undivided attention. The first five months, Mohan rushed to buy medicines for her, washed the baby's clothes and scoured the utensils until they gleamed like newly minted coins. With their second child, Mohan seems to have taken a discernible step back. The light in his eyes for her has dimmed and his face has grown sullen. He frowns often, worries more and snaps at will. He does not neglect his children, though. Mohan looks after Sugi, cradling her in his arms and taking her at once to a clinic whenever she falls sick. He promptly buys all the medicines for his children. Mohan is an attentive parent, Twinkle says. She cannot fault him for that.

The heavy energy stagnating between the two of them, however, has begun feeding into Twinkle's loneliness. Her mother-in-law loathes her, as do her brothers-in-law. And ever since the strange illness took over Kamala Devi in August 2021, even Mohan has begun showing signs of contempt towards Twinkle. Perhaps it is her constant dissent all these years against his mother that has made him tire of his second wife. His mother's illness has turned

Mohan into a doting son, desperate to cling to the last vestiges of what his mother had once been, not what she has become. It is as though shouting at Twinkle and telling her off is a way of letting his mother know that he is on *her* side. That he will always remain her little boy.

Twinkle's own body seems to be failing her: her breasts went dry after nursing her newborn for just two months. When Mohani was born, Twinkle's body was healthier and was able to produce sufficient milk. Now, her milk is not enough to fill her newborn's stomach; Sugi's hungry wails leave Twinkle feeling tense, incompetent. Mohan buys buffalo milk for the infant, who has learnt to suckle on the plastic nipple of a market-bought bottle.

Twinkle feels trapped. When her toddler, Mohani, runs up to her and demands that she strap sandals onto her tiny feet, Twinkle does so, all the while watching an insect lodged in a crevice in the floor, writhing desperately.

By January 2022, Kamala Devi's health had taken a turn for the worse. The cancer was spreading rapidly through her body. Fevers would visit her in terrifying flashes at night, and she would fitfully utter garbled sounds in pain. Yet, even in the biting cold, she refused to button herself up in a sweater, find warmth in a knitted cap or slip on socks. The women in the community wore shawls. They found socks itchy and uncomfortable. The tight elastic bit into their flesh and they often became soaking wet while washing the dishes. The women did not wear them, nor would Kamala Devi. Ill or not, she did not see any reason to upset her way of living.

When Kamala Devi finally began feeling slightly better, Bhola, who had returned to Chand Ghat to take care of her, promptly started her on radiotherapy sessions. She did not know what was wrong with her, but she could sense that her mind was occasionally slipping into dark chasms of forgetfulness. Her legs had become useless and her tongue took time constructing sentences. For a woman who was used to climbing a precarious ladder at home several times a day, Kamala Devi now felt out of breath and overwhelmingly tired. Even a short walk to the lavatory a few stairs below, situated in Twinkle's part of the house, made Kamala Devi feel as though someone was jabbing aggressively at her lungs. When she needed to use the bathroom, Bhola would squat behind her and wrap his arms around her, before allowing her to lean back against him so that she could stand with his support.

No one in the neighbourhood had been told about Kamala Devi's disease. People in the community were known to harbour the misconception that cancer was contagious. When anyone asked, the family said that her sudden convulsions were due to old age. Sometimes, Kamala Devi confided in Bhola about the pesky neighbours who would visit her under the pretext of asking about her health. She felt that they wanted to see the 'mad woman' she had become. 'If people come here, they will make fun of me,' he remembers her telling him. Thereafter, such 'friendly' visits were banned.

One day, at home, while Bhola was making her take small sips from a bowl of *dal ka paani*—a warm, almost colourless lentil broth, which was the only meal she could subsist on lately—she absentmindedly ran her fingers through her hair. Like clumps of wool, her grey hair fell limply into her palms without a fight.

Trips to the hospital were draining. Nonetheless, with a disposable mask looped behind her ears, Kamala Devi would agree to go to the hospital on Bhola's insistence to get all sorts of 'strange' tests and treatments. She would reluctantly wear a patient's smock over her petticoat, push her fingers into sterile gloves and wear a scrub cap to cover her patchy scalp. She would sit on the patients' bench with Bhola in silence, staring at the smooth, disinfectant-mopped floor, until they were called in. Technicians would draw tubes and tubes of blood. 'Everything will be okay, mata ji,' they told her. Kamala Devi looked at them with a perplexed expression. She was a woman who did not want to be consoled; she wanted things explained. *Was it old age? Was it something in her bones? Was this the end?* Bhola refused to tell his mother the name of her disease, as if doing so would make matters worse.

Being able to enter the premises of the cancer hospital was a long waiting game. Sometimes, Shortcut helped by getting there early in the morning and standing in the serpentine queue outside the gate. 'If two people went, things got done quickly,' he explains. While waiting, he would admire the imposing complex of the hospital, feeling the smallness of his being. As soon as Shortcut came closer to the entrance, Bhola would arrive with his mother in a wheelchair, and the three of them would proceed inside together.

There were many queues. First, one had to stand outside the hospital; then, one had to wait inside to see the doctor. Then, one had to stand in front of the in-house pharmacy to procure the medicines scrawled on the prescription by the doctor. The visit—from waiting in the queues to meeting the doctor to buying the medicines—swallowed an entire day.

Inside, amidst the harrowing wails of patients and the hurried activities of hospital care, of nurses shuttling across long, brightly lit corridors and taking instructions from doctors, Shortcut noticed hundreds of people ailing, with all forms of incapacitating maladies. There were patients with tumours growing out of their necks or bulbous cysts sprouting on their limbs. Shortcut would reel back in disgust when he saw people with distorted jaws, bleeding gums and lips that looked as though they had melted away—patients who were once addicted to chewing or smoking tobacco. To ensure that Kamala Devi did not see such sights and get scared, Bhola would pull down his mother's veil to her shoulders and tell her to doze off.

Back home, Kamala Devi's four daughters had routinely begun visiting their mother, taking turns among themselves, and staying over to help for as long as their husbands permitted. When they came, Kamala Devi looked better, felt better, as though the strange heaviness pressing against her lungs and skull had temporarily dissipated. The daughters carried out the daily chores, chatted and giggled, chopped vegetables, massaged their mother's head and calves, and did everything Kamala Devi had done before the cancer colonized her body. Every time a daughter left, however, her body stiffened. Loneliness arrived in waves before consuming her completely.

———

One late February morning in 2022, Twinkle, who was still recuperating in her mother's home after giving birth to Sugi in

January, watched a harried Mohan burst through the door. With his hair in disarray, he commanded his wife to return to his house. One of his sisters had just left and someone needed to take over the household duties while Kamala Devi was recovering. Twinkle was the only able woman now.

Yet, even after Twinkle reluctantly returned to Mohan's home before the month ended, she felt that no respect was accorded to her for her conscientiousness. 'In front of his mother and brothers, he gave me the status of a dog,' she tells me.

By the time March arrived, things became more trying. Twinkle had a sickly newborn fussing in her arms, an ailing mother-in-law, a disgruntled husband and a meal spread to prepare for his brothers. She was expected to wash and dry their clothes, sweep the insides of their home, collect water in buckets between 4 p.m. and 10 p.m., feed her daughters and massage her mother-in-law's body, among many other things.

During the state elections, when Prime Minister Narendra Modi visited the city, the shops were shuttered and the streets had swollen up with people, their voices cheering and roaring in unison. The hullabaloo of elections bothered Twinkle, because while the men from the community had gone to witness the spectacle, Twinkle could not step out even if she wanted to.

On voting day, Mohan went off to vote. Twinkle was miffed—she had wanted to get her fingernail stained with ink too. Instead, she was sitting in front of a lit stove, cutting up a pumpkin into uneven cubes, picking out peas from their bottle-green jackets, stirring dal and watching the overwatered rice boil and turn to mush. Despite her repeated requests, her husband hadn't got a Voter ID Card made in her name. Yet, Twinkle kept herself abreast of what was happening in the country. She felt intellectually superior to her husband—and everyone else in the family.

A year ago, in 2021, the late Dom Raja Jagdish Chaudhary, was posthumously awarded the Padma Shri.[1] The Dom Raja was, literally, the king of the Dom community, who had lived in a sprawling, albeit dilapidated, bungalow in Man Mandir Ghat, with milk-giving cows tethered within its premises. Locally, the bungalow was known as the 'sher-wali kothi'—the 'tiger bungalow'. The home had a grand balcony with a marvellous view, and two memorable and well-photographed tiger statues on its balustrades that overlooked the holy river. The balcony was where the women of the house gathered to talk and soak up the sun, and where the men, with their well-greased heads, stretched out their legs on the charpoys. The Dom Raja's home even had its very own wrestling pit, where only decades ago, pehelwans threw each other to the ground and played for glory. When Jagdish Chaudhary was awarded the Padma Shri, his teenage son Hariom declared that the Dom community had finally been given the 'honour' it deserved on a national platform.[2]

All that was very good, Twinkle said, but that respect had not translated on the ground into any development for the community at large. For the Dom labourers, 'vikas', progress, was yet to arrive. If anything, progress, in the form of the Corridor, had built up a scare within her. Her mother-in-law, in her half-delirious state, was sure that their basti would be broken down and had aggressively begun to push her sons to buy a plot of land elsewhere. The same fear had slowly begun to infiltrate Twinkle's thoughts as well: Would they be compelled to relocate too?

The likes of Lakshaya might have had the right documents to be monetarily compensated but all her family had was hope—

hope that their residence would be spared. But hope alone was not enough in this dog-eat-dog world. Where would they go scouting for a new home in worried haste? Most dwellings near the ghats had already been demolished; what remained would either be caste-ridden or beyond their budget. If they were to rent a room far away from Manikarnika Ghat, how would her husband travel to work every day? They would end up spending more money than they earned.

Amidst all this worry, Twinkle struggled to brush aside the discontent she received from Mohan every day. There was nothing wrong with her, she assured herself, and she would not let her husband convince her otherwise.

One day, Mohan returned home unannounced in the middle of the day, drunk. A terrible brawl at the ghat had made him quit work midway. The resentment seething inside Twinkle's belly for months came out in a bitter tirade: 'Your job is to fight,' she hissed. 'You fight with *everyone*. Now you've left your work and are sitting here idle. How will we survive? We'll have to eat someone else's jhootha, their leftovers. I live like a dog already, and now so will you.'

Twinkle recalls how Mohan had picked up the heavy lid of a big steel container and had flung it, and all his frustrations, at her. The blow left behind a nasty swelling on her leg that took on the colour of aubergine. The swelling didn't subside for days. Twinkle, who had been forced to quit school and smother her aspirations for the sake of a 'happy' marriage, had never thought about escaping Chand Ghat until that day. She had been squirrelling money away—small portions of the funds that Mohan gave her for household expenses. She squeezed crumpled notes into her blouse, shoved them into dry kitchen containers and under the mattress when no one was looking. Now, she began fantasizing about whisking her children away, in a planned but hurried fashion, to a distant, modern city. She would find a job, she told herself. She would earn and feed her daughters respectably. Twinkle would do anything to survive, except get married again.

Could she really do it, though? Where would she go? Mumbai? Delhi?

What happened next, however, made her reconsider everything.

38

The Final Chapter

July 2022

IT HAD BEEN almost a year since Kamala Devi's family had learnt about the hungry, devouring illness that had taken control of her body. Bit by bit, it was stripping away every sense of her being.

Bhola had watched his mother apologize profusely to him and his brothers when she accidentally soiled her sari in front of them. 'Look what has become of me,' she would say weakly. 'What has happened to me that I have to see such a day in front of all of you?' Later, Twinkle would dutifully grab a washcloth and scrub her mother-in-law clean. She would wash Kamala Devi's sari and promptly disinfect the unwieldy, heavy mattress in the sun.

―――

On 25 July 2022, at 6.30 a.m., red-eyed and groggy, Bhola stood in a queue at the cancer hospital in Banaras, hoping to get an appointment for his mother's chemotherapy treatment. Kamala

Devi was at home, resting and waiting. It had been decided that once Bhola obtained an appointment slot for her, one of his younger brothers, Raja, would whisk her off to the cancer ward in a wheelchair. Until then, Raja had promised to keep a watchful eye on her at home. He would give Kamala Devi her medicines and feed her breakfast on time.

Bhola's head ached. He was tired of these hospital visits. He was tired of watching his mother throw the bowl of watery dal from his hand on days she did not want to eat. The steel utensil always clanked ominously against the ground. He was tired of his brothers' spiteful remarks about 'acting like a leader' whenever Bhola demanded that they needed to pitch in. He was tired of paying the mounting medical bills that had consumed his savings. He was tired of his employer grumbling from Chennai, accusing him of not working 'hard enough'. The employer deducted a considerable portion from Bhola's monthly salary under the pretext that he was taking 'too many holidays'.

'There are days when I cry by myself,' Bhola admits. 'The pressure is too much.'

He bemoaned the pointless expenses too. When guests arrived from far-off villages, chicken was specially bought from the market, even when it was unaffordable. When there was a wedding in the community, they could not attend it empty-handed. When Twinkle arrived home with her newborn, Bhola, on the insistence of his mother, half-heartedly gave Twinkle Rs 500 as a gift.

That day, around 8 a.m., as Bhola observed the patients and their caregivers spill in and out of the hospital, he briefly sensed something ominous. Something told him to call his brother and check in, but he did not act on it. Instead, he waited in line—

browsing on his phone, tapping his foot, watching the hospital staff converse in coded medical talk, hoping his queue would shorten faster.

His phone rang suddenly. Moments later Bhola had given up his hard-earned spot in the line and was running towards the exit in a wild panic.

When Kamala Devi awoke that morning, the first thing she did was ask for Bhola. Her son Raja told her that Bhola was away. For the last ten days, she had been sleeping in Mohan's home, on Mohan's bed, since it was the closest to the lavatory. Initially, Twinkle had protested, but she eventually gave up and began sleeping in Kamala Devi's room instead.

Raja offered his mother some sweet tea and biscuits. Shortly after, when he attempted to lift Kamala Devi from the plastic chair on which she was sitting to take her to the bathroom, he failed. Her body was too weak, too heavy, too sore. Her feet had not been firmly planted on the ground. Her legs were like jelly. When he picked her up, Kamala Devi swayed momentarily and lost her balance.

Raja was not used to being the caregiver. He spent a majority of his hours working at a sari shop, unravelling brightly coloured Banarasi saris before customers, bargaining for the 'right price' and then carefully placing the same, crisply folded saris in plastic bags once they were sold. When Bhola came back to Banaras to look after their mother, Raja and his other brothers willingly stepped back. Bhola took over: thoroughly reading hastily scribbled prescriptions, keeping track of their mother's medicine routine, securing appointments for biopsy tests, MRI scans, radiotherapy and chemo. His brothers let him handle it all since Bhola was quick and aware, and held more sway at hospitals, often rattling off in English at the busy and cold hospital staff if they did not pay attention.

'They take me more seriously when I speak in English,' Bhola later said. On the other hand, Mohan, in his masaan clothes and with his unshaved chin and mumbled drawl, was often ignored or overlooked whenever he stood inside the large, packed hospital. In such unfamiliar spaces, Mohan was invisible, while Bhola sought and demanded attention.

On the morning of 25 July, Twinkle was upstairs, preparing food. Mohan had left for the masaan. Kamala Devi's eldest daughter, who had been staying with them, had left the night before. She had to return to her in-laws' home, since her children had school the next day.

A hassled Raja tried once again to lift Kamala Devi up from the chair, but his method was wrong and awkward. She slipped again. *Thump.* Then again. *Thump.* Kamala Devi looked at her son blankly for a few seconds, before panic overwhelmed her and she began heaving, desperately gasping for air. Raja frantically settled next to her. The first medicine was fed quickly. He brought a cup of water near her mouth and forced her to swallow. Kamala Devi was too exhausted, too defeated. She gestured to her son to continue giving her the medicines. 'Feed me more. More. Give all of them to me!' Kamala Devi had had enough.

Raja ignored her demand. He, however, still needed to give her the required number of pills. By the time a flustered Raja placed the third pill on her tongue, he noticed that her feet had turned cold. Harrowed, Kamala Devi insisted that Raja went on with his day. Unable to argue with his mother, Raja listened to her and went to the bathroom to wash up.

'It was as though she did not want anyone to see her go,' Raja would tell me later.

When Raja returned from the bathroom, he noticed something terribly awry. He rushed to give Kamala Devi water, but her mouth had unclenched, and the water dribbled to her chin. He called Bhola.

It was just after 8 a.m.

'She's not well. Come home!'

'If she is not well, bring her here to the hospital quickly. I am waiting in the line. The doctors can help her!' Bhola screamed desperately into the phone.

'Just come,' his brother told him.

Outside, the sky had broken, flinging hard pellets of rain onto the ground. It was a Monday—Lord Shiva's day—and pilgrims were thronging to the Kashi Vishwanath temple to receive the god's blessings. All routes leading home were clogged. Bhola searched for a vehicle to take him to his mother but all the autorickshaws and cycle-rickshaws plying the roads were full. Stumbling over puddles, he began hailing strangers riding motorbikes. Finally, someone pulled over and allowed him to ride pillion for a part of the way. From there, Bhola ran home as fast as he could.

Grief moves differently in people. Some of us are broken and inconsolable, and some have unsettling emotional outbursts.

Then, there are those who build walls. They talk calmly, make the necessary decisions, focus on what needs to be done but refuse to sink into the black hole of shock, anger, guilt, or denial. Bhola is one of them. He moved quickly, took logistic calls, and did not allow his mind to derail.

At home, Bhola played a soothing chant—'*Om, om, om*'—on a loop on his phone and placed it near his mother's ear, hoping that her soul would get peace. He directed Shortcut to purchase 5 kilograms of desi ghee from the market.

Bhola's sisters were inconsolable that July morning. They were keening, fainting, momentarily stabilizing before spiralling again. Twice, he had to sprinkle water on Mitthoo's face. The others waited until Kamala Devi's sister-in-law arrived. In the community, it is customary for a female relative from the deceased woman's paternal home to perform the task of cleansing and clothing the body.

Kamala Devi's sister-in-law gently bathed and draped her in a white light-cotton sari with tiny flowers printed on it. Other women in the family offered saris and shawls to Kamala Devi as parting gifts, placing the garments on her body in turn. She was then taken to the cremation ground.

Bhola had already booked a spot at a higher platform at Manikarnika Ghat. Decades ago, this area was reserved only for the rich 'upper castes' but today, it is available to anyone who has clout and the money to spend. Bhola booked it for Rs 5,000, but by the time Kamala Devi's body arrived at the ghat, the spot had been given to someone else. Bhola did not have the energy to fight, and so her body would have to be cremated on the common masaan ground.

A coloured shroud did not cover the corpse; this was as per the Dom tradition. And since it was a death within the Dom community, wood was given by the community members as offerings to the deceased.

Locals claim that when the Dom Raja Jagdish Chaudhary passed away in August 2020, his pyre was built using approximately 551 mann of wood. For Kamala Devi's funeral, about 21 mann of dry and wet timber was used. On her pyre, they placed all the things she liked to eat: thick, white cream nestled in an earthen kulhad, pieces of fresh paan, and some alcohol because she occasionally liked to drink.

Standing near her pyre, Bhola spoke quickly to his distant relatives, unwilling to trip into pockets of silence, as though the moment he tumbled, it would loosen the stoic grip he had on himself and he would fall apart. His voice remained flat and uncoloured. When it broke momentarily, Bhola masked it, saying that something was scraping against his throat.

Around 8.30 p.m., a broken-down Mohan with a freshly shaved head, finally lit his mother's pyre. The corpse burners then gathered around in a synchronized fashion, taking turns to stoke the pyre and arrange more wood to keep the fire alive. Mohan quietly stared at the fire and thought of the ordained violence it inflicted on his mother's body: how it ate her so hungrily, so cruelly. He watched her face blacken and shrivel, heard her bones crack, break away and fall—the very bones that had once held her upright and allowed her to run after him when he was a little boy.

He thought to himself: 'This body, it belonged to my mother who took care of me all my life. Now look at it. Look how it's burning and turning to ash.'

A few hours later, all of Kamala Devi's ashes were swept into the river by the five brothers.

––––•––––

When they returned home after the cremation, Mohan's brothers refused to sleep in the room where Kamala Devi had died. His youngest brother declared the possibility of her spirit haunting them and slipping into one of their bodies in the dark. Mohan settled them down and went to sleep alone in his room—the room where his mother breathed her last.

After some days, Bhola scoured his phone and brothers' phones for a photograph of a smiling Kamala Devi. He wanted to get it blown up, printed, framed and wreathed for their home. Then, he would deliberate leaving.

'*Mummy ke jaaney ke baad, ghar pura khatam ho gaya.* After her passing, it felt like my home had been completely destroyed,' Bhola says.

The loss of a parent cannot be expressed in words. Kamala Devi had held the family together in her lifetime. For Bhola, she had been the solitary reason that kept bringing him back to Banaras. Her death unbraided the only relationship he had wanted to keep with the city.

Before the calendar marked two weeks from her death, he booked a train ticket to Delhi, desperate to remove himself from the thicket of pain, sadness and emptiness that had invaded his home. He needed to move on. Work would be a necessary distraction, the perfect balm that would hopefully help him heal. Within the next six months, he would land a job that he had been wanting for two years, leave Delhi and move to Chennai, promising himself never to make Banaras his home again.

Afterword

2022–23

In MARCH 2019, Prime Minister Narendra Modi laid the foundation of the Kashi Vishwanath Dham project. Work on this project had not been deterred by the pandemic. It was completed in record time, and in December 2021, the Prime Minister inaugurated the Corridor.

Chand Ghat residents who had feared that their dwellings would be razed to the ground by the Corridor and thought that they would be displaced were relieved: their homes had remained intact.

Shortcut says that since the Corridor was built, there had been a deluge of visitors to Banaras: from politicians to actors and television celebrities. He claims to have seen the 1980s hero Govinda, talk-show host Kapil Sharma and modern-day superstars Alia Bhatt and Ranbir Kapoor in Banaras.

After the COVID-19 restrictions began to ease up in the second half of 2021, Lakshaya helped Shortcut, who was unemployed and desperate, acquire a job as a tourist guide.

Still, Shortcut struggled under the pressure to earn. In January 2022, his elder brother Bunty, in a wild, jealous fit, had fought with his parents, insinuating that they coddled their youngest more than necessary. Bunty threw his hands up and said he no longer wanted the responsibility of looking after his parents. He challenged Shortcut to earn enough to provide for them. Days later, a brick wall was built, dividing their small home into two. A portion of it was occupied by Bunty, his wife and their children, while the other by Shortcut and his parents. If Shortcut sat with his back against the partitioning wall and splayed his legs, his toes could easily touch the adjacent walls. In life too, he felt as though the walls were closing in on him.

After failing the twelfth standard, Shortcut had miserably flitted between jobs, working as an electrician and later turning to tourism. But the competition among the local guides in a city that thrived on religious tourism was cut-throat. There were days when Shortcut returned home with zero earnings.

'*Main bahut pareshaan rehta hoon,* I stress a lot,' he tells me.

Shortcut wanted a long-term career that could provide a stable salary. He knew it was possible. He had seen Bhola do it. 'I want a career so that I can change my background, move away from this mahaul, this environment.'

Shortcut had watched Bhola steadily ascend professionally and receive a big salary packet, which had allowed him to leave Chand Ghat for good. It had finally dawned on him that Bhola was able to do so because he had remained steadfast in his vision and completed his college education, despite facing multiple setbacks.

As though he had manifested his wish, Shortcut was able to find and approach an NGO that offered financial aid to underprivileged students and enabled them to complete their education. The NGO provided him the assistance he needed to sit for his twelfth standard Board exams again through the National Institute of Open Schooling (NIOS) in April 2023.

Shortcut poured all his time and energy into studying and hustling. He would wake up at 5 a.m., bathe and head to work, then return home around 9 p.m., eat dinner and diligently study until midnight. He wanted to do well in the exams and, eventually, get a job that would give him a certain kind of social standing.

'*Koi bhi job mil jaye. Mujhe bas yeh tag chahiye ki, "ladka service kar raha hai". Kuch paisa kum hi miley, bas main basti chordh ke nikal jaun.* Any job will do. I just want a tag that says, "The boy is in government service." I am willing to earn a little less, as long as I can leave my neighbourhood,' he says.

As of May 2023, Shortcut has achieved a part of his dream. He cleared the Board exams with 64 per cent marks. His voice is full of hope and elation when he shares the news with me on the phone. The next step, he says, is to enrol in a part-time B.A. programme in college that will enable him to study while he continues his work as a tour guide.

———

Komal and Lakshaya are more than happy as a married couple. Lakshaya routinely takes Komal out on dates on his motorbike. As often as they can, they try catching a first-day-first-show of new Bollywood releases or go to eat at a nearby chaat shop. Komal recently sent a photograph of both of them seated on a motorbike. In the photograph, Lakshaya is grinning from ear to ear, wearing a pale-coloured shirt. Komal is smiling too. Her hair is loose and a thick line of vermilion streaks the parting of her hair. She is wearing a T-shirt and jeans, and has an ice cream in her hand.

What delights Komal is the immense degree of freedom she is now experiencing—something she never could when she was unmarried. She can choose not to cook if she doesn't want to; she can wear the clothes she wants to; and explore the city with Lakshaya long after 8 p.m. When Lakshaya is at home, he washes the dishes alongside Komal. When he goes to work, Komal invites her friends over. They sit and chat over cold drinks and popcorn. Komal has also begun offering tuitions, teaching young school kids. This keeps her busy on most days.

'*Bahut mehnat kiye hain usko paaney ke liye, uske poore family ko mananey ke liye.* It has taken immense hard work to have her in my life, to convince her entire family to accept me,' Lakshaya tells me on the phone one day. 'Think about it. We were in a relationship for many years but we never did anything that would make our families hang their heads in shame.'

According to Lakshaya, everyone in Komal's family, including her maternal uncles, have come around and accepted their marriage. He explains that they are warmer towards him since they can see that Komal is being well looked after. 'They saw the things I bought for her, the jewellery I bought for her ...'

'Do you think money changes things?' I catch myself asking.

'Yes, that's exactly the thing. Money talks,' Lakshaya agrees. 'Today, everyone has come around and has accepted us. We are both very happy.'

Dolly, Lakshaya's sister, seems to be doing well too. She has overcome the initial hurdles of managing a shop as a businesswoman. The resentment that seethed within the mohalla against her has subsided, perhaps because she no longer allows anyone to talk down to her.

She does not know this, but her sheer resilience and entrepreneurial instincts have begun to sow optimistic thoughts in the minds of a few women in the community, including one of Bhola's older sisters. They have begun imagining alternative lives for themselves. *Can they muster up the courage to establish small shops like Dolly? Can they too earn on their own?*

Dolly finally recognizes the enormity of what she has been able to accomplish. 'In my caste, I am the only woman who earns,' she says on a video call, acknowledging her own tenacity. As she hands a steaming cup of chai sprinkled with bhujia to her daughter Vidhi, who loves the added crunch, she adds, 'Sometimes I think of myself as a man. I earn like a father and feed like a mother. I'll continue to battle my fears with strength.'

Dolly tells me that she had a special dream the night before our video call. For the first time since his death, Sekond Lal visited her. In the dream, they were holding hands, laughing together and running in a garden. 'It was the sweetest dream,' she says, with a thrill in her voice.

———

In December 2022, Bhola was in a celebratory mood when he met me in Delhi. He was leaving the next day for Chennai again, where he had been offered a new job. It had a good pay package and there seemed to be scope for tremendous growth. Bhola had applied for the same job once before in 2021 but was rejected at the time. While working at another firm, he had improved his communication skills and prepared with perseverance. He applied again in 2022. This time, he got the job.

Bhola is determined to make a new life for himself. '*Bachpan se maine udaan bharney ke sapney dekhe hain. Matlab, mujhe chahiye.* Since childhood, I've had countless dreams of taking flight. It means, I wanted it, one way or another,' he says, with unwavering confidence. At the same time, Bhola is aware of the sacrifices he has had to make, to pull himself out of his neighbourhood: it was the only way he could soar. 'If you speak to anyone in my mahaul, they can't think beyond Chand Ghat,' Bhola says. 'Living in that mahaul, you cannot do anything. You have to leave. You have to get out of there.'

He intends to return, but only when he has 'become someone', he declares. Sometime in the future, when he has mustered substantial clout, he will return to change the way things are done at Manikarnika Ghat.

Sharing his vision for the community with me, he says, 'If I were to get an audience with the Prime Minister, I would let him know the actual situation we face as a community. The Doms' fire is a very important thing. People come to Manikarnika Ghat for the Doms, not anyone else. Today, however, their value is diminishing.' Bhola feels that this is because the wood sellers belonging to other castes have taken over the negotiations at the cremation ground with the mourners who come to cremate their relatives.

Although concrete steps are still needed to ensure that caste is no longer inextricably associated with the profession of cremating corpses, and focused measures are required to assist the Doms in receiving quality education that will enable them to pick a profession of their choice, Bhola realizes that this will take years. For the moment, he wants the government to intervene by initiating a complete overhaul of the cremation ground and ensuring that the corpse burners are assigned eight-hour shifts (like 9-to-5 jobs) and are given a regular monthly salary. Cremation work, he insists, should be treated as a profession, where the corpse burners are not pushed to work for unreasonably long hours.

Bhola notes how, cognizant of his success, the mindset in Chand Ghat towards education is changing. More parents are now keen on sending their children to school. In early 2023, Bhola brought Imlee and two other nieces to Chennai to put them in school. This was a big step, since parents had never allowed girls to leave Chand Ghat, let alone Banaras—that too for an education.

Bhola knows that it was education that enabled him to arrive where he is today. For that, he remains indebted to Mohan. 'When I get somewhere, become someone, I will not turn my face away from him,' Bhola says. At the same time, he hopes to encourage his sisters (who are stuck in unhappy marriages) to become businesswomen someday, so that they too can be financially independent. When he has earned enough, he will buy a few shops and hand the keys to his sisters.

'Just now my time has not come, but when it does, we will all live like maaliks!' Bhola declares.

Acknowledgements

I AM FOREVER INDEBTED to the families of the Dom community who welcomed me into their homes and lives, and who have taught me invaluable lessons on courage, spirit and will. Without the kindness and support of the individuals in these pages—the true heroes—this book would have never been written. Over the years, I have come to know them, befriend them and learn from them. They have been patient and generous with their responses during our interview sessions, spurred by a desire for the world to know about their community, its aspirations, its disappointments and its sheer resilience. These are the individuals whose contributions have been critical to my reporting. However, in the interest of their privacy and security, I am unable to identify them here. To them, I express my profound gratitude.

I am grateful to Hemali Sodhi for her incredible support and efforts in championing this book from the get go; and to Ambar Sahil Chatterjee, who is my confidant and trusted advisor.

Thank you, Ananth Padmanabhan for your faith in my book and Udayan Mitra for your encouragement. I am grateful to Arcopol Chaudhuri for being among the first to see the potential in this book, Swati Chopra for being a thoughtful and serious editor, and Shatarupa Ghoshal for her excellent copy-edits and fact-checking. I am deeply grateful to Shalin Maria Lawrence for coming on board as a sensitivity reader, for patiently perusing my book and sharing her views. Thank you, Saurav Das, for creating a powerful cover design that left me speechless.

I thank David Hajdu for reading the first few chapters when the book was still in a nascent stage and for his unwavering support. Many thanks to Dr Aakriti Mandhwani for reading my early draft, giving feedback and asking pertinent questions. My deep gratitude to Vikram Mathur (name changed) for sharing his crucial insights and his film. I thank Gal Beckerman for his keen eye and balanced counsel, which helped shape my first report on the community at Columbia University in New York. Special thanks to George Grey (name changed) for always being excited about the book and for his consistent encouragement.

The Sanskriti-Prabha Dutt fellowship aided my research and reporting during the initial stages. I am grateful to Sangam House for the month-long residency in Bangalore, where I began writing the first chapter of my book, and I thank Charles Wallace India Trust and the University of Kent for boarding me as a writer-in-residence in Canterbury, UK, which further enabled me to write for focussed long hours.

This book would have been impossible without the support of my family—the original believers—who constantly reminded me of my potential. Abha Iyengar, my mother, a gifted writer herself, who read every draft, and is my greatest source of strength. My father, Vinod A. Iyengar, who has always had my back and whose avid interest in reportage has seeped into my being. My brother, Adil A. Iyengar, whose advice and wit in equal measure have kept me balanced. My husband, Anindya Choudhury, who kept me calm, focused and motivated throughout, and for his persistent faith in my writing. Atticus, my Golden Retriever, who is my absolute stress-buster.

Dr Ashwani Vasishth, Sunil Bhatia, Shreenu Mukherjee, Samiksha Sharma, Dr Matthew Whittle, Dr Ravi Nandan Singh, Somnath Waghmare, Vicky Kaushal, Shahnaz Siganporia, Amy Sackville—thank you for helping me in your own individual ways.

Author's Note

Please note that the names of the people and places have been changed to protect the individuals' identities.

I FIRST MET BHOLA, Lakshaya, Aakash and Shortcut in 2015, and I knew this wouldn't be our last meeting. In the following years, I would return repeatedly to Chand Ghat, with an unwavering curiosity and interest to learn about the community that cremates the dead. Through these boys, I met people like Dolly who broke tradition by becoming the first woman in her basti to start a small business, and Twinkle, an exceptionally intelligent woman whose early marriage thwarted her personal ambitions.

The stories of the people in this book are a culmination of many hours of interviews that were held between late 2015 and early 2023. Almost all of these were recorded; some were documented on video. On the occasions when certain interviews could not be recorded, they took the form of handwritten notes. During my field visits, I took several photographs as well. These were visual records and aided in describing places, spaces and people.

I was present for many of the events portrayed in this book, including the argument that broke out between Dolly and Aakash. For events that occurred in the past or those that I had not witnessed, I relied on individual retellings, which were supported by their families or those present at the time. The incidents of Komal being harassed in Chand Ghat have been corroborated by both Komal's and Lakshaya's families. Certain scenes, such as the conversations between Lakshaya and Komal, where dialogues have been used, were culled from the retellings of these moments by both of them. The impressions of Saroj have been formed through interviews with Geeta, Shortcut and others. Certain thoughts that have been attributed to individuals in the book, for example, the description of Mohan watching his mother's cremation and what he was experiencing, were recounted by him to me. For my research, I also travelled to the schools where Bhola, Lakshaya and Shortcut studied.

During the pandemic, when travel was impossible and I couldn't be physically present, particularly in 2020 and parts of 2021, I held interviews over video calls and phone. I held follow-up interviews in person with Mohan and others about their experiences during the pandemic, shortly after the lockdown was eased.

When I asked the community members questions about Sekond Lal or the sequence of events that occurred on the night of his death, their answers were heavily dependent on where their allegiances lay. Years had passed since his death, so there was a lot of back and forth in recounting, particularly when I asked for specific details over and over again for fact-checking purposes. Nevertheless, the description of what may, or may not, have happened, has been reconstructed using inputs from various interviews.

There are, of course, many sides to a story. Therefore, in this case, there is no singular truth.

Bunty, who was earlier approachable, began avoiding me the day I started inquiring about Sekond Lal's death. When I bumped into him one day, he was on his way to see a doctor, and then disappeared quickly. Bunty politely refused to see me afterwards.

Whenever I asked about Gopi, it seemed that he was never in the neighbourhood. Gopi is one of the maaliks at Manikarnika Ghat, which means he has reasonable social clout in the Dom basti. When I finally did meet him, it was by chance, when he was walking home after returning from the ghats. Gopi was surprised to see me, and looked at me as though he knew who I was. His demeanour was extremely guarded when I met him. When I inquired whether we could talk, he suggested another day, while also stating that he had nothing to tell me. Then he retreated into a sullen silence before joining his palms together to take his leave.

The next day, I requested Aakash, Gopi's close friend, to facilitate a proper introductory meeting with Gopi. Later, however, Aakash informed me that Gopi had declined to see me.

This is not a work of investigative journalism. For instance, I was not interested in following the accident or the alleged murder, but I wanted to understand the aftermath of it on Dolly's life, and how she dealt with the situation. I was also interested in following her transformation, from a woman who was once called 'naive', into an astute entrepreneur. In addition, I was curious to explore how each individual had slightly, or completely, varied accounts about a singular event—a universal phenomenon.

Over time, I have seen the people I have written about in this book grow up, form opinions, pursue their dreams and achieve their goals. What has remained intact is their tenacity and the strong desire to change their circumstances. However, it is important to note that the story of the Dom community in Chand Ghat is not, and cannot be, fully representative of other Dom bastis in Banaras and anywhere else in the country.

Born into an Iyengar family, I am acutely aware of my privilege. Through my research, I have read, engaged with and tried to understand the complex, larger debates surrounding Dalit representation in literature, cinema and history. I have worked closely with a sensitivity reader for this book. I have taken great care to ensure that the Doms' voices have not been overshadowed by mine. My function is to document their experiences. I only insert my voice to ask crucial questions and to direct the narrative forward.

I paraphrase my former professor Jeroo Mulla (the Head of Department of Mass Communication at SCM Sophia Polytechnic, Mumbai, at the time) who said: We are all here—the caste we belong to, the class we belong to—through the accident of birth. That, the privileges accorded, or not accorded to us, are inextricably linked to the family we are born into.

When I began writing this book, there were moments when I asked myself: Why am I writing this book? Do I need to tell this story? Was it even my place to do so? I was deeply aware that no amount of research, reading, interviewing and storytelling, could relay personally lived experiences.

However, I realized that this book needed to be written for the individuals who had carved out portions from their days to speak to me, and tell me their stories. Over the course of eight years, they had taken out the hours to narrate their accounts and share their first-hand life experiences. It would be a disservice to them, their time, their hopes and energies, if I did not write.

Our interviews would take on different tones. Sometimes our conversations were serious, intense and painful; sometimes these conversations were light and playful. Sometimes, they were just therapeutic. Many of them, particularly the women, wanted someone to listen to them, to hear them, to befriend them, to *see* them. They told me their experiences in the hope that the world would know about them—that they are not just a community of cremators (as is their unidimensional identity in public consciousness at the moment), but that they are real people living real lives.

There was also the immediacy to document Dolly's, Bhola's, Shortcut's, Lakshaya's and Komal's lives—individuals who were going against the grain—and their experiences. If they were not, then no one would know how each of them, despite having the odds stacked against them, had transformed their lives.

I am aware that the labels 'upper' and 'lower', used for describing individuals belonging to a particular caste stratum, are problematic. These terms have been used in my book only due to their widespread usage, and as evidence for providing a history of power and oppression even in contemporary times. I have written this book to the best of my abilities as a journalist, and I personally reject the caste hierarchy's existence, and the discrimination it has engendered.

New Delhi   **Radhika Iyengar**
August 2023

List of Characters

(In order of appearance)

Dolly, *a young widow and a mother of five.*

Sekond Lal, *Dolly's late husband, who died in 2016.*

Vidhi, *Dolly's youngest daughter.*

Aakash, *works at the cremation ground as a corpse burner. He is Dolly's neighbour.*

Lakshaya, *Dolly's younger brother and a tour guide in Banaras.*

Komal, *Lakshaya's girlfriend.*

Aman, *Komal's younger brother.*

Ajay, *Dolly's younger brother, who is older than Lakshaya.*

Mirchi, *Dolly's neighbour.*

Bhola, *the only individual in his community in Chand Ghat to receive a private college education.*

Mohan, *Bhola's older brother. He works as a corpse burner at Manikarnika Ghat.*

Kamala Devi, *Bhola's mother.*

Twinkle, *Mohan's wife.*

Sunny, *a wood seller from the Dom community.*

Imlee, *Mohan's daughter from his first marriage. Imlee is Mohan's eldest daughter.*

Keshav, *Bhola and Mohan's late father. He passed away in 2011.*

Compounder, *the man to whom Dolly is initially betrothed before the engagement is called off.*

Geeta, *Dolly's mother.*

Saroj, *Sekond Lal's mother.*

Shortcut, *Bhola's neighbour and close friend.*

Balram, *Shortcut's cousin.*

Vikram Mathur, *a filmmaker.*

George Grey, *an American who sponsors the children's education.*

Bunty, *Shortcut's older brother.*

Simi and Barkha, *Komal's friends.*

Santosh, *the chief operator at the electric crematorium at Harishchandra Ghat in 2015.*

Vicky, *the chief operator at the gas-powered crematorium.*

Mitthoo, *Bhola's younger sister.*

Mohani, *Mohan and Twinkle's first child.*

Gopi, *Sekond Lal's friend and neighbour.*

Chanchal, *Ajay's wife. She is Dolly and Lakshaya's sister-in-law.*

Suresh, *Lakshaya's cousin.*

Munni, *Suresh's wife.*

Gauri, *one of Lakshaya's sisters.*

Sugi, *Mohan and Twinkle's second child.*

Raja, *one of Bhola's brothers.*

Notes

Epigraph (p. ix)

Essential Kabir, tr. Arvind Krishna Mehrotra (Gurgaon: Hachette India, 2011), p. 35.

1. The Neighbourhood

1. Indira Gandhi was India's former Prime Minister. She was assassinated on 31 October 1984.
2. This is common in many rural and semi-rural parts of India and is not necessarily specific to a particular community.

2. Charcoal, Smoke and Tangerine

1. A savoury and addictive mixture of crushed areca nuts, tobacco and catechu.
2. Diana L. Eck, *Banaras: City of Light* (New York: Alfred A. Knopf Inc., 1982), p. 324.
3. Bhang is made from the leaves of the hemp plant. It is used as an ingredient in certain food and drinks traditionally distributed in India during religious Hindu festivals like Holi.
4. A Jyotirlinga, or a radiant phallus-shaped stone, represents Lord Shiva. It is revered since it is believed to be one that has emerged from the ground itself and is not man-made like the linga. In India, there are twelve Jyotirlingas that have been identified.

5. Mark Twain, *Following the Equator: A Journey around the World* (American Publishing Company, 1897), p. 480.

6. Norman Macleod, *Days in North India* (Philadelphia: J.B. Lippincott, 1870), p. 20.

7. Ibid., p. 31.

8. Ibid., p. 32.

9. Jonathan Parry, 'Ghosts, Greed and Sin: The Occupational Identity of the Benares Funeral Priests', *Man*, vol. 15, no. 1 (1980): 88–111. Today, there are services like Last Journey that offer similar transportation services.

10. Eck, *Banaras,* p. 331.

3. The Monolith of Caste

1. Louis Dumont, *Homo Hierarchicus: The Caste System and Its Implications*, tr. Louis Dumont, Mark Sainsbury, Basia M. Gulati (New Delhi: Oxford University Press, 1980), p. 67.

2. Darpan Singh, 'Who is Dalit or Savarna? Why caste system must go in totality', *India Today*, 18 August 2022.

3. Sujatha Gidla, *Ants Among Elephants: An Untouchable Family and the Making of Modern India* (New York: Farrar, Straus and Giroux, 2017), p. 9.

4. There are, of course, pockets of change. For instance, Punjabi singer Ginni Mahi sings songs about her community with pride. In 2015, she released a song called 'Danger Chamar', which went viral on social media; 'Chamar Studio' is an accessories brand that supports and economically uplifts Dalit artisans. The intention is to reinstate respect in the word 'Chamar', which has been earlier used as a slur.

5. Tejas Harad, 'There's no accurate data on Other Backward Classes. 2021 census should start counting', The Print, 22 May 2018.

6. K. Satyanarayana and Susie Tharu, *The Exercise of Freedom: An Introduction to Dalit Writing* (New Delhi: Navayana, 2013), p. 11. Dalit Panthers was co-founded in May 1972 by Namdeo Dhasal,

Arjun Dangle, Raja Dhale and J.V. Pawar as a radical organization to fight systemic caste oppression.

7. Vinil Baby Paul, 'In His Radiance I Would Be Cleared of My Black Colour: Life and Songs of Dalit Christians in Colonial Kerala', *Nidān: International Journal for Indian Studies*, vol. 4, no. 1 (2019): 150.
8. Ambedkar, *Writings and Speeches, Vol. 5*, p. 30.
9. Sangharakshita, *Ambedkar and Buddhism* (Delhi: Motilal Banarsidass Publishers Private Limited, 2006), pp. 54-55, https://books.google.co.in/books?id=e-b2EzNRxQIC&&pg=PA53&&redir_esc=y.
10. 'Karnataka: After Dalit Woman Drinks from Water Tank, "Upper-Caste" Locals "Clean" It with Cow Urine', The Wire, 21 November 2022.
11. Deep Mukherjee, 'Rajasthan Dalit boy's death: Teacher tried to buy family's silence', *The Indian Express*, 15 August 2022.
12. Dr Babasaheb Ambedkar, *Writings and Speeches, Vol. 17*, eds Hari Narake, Dr M.L. Kasare, N.G. Kamble, Ashok Godghate (Delhi: Dr. Ambedkar Foundation, 2014), p. 53.
13. Dr B.R. Ambedkar, 'Speech delivered at Bombay Presidency Mahar Conference', tr. Vasant Moon, 31 May 1936, http://www.columbia.edu/itc/mealac/pritchett/00ambedkar/txt_ambedkar_salvation.html.
14. The polemical speech, which fiercely attacked the caste infrastructure and Hindu religion, was scheduled to be delivered at the 1936 annual conference held by the Jat-Pat Todak Mandal (Society for the Abolition of the Caste System) in Lahore. After the organizing committee read an advance copy of the speech, they disinvited Ambedkar fearing a violent backlash from conservative Hindus. Ambedkar later published *Annihilation of Caste* himself.
15. Dr Babasaheb Ambedkar, *Writings and Speeches, Vol. 1*, comp. Vasant Moon (Delhi: Dr. Ambedkar Foundation: 2014), p. 63, https://www.mea.gov.in/Images/attach/amb/Volume_01.pdf.
16. The Scheduled Castes and Scheduled Tribes (Prevention of Atrocities) Act, 1989, pp. 2-3, https://tribal.nic.in/actRules/preventionofAtricities.pdf.

17. According to the National Crime Records Bureau report published in 2021, it was reported that between 2018 and 2021, over 1,89,900 cases were registered under crimes against Dalits across India; Uttar Pradesh had the highest number of cases for crimes against Dalits. (Source: 'Over 1.8 lakh cases of crimes against Dalits were registered between 2018 and 2021', Scroll, 22 March 2023.)

4. Modern Love

1. Prachi Salve and Saumya Tewari, 'Just 5% of marriages in India are inter-caste', says report, Scroll, 13 May 2016.
2. 'Gujarat: Dalit Man Killed Allegedly by Wife's Upper-Caste Family', The Wire, 10 July 2019.
3. Jats are traditionally farmers and are recognized as OBC. In states like Haryana and Punjab, however, their agricultural and land ownership has helped them ascend economically, giving them a higher social status vis-à-vis Dalits.
4. Harsh Mander, 'Sonipat: Years after three relatives were murdered for inter-caste marriage, one man seeks justice', Scroll, 4 August 2019.

5. The Transgression

1. 'Manual Scavenging', International Dalit Solidarity Network, https://idsn.org/key-issues/manual-scavenging/.
2. Education is a fundamental right in India. Under the Right of Children to Free and Compulsory Education (RTE) Act, 2009 and the Sarva Shiksha Abhiyan (Education for All campaign), the Government of India made education free and compulsory for all children aged between six and fourteen years, https://www.education.gov.in/sites/upload_files/mhrd/files/upload_document/RTE_Section_wise_rationale_rev_0.pdf.

6. Fleeing the 'Crabs'

1. Across India, there are still countless temples that Dalits are prohibited from entering. They have been humiliated, fined, threatened, thrashed and even murdered for trying to offer prayers at public temples. E.g.:

Harveer Dabas, 'UP: Barred from entering temple, Dalit youth, 17, argues with 4 upper caste men, found shot dead in Amroha', *The Times of India*, 8 June 2020; Nagarjun Dwarakanath, '2-year-old Dalit child runs into temple in Karnataka, family fined Rs 25,000 for "purification ritual"', *India Today*, 22 September 2021.

2. Sharankumar Limbale, *Akkarmashi* (*The Outcaste*), tr. Santosh Bhoomkar (Delhi: Oxford University Press, 2003), p. 4.

3. Ibid.

4. Ibid., p. 6.

5. Omprakash Valmiki, *Joothan: A Dalit's Life*, tr. Arun Prabha Mukherjee (Delhi: Radhakrishna Prakashan Pvt. Ltd., 1997), p. 5.

6. Ibid., p. 65.

7. Ibid., p. 56.

8. Hamza Khan, 'Sweep the floor or we'll give you a TC: Threat to Dalit students in Jaipur school', *The Indian Express*, 8 November 2015, https://indianexpress.com/article/india/india-news-india/sweep-the-floor-or-well-give-you-a-tc-threat-to-dalit-students-in-jaipur-school/; and 'Dalit minor girl made to clean school toilet by headmistress, allege parents', *The New Indian Express*, 15 February 2020, https://www.newindianexpress.com/states/tamil-nadu/2020/feb/15/dalit-minor-girl-made-to-clean-school-toilet-by-headmistress-allege-parents-2103785.html.

9. 'FIR against Bengaluru school headmistress for ill-treating, threatening Dalit kids', *India Today*, 17 December 2021, https://www.indiatoday.in/cities/bengaluru/story/fir-against-bengaluru-school-headmistress-for-ill-treating-threatening-dalit-kids-1888987-2021-12-17.

10. Milind R. Lashkari, 'Dalit girl made to do 500 sit-ups for refusing to clean toilet', *Hindustan Times*, 19 August 2013, https://www.hindustantimes.com/india/dalit-girl-made-to-do-500-sit-ups-for-refusing-to-clean-toilet/story-6gbWfhMpmSJtsnvnbFiMlJ.html

11. Yashica Dutt, 'The IITs have a long history of systematically othering Dalit students', The Print, 17 February 2019; and Shadab Moizee, 'Why Are Dalit Students Dying by Suicide at India's Prestigious Universities?', The Quint, 10 March 2023.

12. 'My birth is my fatal accident: Full text of Dalit student Rohith's suicide letter', *The Indian Express*, 19 January 2016, https://indianexpress.com/article/india/india-news-india/dalit-student-suicide-full-text-of-suicide-letter-hyderabad/.

13. Divya Karthikeyan, 'JNU student's alleged suicide brings back memories of Rohith Vemula', Scroll, 14 March 2017, https://scroll.in/article/831741/jnu-students-alleged-suicide-brings-back-memories-of-rohith-vemula.

14. Sravani Sarkar, 'MP: Dalit girl stopped from going to school; family beaten up', *The Week*, 26 July 2022, https://www.theweek.in/news/india/2022/07/26/mp-dalit-girl-stopped-from-going-to-school-family-beaten-up.html.

15. In Hindi, 'saale' or 'saala' means wife's brother. It is colloquially used as an insult, insinuating that the insulter has been sleeping with the insulted person's sister.

8. The Rumour

1. Lord Shiva.

9. The Most Beautiful Girl

1. Lord Shiva's day. Shiva is often depicted with a snake around his neck. In Hindu religion, a snake symbolically represents the boundless cycle of death and rebirth. Monday is considered an auspicious day of worship for Shiva's disciples.

2. In India, giving birth to a son has been traditionally cherished over raising daughters in the family. This is largely because many view sons as potential breadwinners, while daughters are thought to be wealth-diminishers: their marriages require hefty sums of money to be given away as dowries.

11. A Five-Rupee Coin

1. 'Ways to curb drug addiction among street children', Save the Children, 23 November 2017, https://www.savethechildren.in/child-protection/ways-to-curb-drug-addiction-among-street-children/.

12. Hunger

1. *Isn't This Plate Indian? Dalit Histories and Memories of Food,* a pioneering book by Deepa Tak, Sharmila Rege, Sangita Thosar, Tina Aranha and the students of KSP Women's Studies Centre, Pune University, compiled food histories and food memories of Dalit communities.
2. Omprakash Valmiki, *Joothan,* pp. 8-9.
3. Ibid, p. 10.
4. Dr Babasaheb Ambedkar, *Writings and Speeches Vol. 5,* comp. Vasant Moon (Delhi: Dr. Ambedkar Foundation, 2014), p. 24, https://www.mea.gov.in/Images/attach/amb/Volume_05.pdf.
5. Sharankumar Limbale, *Akkarmashi (The Outcaste),* p. 10.
6. Ibid., p. 11.
7. Neo-Buddhists: In what came to be considered an act of religious mass conversion in India, Ambedkar and lakhs of his followers embraced Buddhism and became Buddhists in Nagpur, Maharashtra, in 1956.
8. Daya Pawar, *Baluta,* tr. Jerry Pinto (Delhi: Speaking Tiger Books, 2015), p. 73. At the time of its publication in 1978 in Marathi, *Baluta* was the first Dalit autobiography ever to be published.
9. Chandra Bhan Prasad, 'It's Justified', *The Pioneer,* 7 April 2013.
10. Mota chawal: The quality of rice in Indian households is also a social marker. The upper and middle classes often consume polished, fine-grained rice, while lower-income kitchens store coarser rice grains.

14. The Naysayers and the Believers

1. Virendra Singh Rawat, 'Akhilesh govt logs out free laptop scheme for 2017 polls', *Business Standard,* 13 April 2016, https://www.business-standard.com/article/politics/akhilesh-govt-logs-out-free-laptop-scheme-for-2017-polls-116041300693_1.html; and 'Uttar Pradesh government to give free laptops to class X, XII pass out students', *The Indian Express,* 24 June 2015, https://indianexpress.com/article/cities/lucknow/uttar-pradesh-government-to-give-free-laptops-to-class-x-xii-pass-out-students/.

17. 'No One Will Touch You'

1. Uma Chakravarti, *Gendering Caste: Through a Feminist Lens* (New Delhi: Sage Publications, 2018), p. 63.
2. Ibid. p. 51.
3. Ibid.
4. Ibid., p. 52.
5. Ibid., pp. 52, 63.

19. Business as Usual

1. Another legend popularized by the Doms is that they have descended from Kalu Dom, the Dom Raja under whom Raja Harishchandra, known for being honest and honourable, worked as an apprentice.
2. Historically, in the case of the deceased, the male member of the family (usually the eldest son) performs this role. However, of late, women are participating in the last rite rituals as well, from performing the role of chief mourners to being pallbearers.
3. Suraj Yengde, *Caste Matters* (Gurugram: Penguin Random House, 2019), p. 136.
4. Ibid., pp. 136-37.

20. A Dom's Duty

1. Once the pyre is lit, a cremator uses a strong bamboo stick to break the corpse's skull. This is a ritual known as 'kapal kriya'. It is believed that through this act, the soul can finally leave the body.

21. Glass, Nails and Gold

1. A tasla resembles a wok without handles.
2. Victor Mallet, 'The Ganges: Holy, deadly river', *Financial Times*, 13 February 2015, https://www.ft.com/content/dadfae24-b23e-11e4-b380-00144feab7de.
3. MPN means Most Probable Number. The MPN technique is used to estimate microorganism populations in soil, water and agricultural products. Kenneth John, 'Bacterial pollution in Ganga highest in Kanpur, Varanasi: Report', *Hindustan Times*, 28

May 2019, https://www.hindustantimes.com/lucknow/bacterial-pollution-in-ganga-highest-in-kanpur-varanasi-report/story-7MZDlfqvaksd0sWXrw7mBP.html#:~:text=The%20survey%20report%20revealed%20as,coliform%20bacteria%20in%20the%20Ganga.

4. V.K. Tripathi, 'Scientists find hazardous chemicals in Ganga between Varanasi and Bihar's Begusarai', *The Times of India*, 12 April 2023, https://timesofindia.indiatimes.com/city/patna/scientists-find-hazardous-chemicals-in-ganga/articleshow/99418746.cms?from=mdr#:~:text=Scientists%20find%20hazardous%20chemicals%20in%20Ganga%20between%20Varanasi%20and%20Bihar%27s%20Begusarai,-VK%20Tripathi%20%2F%20TNN&text=PATNA%3A%20Scientists%20have%20found%2051,Pradesh%20and%20Begusarai%20in%20Bihar.

22. Mohan's New Bride

1. Rupsa Chakraborty, 'Mumbai: Survey reveals using fairness cream is leading to rise in mental illness', *Mid-Day*, 12 August 2018, https://www.mid-day.com/mumbai/mumbai-news/article/mumbai-tiss-survey-reveals-using-fairness-cream-is-leading-to-rise-in-mental-illness-19694169.

23. The Great Makeover

1. '"Demolition" of temples in Varanasi figures in UP legislature', *Business Standard*, 20 December 2018, https://www.business-standard.com/article/pti-stories/demolition-of-temples-in-varanasi-figures-in-up-legislature-118122000606_1.html; Omar Rashid, 'Kashi demolitions reveal communal faultlines', *The Hindu*, 20 January 2019, https://www.thehindu.com/news/national/other-states/kashi-demolitions-reveal-faultlines/article26039411.ece; and 'Kashi corridor: Section of locals unhappy over "lost homes", demolition of iconic buildings', *The Indian Express*, 15 December 2021, https://indianexpress.com/article/cities/lucknow/kashi-corridor-locals-lost-homes-demolition-iconic-buildings-7674248/.

2. '5,000 hectares, Rs 399 cr: What the Kashi Vishwanath Corridor Project entails in numbers', Firstpost, 13 December 2021, https://www.firstpost.com/india/5000-hectares-rs-399-cr-what-kashi-vishwanath-corridor-project-that-pm-modi-will-inaugurate-is-all-about-10206331.html.

3. Ullekh N.P., 'Kashi Vishwanath Temple: The Grand Makeover', *Open Magazine*, 17 December 2021, https://openthemagazine.com/cover-story/kashi-vishwanath-temple-the-grand-makeover/; and Sudhir Kumar, 'Kashi Vishwanath Corridor: Sacred site gets a mega facelift', *Hindustan Times*, 12 December 2021, https://www.hindustantimes.com/india-news/kashi-vishwanath-corridor-sacred-site-gets-a-mega-facelift-101639333323745.html.

4. 'PM Modi's plan to transform Varanasi into Kyoto-style city: People both hopeful & apprehensive', *The Economic Times*, 18 December 2014, https://economictimes.indiatimes.com/news/politics-and-nation/pm-modis-plan-to-transform-varanasi-into-kyoto-style-city-people-both-hopeful-apprehensive/articleshow/45506439.cms.

5. Damini Nath, 'PM to open Kashi Vishwanath Corridor today', *The Hindu*, 13 December 2021, https://www.thehindu.com/news/national/pm-to-open-kashi-vishwanath-corridor-today/article37941370.ece.

6. 'The rejuvenation of Indian pride', Yogi Adityanath, 15 December 2021, Government of India, https://blog.mygov.in/editorial/the-rejuvenation-of-indian-pride/.

7. Nath, 'PM to open Kashi Vishwanath', *The Hindu*, 13 December 2021.

8. Siddhant Mohan, 'Varanasi: Yogi Adityanath worse than Aurangzeb, claims senior journalist; threatens to commit suicide', Two Circles, 31 January 2018, http://twocircles.net/2018jan31/420440.html.

9. Kabir Agarwal, 'In Modi's Varanasi, the Vishwanath Corridor Is Trampling Kashi's Soul', The Wire, 8 March 2019, https://thewire.in/politics/kashi-vishwanath-corridor-up-bjp; and Subhendu Sarkar, 'In Pics: Modi's Varanasi Kashi Project Faces Local Resentment', The Quint, 30 January 2019, https://www.thequint.com/photos/kashi-vishwanath-corridor-project-demolition-in-varanasi

10. 'Petition filed in High Court against Kashi Vishwanath Temple Corridor', *Amar Ujala*, 11 May 2018, https://www-amarujala-com.translate.goog/uttar-pradesh/varanasi/petition-file-allahbad-highcourt-for-kashi-vishwanath-corridor?_x_tr_sl=hi&&_x_tr_tl=en&&_x_tr_hl=en&&_x_tr_pto=sc.

11. 'People came out on the road in Banaras to protest against this grand plan of PM Modi', *Patrika*, 18 February 2018, https://www-patrika-com.translate.goog/varanasi-news/protest-against-vishwanath-temple-corridor-in-varanasi-2385087/?_x_tr_sl=hi&&_x_tr_tl=en&&_x_tr_hl=en&&_x_tr_pto=sc.

12. 'Padyatra against Kashi Vishwanath Corridor', *Varanasi Jagran*, 8 May 2018, https://www-jagran-com.translate.goog/uttar-pradesh/varanasi-city-pedestrian-protest-against-kashi-vishwanath-corridor-17924906.html?_x_tr_sl=hi&&_x_tr_tl=en&&_x_tr_hl=en&&_x_tr_pto=sc.

13. Faisal Fareed, 'In Varanasi, a plan to build corridor from Kashi Vishwanath temple to river Ganga sparks anger', Scroll, 10 February 2018, https://scroll.in/article/868178/destruction-not-development-plan-for-varanasis-kashi-vishwanath-temple-sparks-protests.

14. Mahatma Gandhi's speech at Banaras Hindu University Speech, 4 February 1916, https://www.mkgandhi.org/speeches/bhu.htm.

15. PM Modi's speech at the Kashi Vishwanath Temple in Varanasi, Uttar Pradesh, 05:24, 02:30, 08:22, 8 March 2019, https://www.youtube.com/watch?v=Lm4IeAHHWNg.

16. Bishwanath Ghosh, 'Beautification plan destroys oldest neighbourhoods in Varanasi', *The Hindu*, 9 December 2018, https://www.thehindu.com/news/national/other-states/beautification-plan-destroys-oldest-neighbourhoods-in-varanasi/article25704389.ece.

17. Adrija Roychowdhury, 'In Varanasi, as Kashi Vishwanath corridor rises, a Dalit colony goes under the rubble', *The Indian Express*, 4 April 2019.

18. Agarwal, 'In Modi's Varanasi', The Wire, 8 March 2019.

19. Roychowdhury, 'In Varanasi', *The Indian Express*, 4 April 2019, https://indianexpress.com/article/india/n-varanasi-a-dalit-colony-reluctantly-makes-way-for-kashi-vishwanath-corridor/.

20. Rashme Sehgal, 'In Narendra Modi's constituency of Varanasi, demolition of 250-year-old buildings for religious corridor creates resentment', Firstpost, 15 April 2019, https://www.firstpost.com/india/in-narendra-modis-constituency-of-varanasi-demolition-of-250-year-old-buildings-for-religious-corridor-creates-resentment-6452181.html.
21. Ullekh, 'Kashi Vishwanath Temple', Open Magazine, 17 December 2021.

24. City of Death

1. Prime Minister's Office, 'PM calls for complete lockdown of entire nation for 21 days', Press Information Bureau, Government of India, 24 March 2020, https://pib.gov.in/newsite/PrintRelease.aspx?relid=200658.
2. 'Unlock 5.0: Schools to reopen in some states from November 16, check details here', DNA India, 3 November 2020, https://www.dnaindia.com/india/report-unlock-50-schools-to-reopen-in-some-states-from-november-16-check-details-here-2854131; and 'Maharashtra: Devotees throng temples as religious places reopen amid easing of restrictions', ANI News, 16 November 2020, https://www.aninews.in/news/national/general-news/maharashtra-devotees-throng-temples-as-religious-places-reopen-amid-easing-of-restrictions20201116131959/.
3. 'Delhi weddings can now host up to 200 guests, The Indian Express, 1 November 2020, https://indianexpress.com/article/cities/delhi/delhi-weddings-can-now-host-up-to-200-guests-6911869/.
4. Infection prevention and control for the safe management of a dead body in the context of COVID-19, World Health Organization, 24 March 2020, pp. 1, 3, https://www.who.int/publications/i/item/infection-prevention-and-control-for-the-safe-management-of-a-dead-body-in-the-context-of-covid-19-interim-guidance.
5. National Directives of COVID-19 Management, Ministry of Home Affairs, Government of India, 23 March 2021, p. 5, https://www.mha.gov.in/sites/default/files/MHAOrder_23032021_0.pdf.

6. 'COVID-19: Uttar Pradesh reports 8,490 new cases, imposes night curfew in many districts', *Mint*, 8 April 2021, https://www.livemint.com/news/india/covid19-uttar-pradesh-reports-8-490-new-cases-imposes-night-curfew-in-many-districts-11617880936912.html.

7. 'India sees 2.34 lakh cases in new daily record; caseload surges over 1.45 crore', *India Today*, 17 April 2021, https://www.indiatoday.in/coronavirus-outbreak/story/india-covid19-fresh-record-2-34-lakh-cases-caseload-surges-over-1-45-crore-1791944-2021-04-17.

8. Ibid.

9. 'Queues continue to crank up the heat outside hospitals', *The Times of India*, 21 April 2021, https://timesofindia.indiatimes.com/city/rajkot/queues-continue-to-crank-up-the-heat-outside-hospitals/articleshow/82167920.cms; Nolan Pinto, 'Covid positive woman found lying on bench outside Bengaluru hospital waiting for ambulance', *India Today*, 14 April 2021, https://www.indiatoday.in/coronavirus-covid-19-outbreak/video/covid-patient-in-bengaluru-seen-lying-on-bench-outside-bengaluru-hospital-1790843-2021-04-14; Jignasa Sinha, 'With a single oxygen cylinder between them, three patients without a bed wait outside Delhi's GTB Hospital', *The Indian Express*, 24 April 2021, https://indianexpress.com/article/india/delhi-covid-19-gtb-hospital-oxygen-7286649/; and Soniya Agarwal, 'Gasping patients wait in ambulances, Ahmedabad's largest Covid facility has no bed for them', The Print, 14 April 2021, https://theprint.in/health/gasping-patients-wait-in-ambulances-ahmedabads-largest-covid-facility-has-no-bed-for-them/639734/.

10. 'DMK leader Kanimozhi holds road show in Ariyalur ahead of state election', India TV, 25 March 2021, https://aninews.in/videos/national/dmk-leader-kanimozhi-holds-road-show-ariyalur-ahead-state-election/; 'Home Minister Amit Shah holds road show in Chennai ahead of 6 April Assembly elections', The Print, 3 April 2021, https://theprint.in/politics/home-minister-amit-shah-holds-road-show-in-chennai-ahead-of-6-april-assembly-elections/633447/; and 'Have witnessed such a rally for the first time: PM Modi in Bengal',

NDTV, 18 April 2021, https://www.ndtv.com/india-news/west-bengal-assembly-election-2021-prime-minister-narendra-modi-in-west-bengal-have-witnessed-such-a-rally-for-the-first-time-2416162.

11. 'Here's a list of politicians who tested positive for Covid-19 recently', *The Indian Express*, 15 April 2021, https://indianexpress.com/photos/india-news/yogi-adityanath-pinarayi-vijayan-akhilesh-yadav-biplab-deb-covid-19-politicians-7274668/.

12. Sanjeev Miglani, Neha Arora, Aditya Kalra, Rajendra Jhadav, Aditi Shah, 'Indian COVID-19 patients die as ventilators run out of oxygen; infections surge', Reuters, 21 April 2021, https://indianexpress.com/photos/india-news/yogi-adityanath-pinarayi-vijayan-akhilesh-yadav-biplab-deb-covid-19-politicians-7274668/.

13. 'A nightmare on repeat: India is running out of oxygen again', BBC, 23 April 2021, https://www.bbc.com/news/uk-56841381.

14. BBC, Yogita Limaye, 25 April 2021, https://twitter.com/yogital/status/1386306578639323145?lang=en.

15. Sakshi Dayal, 'Gurgaon: 4 arrested for selling cylinders for 90k', *The Indian Express*, 24 April 2021, https://indianexpress.com/article/india/gurgaon-4-arrested-for-black-marketing-of-oxygen-cylinders-7286467/.

16. NDTV, 'Two sold fire extinguisher as oxygen cylinder to Delhi woman, arrested', 29 April 2021, https://www.ndtv.com/india-news/2-sold-fire-extinguisher-as-oxygen-cylinder-to-delhi-woman-arrested-2424770.

17. Ismat Ara, 'Mother of Man seen pleading for oxygen to not be taken away dies; cops say video "misleading"', The Wire, 29 April 2021, https://thewire.in/rights/uttar-pradesh-agra-oxygen-cylinder-police.

18. 'India becomes the first country in the world to report over 4 lakh new cases in a single day on April 30, 2021', *The Hindu*, 30 April 2021, https://www.thehindu.com/news/national/coronavirus-india-becomes-first-country-in-the-world-to-report-over-400000-new-cases-on-april-30-2021/article61817889.ece.

19. Kamal Khan, 'Covid deaths in Lucknow underreported? Cremations vs Government Data', NDTV, 15 April 2021, https://www.ndtv.com/india-news/uttar-pradesh-coronavirus-covid-deaths-

in-lucknow-underreported-cremations-vs-government-data-2413690#:~:text=This%20means%20the%20deaths%20of,the%20 official%20figure%20was%2021.

20. Ismat Ara, 'Varanasi: About Half of COVID-19 Deaths at Crematoria, Graveyards Not Recorded', The Wire, 18 April 2021, https://science. thewire.in/uncategorised/varanasi-about-half-of-covid-19-deaths-at-crematoria-graveyards-not-recorded/.

21. News24, Twitter, 15 April 2021, https://twitter.com/news24tvchannel/ status/1382745545278513156?ref_src=twsrc%5Etfw%7Ctwcam p%5Etweetembed%7Ctwterm%5E1382745545278513156%7C twgr%5E%7Ctwcon%5Es1_&ref_url=https%3A%2F%2Fscroll. in%2Fvideo%2F992414%2Fnever-seen-such-a-fearful-sight-corp.

22. W.F. Gatacre, Bombay Plague Committee, *Report on the Bubonic Plague in Bombay* (National Library of Scotland, 1896-97), p. 2, https://www.jstor.org/stable/pdf/community.27572874. pdf?refreqid=fastly-default:aea3b5ba483f075de30b2c62a8bf90a1 &&ab_segments=0/SYC-6704_basic_search/test-1.

23. Ibid., pp. 185, 188–91.

24. W.B. Bannerman, 'The spread of plague in India', *The Journal of Hygiene*, vol. 6, no. 2 (April 1906): 187, https://www.jstor.org/ stable/pdf/3858816.pdf?refreqid=fastly-default:ee0d0a3d7edcef667 97d4566f8c3184a&&ab_segments=0/SYC-6704_basic_search/test-1&&origin=search-results.

25. 'India's "untouchables" gather tsunami dead', ABC News, 3 January 2005, https://www.abc.net.au/news/2005-01-03/indias-untouchables-gather-tsunami-dead/612178.

26. 'Making Things Worse: How "caste blindness" in Indian tsunami recovery exacerbates vulnerability', International Dalit Solidarity Network, December 2006, pp. 1, 11, https://idsn.org/uploads/ media/Making_Things_Worse_report.pdf.

27. S. Prasad, 'Study reveals discrimination against Dalits at relief camps', *The Hindu,* 12 December 2018, https://www.thehindu. com/news/cities/puducherry/study-reveals-discrimination-against-dalits-at-relief-camps/article25720978.ece#:~:text=%27Not%20 allowed%20into%20faciliites%20with%20dominant%20

castes%27&text=A%20Damage%20Assessment%20Study%20 by,the%20cyclone%2Dravaged%20Nagapattinam%20district; and Mahima A. Jain, 'Why disaster rehab must focus on landless Dalit farmers', Scroll and IndiaSpend, 25 October 2019, https://www. indiaspend.com/why-disaster-rehab-must-focus-on-landless-dalit-farmers/#:~:text=But%20they%20own%20only%209,lay%20 claim%20to%2C%20we%20found.

28. News platforms like The Wire also reported that the number of cremations at Manikarnika Ghat had increased, which had made people 'suspect [that] many of the bodies [were] of COVID-19 victims', while *Frontline* reported that the locals noticed 'an exponential increase in the number of bodies brought for cremation' to Manikarnika Ghat. Sources: Ismat Ara, 'Varanasi: Cremation, Burial Grounds Show About 50% of COVID-19 Deaths Aren't Officially Recorded', The Wire, 17 April 2021, https://thewire.in/ health/varanasi-cremation-burial-grounds-show-about-50-of-covid-19-deaths-arent-officially-recorded; and Venkitesh Ramakrishnan, 'Fudging the death count in Varanasi', *Frontline*, 4 June 2021, https://frontline.thehindu.com/covid-19/fudging-covid19-death-count-varanasi-uttar-pradesh-yogi-govt/article34717167.ece.

29. Kamal Khan, 'Sunday lockdown in UP, Up to Rs 10,000 fine for second mask violation', NDTV, 17 April 2021, https:// www.ndtv.com/india-news/sunday-lockdown-in-up-rs-1-000-fine-for-not-wearing-mask-rs-10-000-for-second-violation-2415011#:~:text=Those%20caught%20without%20a%20 mask,and%20%2010%2C000%20the%20next.

30. Jacob Koshy, 'Vaccines for all above 18 from May 1; States can buy directly', *The Hindu*, 19 April 2021, https://www.thehindu.com/ news/national/from-may-1-everyone-over-18-years-eligible-for-covid-19-vaccination-government/article34359940.ece.

31. Shailesh Menon, 'Cost of death: How and why funeral rates have gone up across this Covid-wracked country', *The Economic Times*, 22 May 2021, https://economictimes.indiatimes.com/news/india/ cost-of-death-how-and-why-funeral-rates-have-gone-up-across-this-covid-wracked-country/articleshow/82862979.cms?from=mdr.

32. *National Family Health Survey* (2019–21), Ministry of Health and Family Welfare, Government of India, p. 47, http://rchiips. org/nfhs/nfhs-4Reports/India.pdf; and Parvathi Benu, 'Stark rural-urban divide reveals most Indians do not possess washing machines, refrigerators', *The Hindu Business Line*, 16 August 2022, https://www.thehindubusinessline.com/data-stories/data-focus/with-the-stark-rural-urban-divide-most-indians-do-not-own-washing-machines-and-refrigerators/article65771260. ece#:~:text=Urban%2Drural%20divide&text=In%20 2021%2C%20just%209%20per,the%20urban%20 populace%20possessed%20this.

33. Tadit Kundu, Pramit Bhattacharya, 'One in three Indians own a refrigerator, a fifth own an AC or cooler: NFHS data', *Mint*, 9 August 2018, https://www.livemint.com/Industry/V7wX0BAvKiko83S4 atfV0I/Consumerdurablesmarketgrowin grapidlyData.html.

34. Rajendra Jadhav and Saurabh Sharma, 'India's Covid-19 crisis pushes up the cost of living—and dying', Reuters, 14 May 2021, https:// www.reuters.com/world/india/indias-covid-crisis-pushes-up-cost-living-dying-2021-05-14/.

35. Alok Pandey, 'Shocking Video Shows Covid Patient's Body Being Thrown in River in UP', NDTV, 30 May 2021, https://www. youtube.com/watch?v=q3-g0ROtBG8.

36. 'Covid: Bodies found buried in sand on banks of Ganga in UP's Prayagraj', *Business Standard*, 16 May 2021, https://www.business-standard.com/article/current-affairs/covid-bodies-found-buried-in-sand-on-banks-of-ganga-in-up-s-prayagraj-121051600343_1. html; and 'Bodies Found Buried in Sand by Ganga River in Uttar Pradesh's Unnao', *Hindustan Times*, 13 March 2021, https:// www.hindustantimes.com/india-news/bodies-found-buried-in-sand-near-ganga-in-uttar-pradesh-s-unnao-101620893824088. html#:~:text=Days%20after%20bodies%20of%20suspected,in%20 the%20sand%20in%20Unnao.&text=PTI%20representative%20 image)-,A%20team%20of%20the%20local%20police%20is%20 in%20the%20process,being%20conducted%20for%20more%20 bodies.

37. Sajid Ali, 'Horror of 71 bodies floating down Ganga was "hell" for residents of Bihar's Chausa', The Print, 12 May 2021, https://www.youtube.com/watch?v=3xDXsMP-Q_I.

38. Geeta Pandey, 'Covid-19: India's holiest river is swollen with bodies', BBC, 19 May 2021, https://www.bbc.com/news/world-asia-india-57154564.

39. 'Bihar: Jalane ko lakdiyaan nahi to Ganga nadi mein phenk rahe shav? Chausa ke Mahadev Ghat par mile 45 shavon se macha hadkamp', Outlook Hindi, 10 May 2021, https://www-outlookhindi-com.translate.goog/country/general/bihar-if-not-wood-to-burn-bodies-are-being-thrown-in-the-ganges-river-45-body-found-in-mahadev-ghat-in-chausa-58195?_x_tr_sl=hi&_x_tr_tl=en&_x_tr_hl=en&_x_tr_pto=sc.

40. Haidar Naqvi, 'More shallow graves found on Ganga bank', Hindustan Times, 17 May 2021, https://www.hindustantimes.com/india-news/shallow-graves-on-ganga-bank-in-up-villagers-say-burials-spiked-recently-101620847125584.html.

41. 'Seven more bodies seen floating in Ganga in UP's Ballia; total count 52', The Times of India, 12 May 2021, https://timesofindia.indiatimes.com/city/varanasi/seven-more-bodies-seen-floating-in-ganga-in-ups-ballia-total-count-52/articleshow/82572714.cms.

42. Ali, 'Horror of 71 bodies', The Print, 12 May 2021.

43. Rajeev Dikshit, 'Bodies spotted in river Ganga, trigger panic across Ghazipur villages in Varanasi', The Times of India, 12 May 2021, https://timesofindia.indiatimes.com/city/varanasi/bodies-spotted-in-river-ganga-trigger-panic-across-ghazipur-villages/articleshow/82560352.cms.

44. 'Discarded masks biggest potential carriers of coronavirus, say experts', The New Indian Express, 18 April 2020, https://www.newindianexpress.com/cities/vijayawada/2020/apr/18/discarded-masks-biggest-potential-carriers-of-coronavirus-say-experts-2131765.html.

45. Akshay Kumar Dongare, 'Coronavirus Safety Gear Dumped at Delhi Crematorium, Poses Serious Risk', NDTV, 22 June 2020, https://www.ndtv.com/delhi-news/coronavirus-cases-delhi-lodhi-

crematorium-ppe-kits-lie-discarded-at-delhi-crematorium-raising-fears-of-virus-spreading-2250387.

46. Ibid.

47. 'World Environment Day: PPE, masks and shields ... pandemic detritus adds to waste crisis', *The Economic Times*, 4 June 2021, https://economictimes.indiatimes.com/news/india/world-environment-day-ppe-masks-and-shields-pandemic-detritus-adds-to-waste-crisis/articleshow/83233597.cms?from=mdr.

25. The Electric Crematorium

1. Sumit Mitra, 'Dom raja protests against installation of electric crematorium at Varanasi ghats', *India Today*, 15 April 1983, https://www.indiatoday.in/magazine/religion/story/19830415-dom-raja-protests-against-installation-of-electric-crematorium-at-varanasi-ghats-770619-2013-07-25.

2. Johnathan Parry, *Death in Banaras* (Cambridge: Cambridge University Press, 1994), p. 67.

3. Ibid., p 67.

4. Swati Chandra, 'Electric crematorium has few takers in Varanasi', *The Times of India*, 3 August 2012.

5. He is referring to Baba Masan Nath, who is another form of Lord Shiva.

27. The Way Things Have Always Been Done

1. According to the World Health Organization, household air pollution caused lung cancer, heart diseases and several other ailments, leading to 3.2 million deaths globally in 2020. Source: World Health Organization, 27 July 2022, https://www.who.int/news-room/fact-sheets/detail/household-air-pollution-and-health.

2. Anuja Jaiswal, 'Giving cellphones to girls leads to rape, says UP State Women's Commission member', *The Times of India*, 10 June 2021, https://timesofindia.indiatimes.com/city/agra/dont-give-girls-cellphones-it-leads-to-rape-up-state-womens-commission-member/articleshow/83379559.cms.

3. Himanshi Dhawan, 'No phone of their own: How Indian women have to share mobiles', *The Times of India*, 12 July 2023, https://timesofindia.indiatimes.com/india/no-phone-of-their-own-how-indian-women-have-to-share-mobiles/articleshow/101692465.cms.

4. This is not an anomaly, of course. In many parts of the country, women's clothes are policed. In Uttar Pradesh's Savreji Kharg village in Devariya district, for instance, in 2021, a seventeen-year-old girl was beaten to death by her grandfather and uncles because she was wearing jeans. Source: Santosh Kumar, 'Relatives kill 17-year-old UP girl over wearing jeans, try to throw body from bridge; 2 arrested', *India Today*, 22 July 2021, https://www.indiatoday.in/india/story/relatives-kill-17-year-old-up-girl-over-wearing-jeans-try-to-throw-body-from-bridge-2-arrested-1831327-2021-07-22; and Kalpana Sunder, 'In India, wearing jeans can be liberating—or deadly—for women', SCMP, 12 August 2021, https://www.scmp.com/week-asia/lifestyle-culture/article/3144677/india-wearing-jeans-can-be-liberating-or-deadly-women.

30. Aakash's Version

1. *British Indian Railway—On Tracks of Empire, Part 4*, (05:33, 04:26), John Sergeant, BBC, https://www.youtube.com/watch?v=xbjbUnooLCo..

2. Frederick Thomas Granville Walton, 'The Construction of the Dufferin Bridge over the Ganges', *Minutes of Proceedings of the Institution of Civil Engineering*, p. 24.

3. *British Indian Railway—On Tracks of Empire, Part 4*, (07:20), John Sergeant, BBC.

4. 'Cops suspect foul play in man's disappearance', *The Times of India*, 31 January 2013, https://timesofindia.indiatimes.com/city/varanasi/cops-suspect-foul-play-in-mans-disappearance/articleshow/18263803.cms; Abhishek Sharma, 'Couple jumps from Rajghat bridge in Varanasi into river Ganga, Pulsar bike found on Rajghat bridge', *Jagran*, 17 September 2021, https://www-jagran-com.

translate.goog/uttar-pradesh/varanasi-city-lovers-couple-jumped-into-ganga-river-from-rajghat-bridge-in-varanasi-pulsar-bike-found-on-rajghat-bridge-22030242.html?_x_tr_sl=hi&_x_tr_tl=en&_x_tr_hl=en&_x_tr_pto=sc&_x_tr_hist=true.

5. Rakesh Ranjan, 'More than 6,500 bridges on Indian highways in "distressed" condition, deadly ones to be shut soon', *India Today*, 31 December 2017, https://www.indiatoday.in/mail-today/story/more-than-6500-bridges-on-indian-highways-in-distressed-condition-deadly-ones-to-be-shut-soon-1119284-2017-12-31.

6. Amrita Nayak Dutta, 'On national highways alone, UP has 226 distressed bridges that need attention', The Print, 17 May 2018, https://theprint.in/india/governance/on-national-highways-alone-up-has-226-distressed-bridges-that-need-attention/59472/.

7. 'Varanasi stampede victims followers of affluent "godman" Jai Gurudev', *Hindustan Times*, 16 October 2016, https://www.hindustantimes.com/india-news/varanasi-stampede-victims-followers-of-affluent-godman-jai-gurudev/story-vR3wvPhVJvI4pJPZqn7ZhP.html.

8. 'Varanasi LIVE: 19 killed, several injured in stampede during Baba Jai Gurudev's sabha', ABP Live, 15 October 2016, https://news.abplive.com/news/varanasi-live-19-killed-several-injured-in-stampede-during-baba-jai-gurudevs-sabha-431600.

9. Binay Singh, 'Varanasi stampede: Toll rises to 25, no action against organizers', *The Times of India*, 16 October 2016, https://timesofindia.indiatimes.com/city/varanasi/varanasi-stampede-toll-rises-to-25-no-action-against-organizers/articleshow/54883285.cms.

10. 'Varanasi Stampede: Rumour "Rajghat bridge broke" made people run for their lives', ABP News, 15 October 2016, https://news.abplive.com/news/varanasi-stampede-rumour-rajghat-bridge-broke-made-people-run-for-their-lives-431735.

11. 'Accidental Deaths and Suicides in India', National Crime Records Bureau, Ministry of Home Affairs,' 2016, pp. 130, 132, https://ncrb.gov.in/sites/default/files/ADSI-2016-FULL-REPORT-2016.pdf.

37. Clumps of Hair

1. Jagdish Chaudhary's son Hariom Chaudhary received the award on his father's behalf.
2. Rajeev Dikshit, 'No one ever honoured us like PM, says Padma awardee Dom Raja's son', *The Times of India*, 26 January 2021, https://timesofindia.indiatimes.com/city/lucknow/no-one-ever-honoured-us-like-pm-says-padma-awardee-dom-rajas-son/articleshow/80457433.cms. In 2019, the Dom Raja Jagdish Chaudhary (in some places spelled 'Chowdhary') had given full support to Prime Minister Narendra Modi during the 2019 Indian general elections, being a proposer for his candidature.

About the Author

RADHIKA IYENGAR is an award-winning journalist with a Master's degree in journalism from Columbia University Graduate School of Journalism, New York. She won the Red Ink Award for Excellence in Indian Journalism (2018). In 2020, she was awarded the Charles Wallace India Trust fellowship at University of Kent, UK. She received the Bianca Pancoat Patton Fellowship in 2019 and was a recipient of the Sanskriti-Prabha Dutt Fellowship (2016–17).

Fire on the Ganges is her first book.

Follow her on Instagram and Twitter: @radhika_iy